INDIAN BIOGRAPHY

PISCHEL YEARBOOKS
A DIVISION OF HERFF JONES
P.O. BOX 36, MARCELINE, MISSOURI 64658 816—376-3523

INDIAN BIOGRAPHY

OR

AN HISTORICAL ACCOUNT

OF THOSE

INDIVIDUALS WHO HAVE BEEN DISTINGUISHED
AMONG THE NORTH AMERICAN NATIVES

AS

ORATORS, WARRIORS, STATESMEN,

AND

OTHER REMARKABLE CHARACTERS

BY

B. B. THATCHER, ESQ.

IN TWO VOLUMES.
VOL. I.

———

With a new scholarly introduction, a new Publisher's
Preface, a new index, new endpaper art and an enlarge-
ment from the original size.

The Rio Grande Press, Inc.

GLORIETA, NEW MEXICO · 87535

First edition from which this edition was
reproduced was supplied by
INTERNATIONAL BOOKFINDERS, Inc.,
P. O. Box 1
Pacific Palisades, Ca. 90272

Library of Congress Cataloging in Publication Data

Thatcher, Benjamin Bussey, 1809-1840.
    Indian biography.

    (A Rio Grande classic)
    Reprint of the 1832 ed. published by J. & J. Harper,
New York; with a new pref. by W. N. Fenton.
    1. Indians of North America--Biography.
2. Indians of North America--History.   I. Title.
E89.T36 1973   970.1'092'2 [B]   73-14660
ISBN 0-87380-089-3

A Rio Grande Classic
First published in 1832

First printing 1973

The Rio Grande Press, Inc.
GLORIETA, NEW MEXICO · 87535

Publisher's Preface

The enthralling and engrossing story of the exploration and settlement of North America is too little known and appreciated these dreary and cynical days. There are those who sneer and say that "history" is "not relevant", yet without history, man is *nothing* and men are *nothing*. Man as he is today is the result of events that extend back through the centuries to the dawn of time. No man could be alive today unless what has happened in the past had happened. The origin and development of mankind is infinitely complex, and infinitely beautiful in its complexity. Why any adult would teach young people that history is "irrelevant" is beyond comprehension; why any adult, in any profession, would passively or actively encourage young people to accept this scurrilous and pernicious idea is beyond belief. It seems to us utterly irrefutable that not only is history "relevant", it is quintessentially revelant. We repeat: Without history, *man is nothing, men are nothing. Nothing.*

These thoughts aside, we submit herewith our 98th title and our 96th beautiful Rio Grande Classic. This one deals with the history of the culture confrontation between the White Man of Europe and his copper-colored cousin in the New World. The time frame lies between the advent of the Jamestown colony (in Virginia) in 1607 and the year of our Lord 1830. In the first three decades of the 19th century, the White Man was lustily engaged in wresting a civilization from the wilderness, and some would say, wresting a continent from its "rightful" owners. Either way, the civilized culture of Europe confronted the aboriginal culture of the New World, and the result is "history".

White Men, up to and early in the 1830's, were preoccupied with surviving in a hostile environment. Some of the elements of that environment were hostile natives. Some of the natives were hostile by virtue of their innately aboriginal human natures; the hostility of others was stimulated by the reciprocal hostility of the White Man. Some of the natives were friendly to the "intruders", and some of the White Men were friendly to the natives. In retrospect, what can the modern historian write but that each man in each group was responding to his own nature, which was (or might have been) hostile or friendly in any other circumstance as well. No purpose is served (that we can see) in judging now why White Men and Red Men were hostile or friendly to each other nearly a century and a half ago. In 1984, we can revise and rewrite history the way we think it should have been, but until Big Brother arrives, we should accept history as it was written. . . in this work, and in all others like it.

All this is to observe that one White Man—in 1832—with perhaps the approval of some of his contemporaries and the disapproval of others, undertook to set forth a sympathetic recounting in a compassionate manner the events of the historic confrontation between the two races from 1607 through about 1830. His name was Benjamin Bussey Thatcher; this is his work. The title he gave it is comprehensive and self-explanatory: *Indian Biography; or, An Historical Account of Those Individuals Who Have Been Distinguished Among the North American Natives as Orators, Warriors, Statesmen and Other Remarkable Characters.*

It is obviously a bibliographic treasure. In his stately but pedantic narrative, the author describes vividly some important moments in American history. Unfortunately, when his book was first published in 1832, it was printed in a format so bad as to make the product nearly unusable. The outer dimensions of the first and all succeeding editions (described in more detail in the following Introduction) was 3¾ inches in width by 6 inches in depth. An average of some 380 words were compressed into a block of copy on each page, 2 1/8 inches by 4¼ inches. Not even young eyes could read and use the text without considerable eyestrain. We have, therefore, photographically enlarged the page size (in reproduction) to an outer dimension of 6 inches in width by 9 inches in depth. This has the effect of enlarging the copy to a very readable size--about a 10 point typeface, as a guess. This also has the effect of increasing the visibility of the type's original imperfections, so there are what might appear to be printing "smudges" on some pages. While these imperfections could not be entirely eliminated, we believe they will not be obvious or obnoxious to the reader.

We present as an illustration immediately following these words an exact-size facsimile of an original random page of copy; the reader can thus more readily perceive why this fine study has been largely by-passed and unused by scholars, students, historians and aficionados of American history since the work was first published in 1832.

Another reason for passing over this study has been that there has never been an index—no previous edition has been indexed. We have had the book indexed by a professional indexer who lives in Albuquerque, a former librarian at the Albuquerque Public Library by name of Katherine McMahon. That gracious lady has done a superb job; users of this edition will be as grateful to her as we are.

A few years ago we came into possession of an edition of this work published in 1900. As a willing and eager student, we are most familiar with that part of American history dealing with the trans-Mississippi west and in particular, with the Great American Southwest. We strained our ageing eyes to read and digest Thatcher's tiny volumes, and our reward was to step backward in time to the wilderness that met the colonists who came to Jamestown in 1607 and elsewhere subsequently. We greatly enjoyed this book, but our traditional and familiar scope of publication was far distant both in time and space. However, in recent years, public interest in the First Americans has waxed mightily; we have published many books, now, dealing with the culture, arts and crafts of the American Indians. Most of them are focussed on the Southwest, a few on the Great Plains and this one--our first--on the Indians that lived east of the Mississippi River. We are, in short, entering and embracing a larger scope of interest than heretofore--this being what we hope will be the forerunner of others outside the Southwest.

But we did not use the 1900 edition to reproduce this edition--we went, as usual, to our cordial and most excellent colleague, Mr. Dick Mohr, President of International Bookfinders, Inc., Box 1, Pacific Palisades, Calif. Seemingly in a trice, he found for us a rare first edition. This we have used in spite of the foxing and age stains on the crumbling old sulphite (wood pulp) paper. With brown filters on the camera lens, we were able to eliminate some of the more obvious flaws and stains.

Keenly aware of our inadequate knowledge of the eastern

American Indians, we searched for several months for an expert who could and would write an Introduction to this work for us. At long last, through the good offices of Dr. Bernard (Bunny) Fontana, of the Arizona State Musuem in Tucson, we reached Dr. William N. Fenton, Department of Anthropology at the State University of New York at Albany. He was pleased to learn of our plans to republish this title, and obligingly wrote for us the excellent Introduction following these pages of ours. From the scholarly viewpoint, Dr. Fenton seems to say, Thatcher's work may not be all that much of a bibliographic milestone. But in today's milieu, it is fitting and proper to restore to usefulness one of the earliest tributes to the First Americans set forth by a White Man. Perhaps that, by itself, justifies reprinting the book. In any event, Dr. Fenton has prepared a meticulous and painstaking "overview" Introduction which places Thatcher's work in an interesting and scholarly perspective. We are most grateful to the distinguished and erudite gentleman from Albany.

We cannot end these words without speaking of the color plates on the endpapers. One of our good friends in the graphic arts business is fine artist Donald J. Mills of Evanston, Ill. We commissioned Mr. Mills to paint two scenes in watercolors, suggesting one as the scene where Pocohantis saves the life of Captain John Smith of the Jamestown colony from the death sentence of her father Chief Powhatan. The other, we suggested, might be an artist's conception of a colonial Thanksgiving Day feast. We gave artist Mills carte blanche to use all the license he chose. However, scholarly as well as artistic, Mr. Mills researched through many art representations and printed descriptions before roughing out the final compositions. After we approved the rough sketches, he went to work. As anyone can plainly see, the finished art was simply magnificent. Mr. Mills lives at 642 Forest Avenue in Evanston, and paints just about anything on commission.

We were reluctant to send the original paintings to the printer through that misnamed United States Postal (dis) Service, so we had them photographed with a Hasselblad camera by one of Santa Fe's most respected professionals, Len Bouche of Bouche Productions. The printing plates were prepared from Mr. Bouche's superb transparencies. We acknowledge his cooperation with our warmest thanks.

We are very proud to restore this fine work to usefulness,

along with Dr. Fenton's scholarly Introduction, Miss McMahon's excellent index and Mr. Mills' splendid paintings. We commend our efforts to the attention of all who are interested in American history, in the culture of the First Americans, and in the adventure of stepping back in time for awhile to a more innocent--and perhaps more worthwhile--milieu. We are, as the gentlemen of yesterday were fond of saying, your most faithful and obedient servants, The Rio Grande Press, Inc.

Robert B. McCoy

La Casa Escuela
Glorieta, N.M. 87535
September 1973

RED JACKET

A facsimile of original page, exact size.

INDIAN BIOGRAPHY.

CHAPTER I.

The Indian tribes of Virginia at the date of the Jamestown settlement: their names, numbers and power—The Powhatan confederacy—The Indian Village of that name—POWHATAN—The circumstances of the first interview between him and the English—OPECHANCANOUGH, his brother—Opitchipan—Reception of Captain Smith by Powhatan—Interposition of POCAHONTAS in his favor—Second visit of the colonists—Third visit, and coronation—Entertainment of Smith by Pocahontas—Contest of ingenuity between Powhatan and Smith : and between the latter and Opechancanough—Smith saved again by Pocahontas—Political manœuvres of Powhatan and Opechancanough—Smith's return to Jamestown.

AT the date of the first permanent settlement effected within the limits of Virginia, and for an unknown period previous to that date, the country from the sea-coast to the Alleghany, and from the most southern waters of James river to Patuxent river (now in the state of Maryland) was occupied by three principal native nations. Each of these nations was a confederacy of larger or smaller tribes; and each tribe was subdivided into towns, families or clans, who lived together.* The three general names by which these communities have been ordinarily known, are the Mannahoacks, the Monacans and the Powhatans.

---

* Jefferson's Notes on Virginia. The author has apparently intended to use the word *family* in its most enlarged sense

B.B. Thatcher's *Indian Biography* (1832).
by William N. Fenton,
[Research Professor of Anthropology,
State University of New York at Albany]

The year 1830 marks the end of an era in American Indian and White relations when Indians ceased to be treated with by the General Government and the States as sovereign powers and after which conflicts over lands were resolved by a policy of removing them west of the Mississippi river. Andrew Jackson, from the back country, became the seventh President the preceding year, and Red Jacket, the Demosthenes of Buffalo Creek, uttered his last prophetic protest against White ways before "going the long trail" to join his ancestors. Red Jacket enjoyed a good press, his speeches were quoted by Hon. Dewitt Clinton, Governor of New York, in a *Discourse delivered before the New-York Historical Society,* 1811 (New York, 1812), and they were reprinted in current periodicals that were read from Charleston to Boston.

Indeed Boston was the center of a rising concern over civil rights–especially over slavery, and of the attempts to remove the native Indians from their historic seats. Several of the missionary societies centered there and received reports from the Seneca country of western New York, from the Cherokee missions in the Great Smokies, and from the old Northwest –places where the land speculators were particularly anxious to have the Indians out of the way, even though substantial progress was being made "toward the civilization of the Indian natives", as Halliday Jackson phrased it in his report on the friendly conduct of the Quaker Missions (Philadelphia, 1830). Not to be outdone by the good works of the Committee on Suffering of the Philadelphia Meeting of the Society of Friends who had been sending young men since 1792 to labor among the Senecas, voices protesting Jacksonian Indian policy sounded from the pulpits of Boston's churches, New England writers contrasted the mistakes of the Puritan founders that led to King Philip's war with the possibility they dreaded that others on the frontier were repeating such historical blunders, and prosperous merchants and manufacturers funded their endeavors to avert a national disgrace.

At that moment when B.B. Thatcher was reading every book and paper on the subject and beginning to write, Emerson was preaching at the Old North Church, and he retired to Concord the year that Thatcher's book appeared. Thoreau, who admired the Indian so much, had not yet entered Harvard, and Francis Parkman who later owned and read Thatcher's *Indian Biography,* was a lad of ten and had not yet projected his classic work on France and England in North America and the role of the Indians in this struggle.

As one reads Thatcher today he may sense how terribly troubled were the intellectuals of his day as they reflected on the history of the relations between the pious New England colonists and their "savage" neighbors whom they dispossesed and exterminated in a series of bloody wars during the seventeenth century. New Englanders looking at their own history in the light of current national issues, like slavery and Indian removal, realized how little man had improved with civilization, and that certain values present in "barbarous societies" --hospitality, generosity, the dignity of men and women, and relative freedom--were somehow being lost. How deeply the New England conscience weighed these issues may be seen in Thatcher's own words which conclude the chapter on the Pequot war: "If it shall be found (as we believe it must be) that under the influence of strong and sincere though fatal excitement, a rashness of the civilized party was the ultimate cause of the ruin of the savage, let the injustice be acknowledged, though it should be with shame and with tears. Let it be atoned for, as far as it may be--in the only way now possible--by the candid judgement of posterity and history, upon the merits and misfortunes of both" (I:265).

And this same theme of atonement is the burden of a long review article by an unknown contemporary in the *North American Review* (of April, 1833: 472-487), in which the reviewer speaks of savage manners producing men with elevated feelings who "in some respects, [were] able to put civilization to shame." He goes on to reflect on the tragedy of men like this being dispossessed from the soil of their fathers to be dispersed as remnants with lost identities and then echoing the eighteenth century idea of progress, and in a way anticipating nineteenth century social evolutionism of L.H. Morgan, the reviewer cautioned that sympathy for native peoples cannot obscure the fact that "Wherever civilization comes in contact with barbarism. . .with a race which has no active principle of improvement within it, it is the order of nature that barbarism shall give way. . . ." Cultivated men need not acquire the habits of the native, nor abandon the country, "for in that case, no room on earth would ever be found for cultivated man." And then he adds that justice and humanity require "that the rights of the weaker party shall be respected. . . ." With this rationalization, tinged with the racism of later evolutionary theory, the reviewer salves his historical conscience: "We do not hold our fathers responsible for the extinction of the Indian race, for we see not how it could have been prevented; but we fear that where were instances, in which they violated the laws of justice and humanity in their dealings with their neighbors, and if so, the other party should not labor under perpetual reproach for the sake of vindicating their reputation" (NAR: 473). Finding some redeeming qualities in the characters of his ancestors, the reviewer congratulates Thatcher for touching "these cases with a delicate and discriminating hand", and notes that in a "popular narrative he could not enter into the subject very largely. . ."; but he asks whether "a work of permanent value as an authority is not required", and indicates that the several "sketches of tribes and individuals. . .might easily be woven into a philosophical history. . ."---- a suggestion, as we shall see, that Thatcher, despite his evident talent, did not live to fulfill.

Thinking that Thatcher might undertake such a work, the reviewer outlined a series of factors implicit in the narrative that were at work in the relations of the New England founders and the native Indians. He was not prepared to admit that the Indians met with such treatment from "our fathers" as they met in later times. "Our fathers meant to do them substantial justice, and if they failed it was owing to jealousy and suspicion. . ." (NAR: 474). The Pilgrims respected land titles, he notes, and invariably tried to extinguish them by deed or purchase. (The interesting thing is that the Indians sometimes gave away land to "friends", but seldom were willing to sell.). Such relations were a trial run, never to be repeated, to which neither culture was prepared to accommodate. Jealousy of the Indians' enormous land holdings was balanced at first by a feeling of weakness, a reluctance to employ force, and then overcompensated as the power relations shifted.

The settlers feared and dreaded the Indians-- a passion which always borders on inhumanity. The reviewer observes how this was powerfully illustrated in the witchcraft hysteria which centered at Salem in the seventeenth century. Both the Indians and the colonists had survived epidemics which reminded the reviewer that ". . .even within the last year, we have seen the fear of pestilential disease lead to acts of gross and enormous inhumanity. . ." Much of what the settlers feared and dreaded in the Indians sprang from ignorance of their numbers, band organization, and territories; a grudging admiration for their energy, cunning, loyalty, and "jealous impatience with wrongs. . ."; an inability to penetrate what A.I. Hallowell has called "the facade of imperturbability" in dealing with their leaders; and, in short, impatience at the thought of learning their languages and understanding their cultures. The rare exceptions-- John Eliot (1604-1690), Roger Williams (1603-1683), and Daniel Gookin--who took Indian manners seriously were all too few at the time; their views did not always prevail, but today their writings preserve some glimpse of the New England Algonquians.

The deeply religious Puritans could not regard the Indians as anything but heathens and savages. They brought with them from western Europe a tradition that hunting peoples of the forests who lived on the margins of civilization were "savages" literally and in fact. This notion prevailed in the nineteenth century when readers of the *North American Review* are not allowed to forget "that the Indians were a savage people" (476). Their virtues were of a warlike kind which made them formidable as enemies and loyal as friends; but "their strongest advocates will not deny, that they had at times a taste for cruelty and torture. . ." Indeed, the reviewer maintains, their true character is not as the philosophers and romantic poets see them from a distance, nor quite as contemporary observers for whom they were too near to regard with much delight, nor perhaps even as depicted in the captivity literature, which, much too personal, stresses treatment of prisoners by extremes of torture or adoption; but rather something *sui generis* that no one was then prepared to grasp. "The country was perpetually ringing with stories of their 'devil worship', and of the torture which they practiced on prisoners. . ." (477). There was then virtually no literature on shamanism (Powwow-ing was an act of deviltry), although torture for obtaining evidence was no stranger to European courts, and burning witches at the stake, beheading political enemies, and hanging thieves were all too familiar.

Three other traits of Indian personality annoyed and bothered the colonists. The Indians regarded themselves as superior to other men, as indeed they were at living and moving in the woods; the idea of "work" as such was completely alien to them; and they had a different concept of time. They attempted to preserve their own independence of action. When asked in one treaty to abstain from labor on the sabbath, they assented "to the arrangement, inasmuch 'as they had not much to do on any day'." (478).

The concept of sovereignty was a more serious problem as it affected all relations between the English colonists and the Indians. Consider the difficulty of communicating the concept of a king across the Atlantic to people who grudgingly yielded power to band leaders and who began to confederate as they perceived the colonists presenting a common threat. How easy it was, too, for the colonists to transfer European ideas of rank and status to the Indians, creating "Indian Kings" of chiefships. We are reminded that, subconsciously if not openly, the colonists, "who could not forebear using the language and manner of condescension", conveyed an attitude of superiority to the Indians "who cannot endure the least approach to contempt" (NAR: 478). The feeling of superiority on both sides inevitably widened the gulf between the two cultures, and as the numbers of English swelled, prevented any real accommodation between the two societies.

Finally, Thatcher's reviewer does not think that any state or nation in modern times could have done much better than the founding fathers two centuries earlier. To test Thatcher's impartiality in treating crucial cases where the colonists dealt severely with the Indians, he confines his selection to concerns of a New England audience and treats only of the regional scene–the Pequot War; the treatment of Miantonomo, the friendly Narragansett; Uncas who got on better with Englishmen than Indians; and King Philip and the coalition that he put together that represented the high-water mark of Indian resistance. In all of these cases the reviewer finds Thatcher's treatment impartial, accurate, sympathetic, and praiseworthy. No space was awarded to the rest of the work.

Since Thatcher never fulfilled the charge to write a philosophical Indian history, some explanation may lie in his career. All that we know about B.B. Thatcher, Esq., as he signs his work, is contained in a brief notice in the *Dictionary of American Biography* (DAB 18: 393).

Benjamin Bussey Thatcher (1809-1840) was born October 8 at Warren, Knox County, Maine, and he died, presumably at Boston, on July 14. He was educated at Bowdoin College, graduating with the Class of 1826, and he then studied and nominally practiced the law; but clearly his real interests were literary, both as editor and author. For a writer who lived but 31 years, he was prolific, and his books and articles quite possibly supported him. His essays appeared in the *North American Review*, which carried advance sections of his *Indian Biography;* but other works, which represent his charitable instincts and social concerns, include: *Memoir of Phyllis Wheatley, a Native African and a Slave* (Boston, 1834), which went through two editions; *Memoir of Rev. S. Osgood Wright, late Missionary to Liberia* (Boston, 1834), again two editions; *Tales of the Indians: being Prominent Passages of the History of the North American Natives, Taken from Authentic Sources* (Boston, 1831), an obvious predecessor of the present book; and *Traits of the Tea Party: being a Memoir of George R.T. Hewes, one of the last of its Survivors; with a History of that Transaction: Reminiscences of the Massacre, and the Siege, and Other Stories of Old Times.* By a Bostonian. (New York: Harper, 1835). One other work relating to the Revolution has been attributed to him (Sabin No. 94253, vol. 24). Clearly Thatcher had a flair for oral history and must have been one of its pioneers in this country, so that it is puzzling that he did not interview some contemporary Indians in his native Maine or as they came to Boston.

He is remembered as prominent in philanthropic work in Boston. He advocated African colonization as a solution to slavery, and he interested himself in helping the blind. He is said to have suffered from ill health, and it is evident that he overworked. He must have known everyone in Boston literary circles of the day, and he is fondly remembered by his fellow Bowdoin alumni, for whom his portrait, now in the Bowdoin Gallery, was painted in England, and he is included among the early worthies of the College. (Nehemiah Cleveland and A.S. Packard, *History of Bowdoin College* (1882). It seems appropriate that he is best known for the *Indian Biography* (1832), which is here reprinted for the first time in more than 50 years. Before discussing its various editions let us see how he worked.

In his Preface, Thatcher is rather explicit about his point of view, or motivation, as if, he says, the work requires an explanation or apology, for if either were true, he would deem it a failure. He is moved to perform historically an act of justice to otherwise unnoticed "patriots, orators, warriors and statesmen" whose deeds and utterances, "barbarians" though they be, coming from leaders of "barbarian communities" are in themselves admirable and deserve mention in the history of America. Uneducated as these men and women were, they exhibit a kind of nobility as natural men, – a view then prevalent in moral philosophy. As a New Englander, Thatcher acknowledges a moral obligation inherited from "our Fathers" who owed so much to the native Indians, man to man, and culturally. On these grounds alone, he thinks, such a work is needed. Moreover, like many authors, he feels that his book is unique-- that no one else has done just this--and he alludes to an "Indian Biographical Dictionary" already in print. This is possibly an early version of Samuel G. Drake's *Biography and History of the Indians of North America,* which came out as *Indian Biography Containing the Lives of More than Two Hundred Chiefs. . .*(Boston, 1832), a work that went through many revisions and reprintings with various titles, attaining its seventh edition by 1837. Thatcher knew the book and cites it late in the second volume, consistent with the fact that it appeared the same year as his own. Drake, however, devotes considerable space in later editions to characters whom Thatcher's preface lists as slighted. Obviously there was feedback between the two men and their books, although possibly some other work is involved that has escaped me.

The 'Life and Times' genre, which combines biography and history in chronological fashion derives from the biographical dictionaries of the preceding century. Drake and Thatcher made it the fashionable way to handle Indian subjects during the nineteenth century, as witness the later writings of W.L. Stone on Joseph Brant (1838) and Red Jacket (1841). Then American ethnology began at mid-century with L.H. Morgan's *League of the Ho-dé-no-sau-nee, or Iroquois* (Rochester, 1851(. But biography revived in this century when Paul Radin introduced the "life history technique" with *Crashing Thunder: the Autobiography of an American Indian* (1926). Although the genre has been modified, it has never really disappeared, but it has vastly improved in Anthony Wallace's early study of Teedyuscung (1949) and his great book on Handsome Lake, the Seneca prophet: *The Death and Rebirth of the Senecas* (1970). The problems of encompassing history and cultures within the biographical medium remain formidable, especially with Indian subjects who leave no personal papers, as contributors to the *Dictionary of Canadian Biography* have come to realize.

In Thatcher's hands the method was to introduce characters in the order of their appearance and then to draw concise summaries of events and periods, as in his précis on King Philip's War (I: 161,162), and of the man himself (I: 176). He would leave the "well known particulars" of the war to others. It was perhaps his ability to sum up whole movements and delineate character in a few strokes that moved his reviewer to hope that he would produce the philosophical history of which he was capable. No author ever quite writes the book that is expected of him or that he projects for himself.

It is amazing to reflect now on the resources that were available to Thatcher in Boston in 1830. Of libraries there was the Athenaeum, the Massachusetts Historical Society (M.H.S.), with its marvelous collections of books and manuscripts already in being, especially the Winthrop Papers to which he refers repeatedly, and in Cambridge the Harvard College Library. (The Boston Public Library was twenty years in the offing.) He also had access to papers that now comprise the Massachusetts Archives, and the records of the Plymouth Colony. Perhaps of even greater importance to a working writer was Daniel G. Drake's "Antiquarian Bookstore", which opened in 1830, first on Market Street and then at 56 Cornhill, for which the proprietor boasted: "this is the first and only establishment of the kind in the country", and like some Washington haberdashers of this century, it was not to be confused with others of similar name. Indeed Thatcher acknowledges the use of manuscripts cited in Drake's *Indian Biography* (I: 322; II: 170). For Drake was the first of that now vanishing breed of bookmen in this country and Thatcher's debt to him was considerable.

Somehow Thatcher managed to get his hands on several

hundred books and manuscripts that comprise most of the then available literature on the American Indians. They covered such topics as travel and exploration, Indian wars, Indian histories, and journals and correspondence of the principal negotiators with the Indians. Besides he looked at colonial records, local histories, broadsides, periodicals, and contemporary newspapers, particularly those published on the frontier and now inaccessible to most readers. These he read, excerpted, and digested. To list in their entirety and identify chapter by chapter (which I undertook in part) the sources that he used is a formidable task that lies beyond the purpose of the present edition. It would mean verifying all of his references, running down the editions that he used (or neglected) in a reference library, and then arranging the sources in a classified bibliography with notes. Only then would we know for certain how carefully he selected, how accurately he quoted, and how much he relied on secondary works, as he sometimes did, that in themselves were copied from other works. We rather have to rely on our own knowledge of the literature of particular subjects that perhaps he knew less well, and point out the virtues and deficiencies for the general reader and for scholars who follow us.

On the Algonquian-speaking Powhatan confederacy of tidewater Virginia (I: chs. 1-iv), he relies on Jefferson's *Notes on Virginia* (1785) for general considerations, and he returns to him later on the Ohio country. His main sources, however, are Capt. John Smith, and the histories of Beverley, Stith, Burk, and Hamer. He refers once to the collections of Hakluyt, mispelling his name (I: 104), and he cites the Journal of Governor Lane. The more important sources on Virginia are now available in critical editions, and works relating to the Indians of the period are listed in Butterfield, Washburn and Fenton's bibliography to my *American Indian and White Relations to 1830* (Chapel Hill, 1957).

On his home ground he is more thorough, discriminating, and critical. The New England Indians, also Algonquian speaking, occupy him for the remainder of Volume One and the first two chapters of Volume Two. Here perhaps the sources are better, he is more familiar with them, having previously published on the 'Pokanoket Sachems' in NAR. He employs a number of critical devices to sustain his own judgements--comparison of sources, compiling synonomies of variant spellings of Indian proper names, compiling his own tables of population statistics and averaging them to test the sources, critique of particular sources, analysis of accounts of wampum payments demonstrating absurd demands, personal field trips to the scenes of the Indian wars, interviewing old people at the scene, and visits to collections of Indian memorabilia. The reader will find his own examples. Thatcher was on the way to a more general statement.

In four New England sources he places greatest confidence: Gov. John Winthrop (1588-1609), his son of the same name (1606-1676), whose papers form one body; Rev. John Eliot (1604-1690) who came out from Cambridge University to translate the Bible into the Massachusetts dialect of Algonquian; Roger Williams (1603-1683) of Rhode Island who had the intellectual curiosity to write *A Key into the Language of America*. . .(1643)-- the lone Englishman of his generation who understood the Narragansett language, treated the native culture with respect, his work reads like an anthropological inquiry, and his letters to the Winthrops comment soberly in the political situation among the Narragansetts when the Plymouth Colony was alarmed and prepared to take up arms against the savages; and the fourth was Daniel Gookin, protector of the Christian Indians and a kind of Indian Commissioner for Massachusetts during King Philip's war, who wrote a memoir on their manners (Mass. Hist. Soc., 1792).

Thatcher used Benjamin Church's *The History of King Philip's War* (1716) (which Drake reissued in 1825); but he impeaches the bias of William Hubbard, *The History of Indian Wars in New England* (1677) (the title from Drake's 1865 edition) as too sympathetic to the prejudices of the colonists and incapable of seeing things in the lights of the Indians. (Vol. I: 139, 143-144, 149, et. seq.) But even Hubbard wrote favorably of Woosamequin of Swanzey who sought in a treaty to protect the native religion from missionary zeal, for according to Rev. Thomas Mahew's rare tract, *The Light appearing more and more towards the perfect Day. . ."* (London, 1651), the Sachem was skeptical of "what earthly good things. . .[the Christianized Indians of Martha's Vineyard]. . .gained by their piety. . ." (II: 139).

For the reader who wants to obtain his own view of Indian affairs in colonial New England, there are happily two excellent fruits of modern historical scholarship, both offering extensive bibliographies: Douglas Edward Leach, *Flintlock and Tomahawk: New England in King Philip's War* (New York: Macmillan, 1958), and Alden T. Vaughan, *New England Frontier: Puritans and Indians, 1620-1675* (Boston: Little, Brown & Co., 1965). Neither felt Thatcher worthy of notice.

Turning to the famous Five Nations of New York, the Iroquois Confederacy, of whom the fierce Mohawks (from *Mauquawogs* or *Mohowawogs,* meaning "Men Eaters" in the Pequot language, as Williams wrote to Wintrop in 1636) were so dreaded in New England by Indian and colonist alike, Thatcher relies mainly on two secondary sources, although the primary sources are extensive. Both were written in a more leisurely day when Governors of New York found time for intellectual discourse. Lt. Gov. Cadwallader Colden, correspondent of the Royal Society of London, first published his *The History of the Five Indian Nations Depending on the Province of New-York in America* (New York, 1727) in defense of the Albany fur trade, and Thatcher used one of the later London editions (1747 or 1750) which include subsequent printed treaties. Colden based his extraordinary book partly on personal observation of the Mohawks who adopted him and his knowledge of official transactions with them; but he also read French sources, particularly Lahontan and Charlevoix, and quite possibly Lafitau's *Moeurs des sauvages amériquians.* . . . (2 vols, Paris, 1724); and his primary materials in English were the New York Indian Records. In 1811, Gov. Dewitt Clinton delivered a "Discourse on the Six Nations" before the New-York Historical Society (New York, 1812), which is a rather remarkable demonstration of scholarly erudition interpreted through personal experience as Governor of New York of dealing with the Six Nations. Clinton faithfully cites his sources who frequently cite each other. Readers who wish to go beyond Thatcher's sketch (Vol. II: chs. iii and iv), may enjoy the writer's "The Iroquois in History" in *North American Indians in Historical Perspective,* E.B. Leacock and N.O. Lurie, eds., (New York: Random House, 1971). He might also look at the chapters by Brasser on the "Coastal Algonquians" and Hickerson on the "Chippewa of the Upper Great Lakes," who are Thatcher's next concerns.

Having reached the mid-eighteenth century according to

his plan, Thatcher next takes up the Ottawas and neighboring Central Algonquians who joined Pontiac in his famous conspiracy to extinguish the English settlements in a single stroke (Vol. II: chs. v-vii). These chapters may be Thatcher's most important contribution as among the first attempts before Parkman to outline the subject from the then-available sources. For an overview of the affair, Thatcher again relies on two "Discourses", one delivered by Gov. Lewis Cass (1782-1866) to the Michigan Historical Society in 1829, and the other by Henry Rowe Schoolcraft (1793-1864), pioneer ethnologist, to the same body the next year. He also read Major Robert Rogers, *Concise Account of North America* (London, 1765), and Alexander Henry's *Travels. . .*, 1760-1766, both contemporary observers of the principals. Thatcher offers his own explanations of Pontiac's motives (II: 78), which he attempts to test in the sources, but his speculations are often ethnocentric and not well-founded (109). He makes good use of contemporary newspapers and periodicals reporting events on the frontier and reprinting letters from Detroit, which lend reality to his account. I like particularly the report of panic as far east as Goshen, N.Y. (113), when partridge hunters missing birds were mistaken for marauding Indians. He finds in the response to the actions of Pontiac the same syndrome of overreaction among the Whites as in response to King Philip's movements a century earlier (114).

One bit of evidence for thinking that Thatcher may have inspired Francis Parkman's interest in Pontiac is that Parkman owned and presumably read the first edition of the work which he later donated with his collection to the Harvard College Library, from which it reached the New York State Library as a duplicate. Parkman nowhere cites Thatcher in *The History of the Conspiracy of Pontiac* (1851), but the approach is similar. Howard H. Peckham, however, in a recent revision of the subject, *Pontiac and the Indian Uprising* (Princeton, 1947), lists Thatcher in his bibliography.

By contrast the treatment of the Delaware shows less originality (II: viii). They were by no means "the most formidable antagonists the Five Nations ever had to contend with" (120; the Susquehannas were far tougher customers. But in discussing factions (Captain White-Eyes vs. Pipe) he touches a topic much in vogue today among political anthropologists. He relies mainly on Heckewelder, *An Account of the History, Manners and Customs of the Indians Nations. . .*

(Philadelphia, 1819), who knew them first hand, and Loskiel, *History of the Mission of the United Brethren. . .*(London, 1794), originally written in German. Again Thatcher employs 'flash-backs' to the New England situation in comparing Heckewelder's *Narrative of the Mission of the United Brethren among the Delaware and Mohegan. . .*(1740-1808 (1820) to the work of John Eliot (II: 143), as reported by Thomas Mahew (See I: 139-140).

There is little that is original in the discussion of the tribes of the Southeast (II: 150 ff.), excepting use of the Charleston, S.C. newspapers. But the destiny of the Cherokee Nation was going to be a major concern in Boston missionary circles whose representatives in Georgia would find the activities of southern politicians particularly reprehensible. (*See* Marion L. Starkey, *The Cherokee Nation* (New York: Knopf, 1946.)

The memory of a series of military disasters during the Federal Period in the territory northwest of the Ohio river was still fresh when Thatcher wrote. General Anthony Wayne had finally erased the disgrace of Harmar and St. Clair, defeating a coalition of Indians at the Battle of Fallen Timbers in 1794, which ended the long dispute with the Indians for the Ohio river boundary line between trans-Allegheny Virginia and Indian territory. The trouble that had begun twenty years earlier in Lord Dunmore's War was finally settled at the Treaty of Greenville, the next year. At the same time Timothy Pickering of Salem was treating with the Six Nations at Canandaigua, N.Y. for a lasting peace with the United States, in which both parties agreed "never to disturb" the other "in the peaceful use and enjoyment thereof". . .The beginning of the long controversy was dramatized in Cresap's murder of the family of Cayuga chief Logan whose pathetic protest Jefferson made an American classic. Thatcher treats this sad affair with great compassion. Besides Drake's materials, which he acknowledges, he quotes first hand accounts from Nile's *Register* (II: 170).

The affairs of the Shawnee, notably Tecumseh and his brothers, one whom was the prophet, occupy four chapters (II: xii-xv). The latter is of especial interest just now because he started and carried out on the frontier one of the first "revitalization movements", to use Anthony Wallace's term, which sought to restore the dignity of the old culture in the face of overwhelming White dominance. Later, Cornplanter's half-brother, who carried the distinguished title of Handsome Lake as one of the Lords of the Iroquois League, was to bring off a requickening of Seneca culture after its disorganization from land losses, drinking, and the decline of the warriors' status following the American Revolution. Cornplanter's prestige as a war leader could not be sustained, he became the friend of Washington and the Quakers, and he soon encountered opposition from Red Jacket of Buffalo Creek whose facility at manipulating the metaphors of the Iroquois oral tradition in satirizing White civilization would raise him up to chieftainship, surround him with a faction, and earn him the envy of Cornplanter's party. The Iroquois reward ability by "raising up a tree", and then soon jealous of power granted look askance at the "antlers of office" they have installed, and begin to look for reasons to "uproot the tree" or "dehorn" the chief. In Red Jacket's case he was charged with witchcraft, but he successfully defended himself with great ability in a famous speech, only to be deposed later in another controversy.

In his final chapter, Thatcher anticipates W.L. Stone's biography, mentioned earlier. The spirit of faction, jealousy of one another, rumor, tendency to listen to prophets, persistent struggle to maintain identity as Indians, retention of grievances, and willingness to fight lost causes however long it takes– are traits that run as themes from Greenville to Buffalo Creek and into modern times.

Readers and viewers of the media today need no reminder of Alcatraz, Plymouth Rock, the Interior Department "rip-off", nor of Wounded Knee. They need but note the success of Dee Brown's *Bury my heart at Wounded Knee* to appreciate how Thatcher's *Indian Biography* was read in the 1830's. In place of the rhetoric that is ascribed to his subjects, and his rather flowery style, we now have Indian writers of the ability of Vine Deloria, the late Professor Edward Dozier of the University of Arizona, and a host of new voices who are writing for the news sheets and periodicals that are springing up like plaintain weed, which the Delawares told Peter Kalm they called "whiteman's foot" because it grew in all the paths. Indian writers have transformed the oral tradition into writing which retains some of the style and flair of their speech.

Thatcher's book was indeed popular and it went through several printings. He evidently wrote it during 1829; parts of it-- on the Massachusetts sachems and Tecumseh--appeared in advance in the *North American Review,* and these pieces were only slightly revised as new information from reading confirmed previous hunches. The Preface is dated September 10, 1832, the year of the first edition. All of the editions that I have seen--1832, 1840, 1900-- were apparently printed from the same plates.

Sabin, *Bibliotheca Americana: A Dictionary of Books Relating to America. . .*(New York, 1868-1936), gives a complete run down on the work. J. & J. Harper of New York issued it as Nos. 45-46 of "The Family Library", or "Harper's Family Library", with the same imprint and date. It was reprinted in 1834 both in New York and in London, and again in New York in 1836, with the same collation as the New York, 1834 edition. By now the firm is Harper and Brothers, at the same address, 82 Cliff Street. It has the same imprint and collation, but one plate was omitted. The 1840 edition is identical. The only addition after 1834 was No. VIII of the Appendix. The 1836 edition was also included in "The Common School Library", 2d, ser., no. 6-7; while the London edition forms Vols. 1 and 2 of "Harper's Miscellany for Young People." All of this reaching out for the market is an indication of the work's popularity among readers. It kept coming out in New York in the years 1841, 1842, 1845, 1848, 1858, 1860, 1869, 1873, 1900; and then from Akron, 1910 and 1917. (Thus until 1850 it appeared almost yearly, then every decade until 1873, etc.) The 1917 edition is entitled "Early American History."

To meet the popular demand, Thatcher prepared in 1833 a juvenile version, *Indian Traits: being Sketches of the Manners, Customs, and Character of the North American Natives,* which Harper, his publisher, brought out in two volumes as VII and VIII of the "Boy's and Girl's Library", and as vols. 16-17 of "The American School Library." The sales must have been large and the royalties not inconsiderable, so for a few years before his untimely death, Thatcher must have lived comfortably from his writing.

Works on the American Indian have enjoyed a perennial popularity in this country, and a near rage in Europe, in Germany particularly. In Thatcher's day there emerged an awareness of the oppression that native peoples suffered at the hands of colonial powers; today it is paralleled by the demand for books that tell the story of the search for a new identity by the American Indian peoples themselves. No longer are the American Indians willing to be interpreted by other writers, either anthropologists or journalists. A new genre of American Indian literature has come into being written by American Indians as a form of social criticism. Thatcher would have welcomed it.

William N. Fenton

"The North Woods"
Keene Valley, New York
June 10, 1973

INDIAN BIOGRAPHY

OR

AN HISTORICAL ACCOUNT

OF THOSE

INDIVIDUALS WHO HAVE BEEN DISTINGUISHED
AMONG THE NORTH AMERICAN NATIVES

AS

ORATORS, WARRIORS, STATESMEN,

AND

OTHER REMARKABLE CHARACTERS

BY

B. B. THATCHER, ESQ.

IN TWO VOLUMES.
VOL. I.

———

A. L. FOWLE
NEW YORK
1832

PREFACE

THE Author does not propose an elaborate explanation, nor an apology of any kind, for the benefit of the following work. If it absolutely requires either, he must even be content to have written it in vain, as no statement or argument can give it any degree of vitality or popularity in the one case or in the other.

He has regarded it, historically, as an act of mere justice to the fame and the memories of many wise, brilliant, brave and generous men,—patriots, orators, warriors and statesmen,—who ruled over barbarian communities, and were indeed themselves barbarians, but whose influence, eloquence and success of every description were *therefore* but the nobler objects of admiration and the worthier subjects for record. Nor can Philosophy look upon them without predilection. Comparatively unopinionated and unaffected as they were,—governed by impulse and guided by native sense,—owing little to circumstances, and struggling much amidst and against them,—their situation was the best possible for developing both genius and principle, and their education at the same time the best for disclosing them. Their Lives, then, should illustrate the true constitution of man. They should have, above all other history, the praise and the interest of ' philosophy teaching by example.'

The strictly moral inducements which have operated on the Author's mind, must be too obvious to require dissertation. We owe, and our Fathers owed, too much to the Indians,—too much from man to man,—too much from race to race,—to deny them the poor restitution of historical justice at least, however the issue may have been or may be with themselves. Nor need it be suggested, that selfishness alone might dictate the policy of a collection such as the Author has endeavored to make this, were it only for the collateral light which it constantly throws on the history and biography of our own nation.

Nothing of the same character is before the public. What may be called an Indian Biographical Dictionary has indeed recently appeared, and to that the Author has gladly referred in the course of his researches ; but the extreme difficulty of doing justice to *any* individuals of the race, and at the same time to *all*, may be inferred from the fact that the writer alluded to has noticed such men as Uncas in some six or eight lines, while he has wholly omitted characters so important as Buckongahelas, White-eyes, Pipe, and Occonostota. On these, and on all their more eminent countrymen, the Author has intended to bestow the notice they deserve, by passing over the vast multitude distinguished only by detached anecdote, or described only in general terms.

In fine, conscious of many imperfections, but also conscious of a strenuous exertion to render them as few and small as might be, the Author submits the Biography to the public, and especially to the candor of those whose own labors, if not the results of them, have shown them the essential fallibility of every composition like this. He will have reason to be satisfied if it do good, as he will assuredly be gratified if it give pleasure.

Boston, Sept. 10, 183.

CONTENTS

CONTENTS.

CONTENTS.

INDIAN BIOGRAPHY.

CHAPTER I.

The Indian tribes of Virginia at the date of the Jamestown settlement: their names, numbers and power—The Powhatan confederacy—The Indian Village of that name—POWHATAN—The circumstances of the first interview between him and the English—OPECHANCANOUGH, his brother—Opitchipan—Reception of Captain Smith by Powhatan—Interposition of POCAHONTAS in his favor—Second visit of the colonists—Third visit, and coronation—Entertainment of Smith by Pocahontas—Contest of ingenuity between Powhatan and Smith : and between the latter and Opechancanough—Smith saved again by Pocahontas—Political manœuvres of Powhatan and Opechancanough—Smith's return to Jamestown.

AT the date of the first permanent settlement effected within the limits of Virginia, and for an unknown period previous to that date, the country from the sea-coast to the Alleghany, and from the most southern waters of James river to Patuxent river (now in the state of Maryland) was occupied by three principal native nations. Each of these nations was a confederacy of larger or smaller tribes ; and each tribe was subdivided into towns, families or clans, who lived together.* The three general names by which these communities have been ordinarily known, are the Mannahoacks, the Monacans and the Powhatans.

---

* Jefferson's Notes on Virginia. The author has apparently ntended to use the word *family* in its most enlarged sense

Of these, the two former might be called highland or mountain Indians. They all lived upon the banks of the various small streams which water the hilly country between the falls of the Atlantic rivers and the Alleghany ridge. The Mannahoacks consisted of eight tribes, five of which were located between the Potomac and Rappahannoc, and three between the last named river and the York. Of the five tribes of the Monacans,* two were between the York and James, and three extended southward from the James to the boundaries of Carolina. The most powerful respectively of the eight and of the five— the Mannahoacks and the Monacans, properly so called—seem to have given their own names to the entire nation or confederacy of which they were members. The former tribe occupied chiefly what are now Stafford and Spotsylvania counties. The latter resided upon James river above the falls.

The Powhatan nation inhabited the lowland tract, extending laterally from the ocean to the falls of the rivers, and from Carolina on the south to the Patuxent on the north. This comprised a much larger number of tribes than either of the others. As many as ten of them (including the Tauxenents, whose chief residence was about Mount Vernon) were settled between the Potomac and Rappahannoc.† Five others extended between the Rappahannoc and York; eight between the York and James and five between the James and the borders of Carolina. Beside these, the Accohanocks and Accomacks, on what is called the Eastern Shore (of Chesapeake Bay) have also been considered a part of this nation.

---

* It may be well to take this occasion of observing, that the author's only rule in the orthography of Indian term has been to follow what appears to be the most approved usage. Stith uses Manakins, instead of Monacans.

† Both these rivers have derived their names from the tribes originally settled on them. The former have been commonly called the Patowomekes.

The territory occupied by the whole of this great confederacy, south of the Potomac, comprehended about 8,000 square miles. Smith tells us in his history,* that within sixty miles of Jamestown were 5,000 natives, of whom 1,500 were warriors. Mr. Jefferson has computed the whole number of Powhatan warriors at 2,400, which, according to the proportions between Smith's estimates (being three to ten) would give an entire population of 8,000, or one to each square mile.

This calculation is probably quite moderate enough. It would leave an average of less than one hundred warriors to each of the thirty tribes. But we find it recorded by an early writer, that three hundred appeared under an Indian chieftain in one body at one time, and seven hundred at another; all of whom were apparently of his own tribe. The Chickahominies alone had between three hundred and four hundred fighting men. The Nansamonds and Chesapeaks showed on one occasion a force of four hundred. And when Smith ascended the Potomac, in June 1608, though he saw no inhabitants for the first thirty miles, he had scarcely entered "a little bayed creeke towards Onawmanient (now Nominy) when he found all the woods roundabout layd with ambuscadoes to the number of *three or four thousand* Savages, so strangely paynted, grimmed and disguised, shouting, yelling and crying as so many spirits from hell could not have shewed more terrible."

It is well known that the valiant Captain was wont to express his opinions in strong terms, but he has rarely been detected in any great inaccuracy. And the circumstances of this case are in his favor: for it has been truly remarked, that the Powhatan confederacy inhabited a country upon which nature had

* A work of which the value is well known to all readers of the early American history. The title is—"The Trve Travels, Adventures and Observations of Captaine Iohn Smith in Europe, Asia, Africke and America, beginning about the yeere 1593, and continued to this present 1629." We copy from the London edition of the date last named.

bestowed singular advantages.   Unlike the natives of
more northern regions, they suffered little from cold,
and less from famine.   Their settlements were mostly on the banks of James, Elizabeth, Nansamond,
York and Chickahominy rivers, all which abounded
with the most delicious fish and fowl.   In his Potomac expedition, Smith met with " that aboundance of
fish, lying so thicke with their heads above the water,
as for want of nets, (our barge driving amongst
them) we attempted to catch them *with a frying-pan.*"
And though the captain naturally enough concluded,
after some trials, that this was a poor instrument for
his purpose, he persists in adding that " neither better
fish, more plentie, nor more varietie for small fish, had
any of vs euer seene in any place so swimming in the
water—but they are not to be caught with frying-
pans."   He found the stingrays in such abundance
among the reeds at the mouth of the Rappahannoc,
that he amused himself by nailing them to the
ground with his sword : " and thus," he observes, " we
tooke more in owne houre than we could eate in a day."
   Vast quantities of corn, too, yearly rewarded even
the simple agriculture of the Indians, bestowed as it
was upon the best portions of a generous soil.   " Great
heapes " of it were seen at Kekoughtan, " and then
they brought him venison, turkies, wild fowle, bread
and what else they had."   In none of his captivities,
or his visits among the natives, did the captain ever
suffer from want of food ; and he often brought off
his boat and his men laden with plenty.   The Nan
samonds gave him 400 baskets-full at one time.   The
Chickahominies, though they complained extremely
of their own wants, yet " fraughted" him with
hundred bushels.   The woods furnished another
inexhaustible supply both of fruits and game : so that
on the whole, it is very easy to believe, that a considerably greater population than Mr. Jefferson's estimate supposes, might have subsisted without much
difficulty on the soil they are known to have occupied.
" And now the winter [of 1607—8] approaching," we

are informed in another passage, " the rivers became so covered with swans, geese, duckes and cranes, that we daily feasted with good bread, Virginia pease, pumpions and putchamins,* fish, fowle, and diverse sorts of wild beasts, so fat as we could eate them ; so that none of our Tuftaffaty humourists desired to go for England." On one occasion, when Smith undertook an exploring tour into the interior, late in the season, a violent storm obliged him and his men to keep Christmas among the savages. "And we were never more merry," he relates, "nor fed on more plenty of good oysters, fish, flesh, wild fowle and good bread, nor ever had better fires in England." In a peaceful interval of a few months, which occurred during the next season, the Indians are said to have brought into Jamestown more than a hundred deer and other beasts daily for several weeks.

It is evident, at least, that the Powhatan confederacy must have been among the most numerous on the continent. It was warlike too ; and though the situation of the Monacans and Mannahoacks among the hills of the back country protected them in some measure, yet nothing but a union of these two nations could assure them of security against their more powerful neighbors on the coast.

The Powhatans proper, who gave their own appellation to the confederacy of which they were leading members, were located in what is now Henrico county, on the banks of the James river, and at the distance of about two days' journey from the English settlement at its mouth. The principal chief—or *emperor*, as the old historians style him—of the thirty tribes of the nation, was found by the first colonists residing with these Indians, and is believed to have been one of their number by birth. His proper name

---

* A species of indigenous plum, which is elsewhere described as growing to a considerable height, with fruit like a medlar, first green, then yellow, and red when ripe. " If it be not ripe, it will draw a man's mouth awry with much torment. If ripe, it is delicious as an apricot."

was Wahunsonacook. He had that of Powhatan,
by which he has been generally designated, from the
town so called, which was the chief seat and metropolis of his hereditary dominions. This town is described as pleasantly situated on a hill. It consisted
of twelve houses, in front of which were three islets
in the river, not far from what in modern times has
been called Mayo's plantation, and a little below the
spot where Richmond now stands. It was considered
by the English both the strongest and pleasantest
place in the whole country ;* and was consequently
named *Nonsuch,* it seems, about two years after the
settlement at Jamestown, when it was purchased of
the emperor by Smith. " The place is very pleasant,"
says the captain in his history, " and strong by nature,
and about it are many cornfields."

The occasion of the first acquaintance which the
colonists had with Powhatan was as follows. The
adventurous and ambitious spirit of Smith had
prompted him to make several journeys and voyages
along the Virginia coast, and into the interior of the
country. Within a few months after the settlement
of Jamestown, among other tribes he discovered the
Chickahominies, and procured a large quantity of
provision from them at a time when the colonists
were in great need of it.

But with the idle and unruly in the colony, this
good fortune served only to produce murmuring.
They complained of his having done so little instead
of applauding him for having done so much ; and
some even of the council undertook to say, that he
ought to have followed up the Chickahominy river
to its source.

Smith was not a man to submit tamely to reproach.
He set off again, therefore, in the winter of 1607—8,
taking with him a crew sufficient to manage a barge
and a smaller boat proper for the navigation of the
upper streams. He ascended the Chickahominy with

---

* Stith's History, p. 105.

the barge, as far as it could be forced up, by dint of great labor in cutting away trees and clearing a passage. Then leaving it in a broad bay or cove, out of reach of the savages on the banks, the captain, with two other whites, and two friendly Indians, proceeded higher up in the smaller boat. Those who were left meanwhile in possession of the barge, were ordered on no occount to go on shore until his return. The order was disobeyed; for he was scarcely out of sight and hearing, when the whole of the crew went ashore. They were very near forfeiting their lives for their rashness. The Indians, to the number of two or three hundred, lay wait for them among the woods on the bank of the river, under the direction of OPECHANCANOUGH, Sachem of the Pamunkies and reputed brother of Powhatan. One George Cassen was taken prisoner; and the savages soon compelled him to tell them which way Smith had gone. They then put him to death in a cruel manner, and continued the pursuit.

The captain, meanwhile, little dreaming of any accident, had gone twenty miles up the river, and was now among the marshes at its source. Here his pursuers came suddenly upon the two Englishmen, who had hauled up their boat, and lain down to sleep by a fire on the dry land, (while Smith himself went out some distance to kill game with his musket for a supper.) The unfortunate wretches were shot full of arrows and despatched. The savages then pressed on after Smith, and at last overtook him. Finding himself beset by the multitude, he coolly bound to his arm, with his garters, the young Indian who had attended him as guide, for a buckler—(what had become of the other, does not appear)—and received the enemy's onset so briskly with his firearms, that he soon laid three of them dead on the spot, and wounded and galled many others so effectually that none appeared anxious to approach him. He was himself wounded slightly in the thigh, and had many arrows sticking in his clothes; but he stil

kept the enemy at bay. His next movement was to
endeavor to sheer off to his boat; but taking more
notice of his foe than his path, as he went, he sud
denly slipped up to his middle in an oozy creek.
Hampered as he was in this awkward position, not
an Indian dared venture near him, until, finding himself almost dead with cold, he threw away his arms
and surrendered. Then drawing him out, they
carried him to the fire where his men had been slain,
carefully chafed his benumbed limbs, and finally restored him to the use of them.

The incidents of the ensuing scene are a striking
illustration both of the sagacity of the prisoner and
the simplicity of his captors. He called for their
chief—through the intervention of his Indian guide,
we suppose—and Opechancanough came forward.
Smith presented him with a round ivory double
compass-dial, which he had carried at his side. The
savages were confounded by the playing of the fly
and needle, especially as the glass prevented them
from touching what they could see so plainly. He
then gave them a sort of astronomical lecture, demonstrating " by that Globe-like Iewell," as he calls
it, the roundness of the earth, the skies, the sphere of
the sun, moon and stars; "and how the sunne did
chase the night round about the world continually;
the greatnesse of the land and sea, the diversitie of
nations, varietie of complexions, and how we were to
them antipodes, and many other such like matters,"
his tawny auditors standing all the while motionless
and dumb with amazement.

But within about an hour they returned to their
original purpose of killing him, as they had killed
three of his comrades. He was tied to a tree, and
the savages drew up in a circle to shoot him. The
arrow was already laid upon a hundred bows. But
at this moment Opechancanough held up the compass. This was a signal of delay, if not of mercy,
and they threw by their arms at once. With great
exultation and parade they then conducted the cap-

tive to Orapakes, a hunting-residence of Pownatan, lying on the north side of Chickahominy swamp, and much frequented by that Sachem and his family, on account of the abundance of game it afforded. The order of procession was a proper *Indian file.* Opechancanough, marching in the centre, had the English swords and muskets carried before him as a trophy. Next followed Smith, led by three stout savages who held him fast by the arm ; while on either side six more marched in file, with their arrows notched, as flank-guards.

On arriving at Orapakes, a village consisting of some thirty to forty mat-houses, the women and children flocked out to gaze at a being so different from any they had ever before seen. The warriors, on the other hand, immediately began a grand war-dance, the best description of which is in Smith's own language. " A good time they continued this exercise, and then cast themselues in a ring dauncing in such severall postures, and singing and yelling out such hellish notes and screeches ; being strangely paynted, every one his quiver of arrowes, and at his backe a club ; on his arme a fox or an otter's skinne, or some such matter for a vambrace ; their heads and shoulders paynted red, with oyle and pocones * mingled together, which scarlet-like color made an exceeding handsome shew ; his bow in his hand, and the skinne of a bird with her wings abroad dryed, tyed on his head ; a peece of copper, a white shell, a long feather, with a small rattle growing at the tayls of their snaks tyed, or some such like toy." Thrice the performers stopped to take breath, and thrice they renewed the dance—Smith and the Sachem mean while standing in the centre. The company then broke up ; and the prisoner was conducted to a

---

* A small root which turned red by being dried and beat into powder. It was used also for swellings, aches, anointing the joints after fatigue and exposure, and painting garments Beverly calls it *puccoon.*

10—2

long matted wigwam, where thirty or forty tall stout savages remained about him as a guard. Ere long, more bread and venison was brought him than would have served twenty men. " I thinke," says the captain himself, " his stomacke at that time was not very good." He ate something, however, and the remainder was put into baskets, and swung from the roof of the wigwam over his head.

About midnight these liberal provisioners set their fare before him again, never tasting a morsel themselves all the while. But, in the morning, when they brought in a fresh reinforcement, they ate the fragments of former meals, and swung up the residue of the last one as before. So little reason had the captain to complain of famine, that he began seriously to believe they were fatting him for the slaughter. He suffered occasionally from the cold, and would have suffered more but for an unexpected relief. An Indian, named Mocasseter, brought him his *goune*, as Smith calls it—perhaps a fur mantle, or a blanket— and gave it to him, professedly in requital of certain beads and toys which Smith had given *him* at Jamestown, immediately after his arrival in Virginia.*

Two days afterwards, he was violently assaulted, and but for his guard would have been killed, by an old Indian whose son had been wounded in the skirmish which took place at his capture. They conducted him to the death-bed of the poor wretch, where he was found breathing his last. Smith told them he had a kind of water at Jamestown which might effect a cure, but they would not permit him to go for it, and the subject was soon forgotten. Within a few days, they began to make great preparations for assaulting the English Colony by surprise. They

---

* A fine illustration of that principle of gratitude which is as proverbially characteristic of the Indians as their revenge, and for similar reasons. No favor is wasted upon them, and no injury or insult is forgiven. The anecdote following this in the text is an instance in point

craved Smith's advice and assistance in that proceeding, offering him not only life and liberty for
his services, but as much land for a settlement and as
many women for wives as he wanted—such an opinion had they formed of his knowledge and prowess.
He did every thing in his power to discourage their
design, by telling them of the mines, the cannon, and
various other stratagems and engines of war, used by
the English. He could only succeed in prevailing
upon several of them to carry a note for him to
Jamestown, (under pretence of getting some toys,) in
which he informed his countrymen of his own situation and the intention of the savages, and requested
them to send him without fail by the bearers certain
articles which he named. These were to be deposited at a particular spot in the woods near Jamestown. The messengers started off, we are told, in as
severe weather as could be of frost and snow, and
arrived at Jamestown. There, seeing men sally out
from the town to meet them, as Smith had told them
would be the case, they were frightened and ran off.
But the note was left behind; and so coming again
in the evening, they found the articles at the appointed place, and then returned homeward in such haste
as to reach Orapakes in three days after they had
left it.

All thoughts of an attack upon the colony being
now extinguished in the astonishment and terror excited by the feats of Smith, they proceeded to lead
him about the country in show and triumph. First
they carried him to the tribe living on the Youghta-
nund, since called the Pamunkey river; then to the
Mattaponies, the Piankatunks, the Nantaughtacunds
on the Rappahannoc, and the Nominies on Potomac
river. Having completed this route, they conducted
him, through several other nations, to Opechancanough's own habitation at Pamunkey; where, with
frightful howlings and many strange ceremonies,
they 'conjured' him three days in order to ascertain,
as they told him, whether he intended them well or

ill.* An idea may be formed of these proceedings, which took place under Opechancanough's inspection, from the exercises for one day as described by the captive himself.

Early in the morning, a great fire was made in a long house, and mats spread upon each side of it, on one of which the prisoner was seated. His body-guard then left the house, "and presently came skipping in a great grim fellow, all paynted over with coale, mingled with oyle; and many snakes and wesels skinnes stuffed with mosse, and all their tayles tyed together, so as they met on the croune of his head in a tassell; and round about the tassell was a coronet of feathers, the skinnes hanging round about his head, backe and shoulders, and in a manner covered his face; with a hellish voyce and a rattle in his hand." This personage commenced his invocation with a great variety of gestures, postures, grimaces and exclamations; and concluded with drawing a circle of meal round the fire. Then rushed in three more performers of the same description, their bodies painted half red and half black, their eyes white and their faces streaked with red patches, apparently in imitation of English whiskers. These three having danced about for a considerable time, made way for three more, with red eyes, and white streaks upon black faces. At length all seated themselves opposite to the prisoner, three on the right hand of the first named functionary (who appeared to be the chief priest, and ringleader) and three on the left. Then a song was commenced, accompanied with a violent use of the rattles; upon which the chief priest laid down five *wheat-corns,*† and began an oration, straining his arms and hands so that he perspired freely, and his veins swelled. At the conclusion, all gave a groan of assent, laid down three

---

* Stith, p. 53.

† An inadvertency, we presume; or the words may be used rather loosely to signify what had as yet no distinctive name Indian corn must be meant.

grains more, and renewed the song. This went
on until the fire was twice encircled. Other ceremonies of the same character ensued, and last of
all was brought on, towards evening, a plentiful
feast of the best provisions they could furnish The
circle of meal was said to signify their country,
the circles of corn the bounds of the sea, and so on.
The world, according to their theory, was round and
flat, like a trencher, and themselves located precisely
in the midst.

After this, they showed Smith a bag of gun-
powder, which had probably been taken from the
boat, and which they were carefully preserving till
the next spring, to plant with their corn—"because
they would be acquainted with the nature of that
seede." OPITCHIPAN, another brother of Powhatan
—of whom we have here the first mention—invited
him to *his* house, and treated him sumptuously ; but
no Indian, on this or any other occasion, would eat
with him. The fragments were put up in baskets ;
and upon his return to Opechancanough's wigwam,
the Sachem's wives and their children flocked about
him for their portions, "as a due by custom, to be
merry with such fragments."

At last they carried him to Werowocomoco, where
was Powhatan himself. This residence of his, lay
on the north side of York river, in Gloster county,
nearly opposite the mouth of Green's creek and about
twenty five miles below the mouth of the river. It
was at this time his favorite village, though afterwards, not coveting the near neighborhood of the
English, he retired to Orapakes. Powhatan, which
gave him his name, was sold to the English in 1609.

On his arrival in the village, Smith was detained
until the emperor (as we shall call him, for convenience,) and his train could prepare themselves to
receive their illustrious captive in proper state · and
meanwhile more than two hundred of these grim
courtiers gathered about him to satisfy their curiosity
with gazing. He was then introduced to the royal

presence, the multitude hailing him with a tremen
dous shout, as he walked in.   Powhatan—a majestic
and finely formed savage, with a marked countenance,
and an air of haughtiness sobered down into gravity
by a life of sixty years—was seated before a fire
upon a seat something like a bedstead, and clothed
in an ample robe of *Rarowcun** skins, with all the
tails hang'ng over him.   On each side sat a young
wench of sixteen or eighteen years old ; and along
each wall of the house, two rows of women in the
rear and two rows of men in front.   All had their
heads and shoulders painted red.   Many had their
hair decked with the white down of birds.   Some
wore a great chain of white beads about their necks.
But no one was without ornament of some kind.

Soon after Smith's entrance, a female of rank,
said to be the queen of Appamattuck, was directed
to bring him water to wash his hands ; and another
brought a bunch of feathers, to answer the purpose
of a towel.   Having then feasted him (as he acknowledges) in the best barbarous manner they
could, a long and solemn consultation was held to
determine his fate.   The decision was against him.
The conclave resumed their silent gravity ; two great
stones were brought in before Powhatan ; and Smith
was dragged before them, and his head laid upon
them, as a preparation for beating out his brains
with clubs.   The fatal weapons were already raised,
and the savage multitude stood silently awaiting the
prisoner's last moment.   But Smith was not destined
thus to perish.   Pocahontas, the beloved daughter
of Powhatan, rushed forward, and earnestiy entreated with tears that the victim might yet be spared.
The royal savage rejected her request, and the exe-
cutioners stood ready for the signal of death.   She
knelt down, put her arms about Smith, and laid her
head over his, declaring she would perish with him
or save him.   The heart of the stern Sachem was

---

* A variation of Racoon, perhaps.

at length melted. The decree was reversed ; and the prisoner was spared for the purpose—as the emperor explained it—of making hatchets for himself, and bells and beads for his daughter.*

This was apparently a mere pretext for concealing the emotions which he thought unworthy of his name as a warrior, and for preventing any jealousy on the part of his counsellors. And subsequent events would lead to the same conclusion. He detained his prisoner but two days. At the end of that time, he caused him to be conducted to a large house in the woods, and there left alone upon a mat by the fire. In a short time, a horrible noise was heard from behind a wide mat which divided the house : and then Powhatan, dressed in the most fantastic manner, with some two hundred followers as much begrimed and disguised as himself, came in and told Smith that now they were friends ; 'and presently he should go to Jamestown to send him two great guns and a grindstone, for which he would give him the country of Capahowsick, and forever esteem him as his own son.' He was accordingly sent off, with twelve guides, to Jamestown. The party quartered in the woods one night, and reached the fort the next morning betimes. The savages were handsomely entertained while they staid. Two demi-culverins and mill-stone were shown them, with other curiosities. They proposed to carry the former to Powhatan ; but finding them somewhat too heavy, contented themselves with a variety of lighter presents. They were excessively frightened by a discharge of the

---

* This celebrated scene is preserved in a beautiful piece of sculpture, over the western door of the Rotunda of the Capitol at Washington. The group consists of five figures, representing the precise moment when Pocahontas, by her interposition, saved Smith from being executed. Smith is attired in the military dress, reclining on his elbow, his body extended, ready to receive the death-blow from the war-mace of an Indian who stands near his head. This is the work we believe, of Capellano, an Italian pupil of Canova

culverins.—Smith, who had political as well as personal motives in view, had loaded them with stones,
and these he fired among the boughs of a tree covered with huge icicles. The effect may easily be imagined.

During the same winter, Smith visited Powhatan,
in company with Captain Newport, a gentleman
newly arrived from England, who had already sent
many presents to the emperor. Attended by a guard
of thirty or forty men, they sailed as far as Werowo-
moco the first day. Here Newport's courage failed
him. He was especially alarmed by the appearance
of various bridges they were obliged to pass over in
crossing the streams ; for these were so loosely made
of poles and bark, that he took them for traps set by
the savages. But Smith, with twenty men, leaving the
boat, undertook to go forward and accomplish the
journey. He accordingly went on, and was soon
met by two or three hundred Indians, who conducted
them into the town. There Powhatan exerted himself to the utmost to give him a royal entertainment.
The people shouted for joy to see Smith ; orations
were addressed to him ; and a plentiful feast provided
to refresh him after the weariness of his voyage. The
emperor received him, reclining upon his bed of
mats, his pillow of dressed skin lying beside him
with its brilliant embroidery of shells and beads, and
his dress consisting chiefly of a handsome fur robe
" as large as an Irish mantell." At his head and feet
were two comely young women as before ; and along
the sides of the house sat twenty other females, each
with her head and shoulders painted red and a great
chain of white beads about her neck. " Before these
sat his chiefest men in like order in his arbor-like
house, and more than fortie platters of fine bread
stood as a guard in two pyles on each side the door.
Foure or fiue hundred people made a guard behinde
them for our passage ; and Proclamation was made,
none vpon paine of death to presume to doe vs any
wrong or discourtesie. With many pretty discourses

to renew their old acquaintance, this great King and our captaine spent the time, till the ebbe left our barge aground. Then renewing their feest with feates, daunсing and singing, and such like mirth, we quartered that night with Powhatan."*

The next day, Newport, who had thought better of his fears, came ashore, and was welcomed in the same hospitable style. An English boy, named Savage, was given to Powhatan at his request; and he returned the favor by presenting Newport with an Indian named Nomontack, a trusty and shrewd servant of his own. One motive for this arrangement was probably the desire of gaining information respecting the English colony. During the three or four days more which were passed in feasting, dancing and trading, the old Sachem manifested so much dignity and so much discretion, as to create a high admiration of his talents in the minds of his guests. In one instance, he came near offending them by the exercise of his shrewdness, although that may be fairly considered their fault rather than his.

Newport, it seems, had brought with him a variety of articles for a barter commerce—such as he supposed would command a high price in corn. And accordingly the Powhatans, generally of the lower class, traded eagerly with him and his men. These, however, were not profitable customers; they dealt upon a small scale; they had not much corn to spare. It was an object therefore to drive a trade with the emperor himself. But this he affected to decline and despise. "Captain Newport," said he, "it is not agreeable to my greatness to truck in this peddling manner for trifles. I am a great Werowance,† and I esteem you the same. Therefore lay me down all your commodities together; what I like I will take, and in return you shall have what I conceive to be

* Smith's History, Richmond Edition, p. 167.
† A Powhatan term of general signification, answering to the Northern *Sachem*, the *Busheba* of Maine, and the English *Chief*.

I.—C

a fair value." This proposal was interpreted to Newport by Smith, who informed him at the same time of the hazard he must incur in accepting it. But Newport was a vain man, and confidently ex pected either to dazzle the emperor with his ostentation, or overcome him with his bounty, so as to gain any request he might make. The event unluckily proved otherwise. Powhatan, after coolly selecting such of Newport's goods as he liked best, valued his own corn at such a rate, that Smith says it might as well have been purchased in old Spain; they received scarcely four bushels where they had counted upon twenty hogsheads.

It was now Smith's turn to try his skill; and he made his experiment, more wisely than his comrade, not upon the sagacity of the emperor but upon his simplicity. He took out various toys and gewgaws, as it were accidentally, and contrived, by glancing them dexterously in the light, to show them to great advantage. It was not long before Powhatan fixed his observing eye upon a string of brilliant blue beads. Presently he became importunate to obtain them. But Smith was very unwilling to part with these precious gems; they being, as he observed, composed of a most rare substance, of the color of the skies, and fit to be worn only by the greatest kings in the world. The savage grew more and more eager to own such jewels, so that finally a bargain was struck, to the perfect satisfaction of all parties, whereby Smith obtained between two and three hundred bushels of corn for a pound or two of blue beads. A similar negotiation was immediately after effected with Opechancanough at Pamunkey. He was furnished with a quantity of this invaluable jewelry at very nearly the same price; and thus the beads grew into such estimation among the Indians far and near, that none but the great werowances, and their wives and children, dared to be seen wearing them. They were imperial symbols of enormous value.

But it was not upon beads only that Powhatan set a high estimate. He perceived the vast advantage which the English possessed over his own men in their weapons; and he became exceedingly anxious to place himself upon equal terms on one side with the colonists, while he should domineer over the less fortunate foreign Indian tribes, as he liked, on the other. When Newport left the country for England, he sent him twenty fine turkeys, and requested in return the favor of as many swords, which that gentleman was inconsiderate enough to furnish him. He subsequently passed the same compliment to Smith; and when the latter gave him no swords in payment, he was highly offended, and is said to have ordered his people to take them wherever they could get them, by stratagem or by force. But Smith soon checked this project in his usual summary manner; and Powhatan, finding that game a desperate one, sent in *Pocahontas* with presents, to excuse himself for the injury done "by some of his disorderly warriors,' and to desire that those who were captive might be liberated for this time on their good behavior. Smith punished them sufficiently, and granted the request of the emperor 'for the sake of Pocahontas. The council were offended at what they considered his cruelty; but Powhatan affected at least to be satisfied.

We hear of the emperor again in September, (1608,) when Captain Newport arrived with a second supply for the colony, and a new commission for himself. By this he was authorized to make an exploring expedition, *for gold*, among the Monacans of the mountain country; and a barge was brought out from England in five pieces, to be carried over the falls, and thence convey the company *to the South Sea*. Smith opposed this sage proposal on the ground of the necessities of the colony; they were especially in want of provision to be laid in for the coming winter. But a large majority were against him. He was even accused of jealousy towards Newport; and

the latter defeated all his opposition, as he thought,
by undertaking to procure a bark-load of corn from
Powhatan, on his proposed route to the South Sea,
at Werowocomoco. He required, however, that one
hundred and twenty men should go with him; he
put no confidence in the friendship of the emperor
or his subjects.

Smith now came forward, and volunteered to carry
the necessary messages to Powhatan himself, and
to invite him to visit Jamestown, for the purpose of
receiving the presents brought over for him by Newport. Among these, it appears, were a splendid ba-
sin and ewer, a bed, bedstead, clothes, and various
other costly novelties; the only effect of which would
be, as Smith alleged, to cause the emperor to over-
rate the importance of his own favor, and to sell
for gold and silver alone what he had heretofore sold
readily for copper and blue beads. Another of the
presents was a royal crown, sent out by his Britannic
Majesty King James I. probably under the expectation of wheedling Powhatan into submission to his
own authority, and at all events with orders to con-
secrate the " divine right" of his royal ally in Virginia
by the ceremonies of a solemn coronation.

Smith took with him four companions only, and
went across the woods, by land, about twelve miles,
to Werowocomoco. Powhatan was then absent, at
the distance of twenty or thirty miles. Pocahontas
immediately sent for him, and meanwhile she and
her women entertained their visiter in a style too
remarkable to be passed by without notice. A fire
was made in a plain open field, and Smith was seated
before it on a mat, with his men about him. Suddenly such a hideous noise was heard in the woods near
by, that the strangers betook themselves hastily to
their arms, and even seized upon two or three old
Indians who were standing near, under the apprehension that Powhatan with all his forces was come upon
them by surprise. But Pocahontas soon made her
appearance; and a little explanation convinced the

captain that, however she might succeed or fail, her
only intention was to gratify and honor him. He
mingled fearlessly therefore with the Indian men,
women and children, already assembled as spectators,
and the ceremonies went on.

"Then presently they were presented with this
anticke. Thirtie young women came naked out of
the woods, only couered behind and before with a
few greene leaves ; their bodies all paynted, some of
one colour, and some of another but all differing.
Their leader had a fayre payre of Buck's hornes on
her head, and an Otter's skinne at her girdle, another
at her arme, a quiuer of arrowes at her backe, a
bow and arrowes in her hand. The next had in her
hand a sword, another a club, another a pot-sticke,
all horned alike ; the rest euery one with their
severall devises. These fiends, with most hellish
shouts and cryes, rushing from among the trees, caste
themselves in a ring about the fire, singing and
dauncing with the most excellent ill varietie, oft
falling into their infernall passions, and solemnly
again to sing and daunce. Having spent neer an
hour in this mascarado, as they entred, in like manner they departed."

" Having reaccomodated themselves, they solemnly
invited him to their lodgings, where he was no sooner
within the house but all these nymphs more tormented him than euer, with crowding, pressing and hanging about him, most tediously crying, Loue you not
me? Loue you not me? This salutation ended,
the feast was set, consisting of all the salvage dainties
they could deuise ; some attending, others singing
and dauncing about them. This mirth being ended,
with fire-brands instead of torches they conducted
him to his lodging.

Thus did they show their feates of armes, and others art in dauncing ;
Some others vs'd there oaten pipe, and others' voyces chaunting."

Powhatan arrived on the following day, and Smith
delivered his message, desiring him to visit " his
father " Newport, at Jamestown, for the purpose of

receiving the newly arrived presents, and also con
certing a campaign in common *against the Monacans.*
The subtle savage replied to this artful proposal with
his accustomed intelligence and independence.   " If
your king has sent me presents," said he with great
composure, " I also am a king, and this is my land—
Here I will stay eight days to receive them. *Your
Father* is to come to me, not I to him, nor yet to
your fort.   I will not bite at such a bait.   As for the
Monacans, I can avenge my own injuries.   As for
Atquanachuck, where you say your brother was
slain, it is a contrary way from those parts you
suppose it.   And as for any salt water beyond the
mountains, the relations you have had from my people are false."   Upon this he began to delineate the
geography of these various regions with a stick upon
the ground.   After some farther discourse upon
general and complimentary subjects, Smith returned
with his answer.   His servant, Namontack, who had
been to England with Newport, was given back to
him upon this occasion.

The presents were sent round to Werowocomoco,
by water ; and the two captains went by land, with
a guard of fifty men.   The parties here agreed upon
the next day for the coronation ; and at that time the
presents were brought in, the bed and furniture set
up, and the scarlet cloak and other apparel put on
the emperor, though with much ado, and only in
consequence of Nomantack's earnest assurance that
they would not injure him.   As for kneeling to receive the crown, which was requested of him, he entirely exhausted the patience of his visiters by his resistance.   They gained their point in the end by
stratagem.   One leaned hard upon his shoulders, so
as to cause him to stoop a little, and three more stood
ready to fix the royal gewgaw on his head ; whereupon, at the discharge of a pistol, the guard were
prepared with such a volley of musketry as a salute,
that the emperor (now a *crowned-head* at least) started
up, as Smith says, in a horrible fear till he saw all

was well. Soon recovering his composure, he generously gave his old shoes and mantle to Newport in acknowledgement of his courtesy. But perceiving that the main object of that gentleman was to discover the Monacans, he labored to divert his resolution, and absolutely refused to lend any of his own men excepting Namontack. Every thing was said and done civilly, however; and, before leaving, Newport was presented with a heap of corn-ears to the amount of seven or eight bushels, in farther return for his politeness and his presents.

For some time after this, little was heard of Powhatan except occasionally through the medium of some of his tribes, who are said to have refused trading with the English in consequence of his orders to that effect. He had become jealous of them, it would seem; and Smith, on the other hand, reciprocated so much of his ill humor, that he at one time thought of falling upon him by surprise, and taking away all his stores. But appearances were still kept up on both sides; and in December, (1608) the emperor invited the captain to visit him—he wanted his assistance in building a house, and if he would bring with him a grindstone, fifty swords, a few muskets, a cock and a hen, with a quantity of beads and copper, he might depend upon getting a ship-load of corn. Smith, always ready for an adventure, accepted the invitation, and set off with a pinnace and two barges, manned by forty-six volunteers The expedition was considered so hazardous that many excused themselves from going, after having engaged to do so; though all knew that if any thing was to be had, Smith was not the man to return disappointed.

Commencing his voyage on the 29th of the month, with victualling for three or four days, he lodged the first night at Warrasqueake. The chief Sachem at this place, being friendly, did all in his power to dissuade the captain from pursuing his journey. " Powhatan will use you kindly," said he, " but he has sen

for you only to cut your throat.   Trust him not, and
give him no opportunity to seize upon your arms."
The next night and several more were passed at
Kekoughtan, where the English were detained by a
severe storm, but found merry cheer, and good fires.
The colonists who were in the habit of travelling
with Smith had learned hardihood. "They were not
curious in any weather, (he informs us,) to lye three
or foure nights together vnder the trees."   They liked
hunting too as they marched, and here was a fine
opportunity ; " an hundred fortie eight foules, the
President, Anthony Bagnall, and Serieant Pising did
kill at three shoots."   It was the 12th of January
when they reached Werowocomoco.

They went ashore, quartered without much ceremony at the first house they found, and sent to
Powhatan for a supply of provisions.   They were
promptly furnished with plenty of bread, venison and
turkeys.   Their liberal host feasted them again the
next day ; but not without inquiring, at the close of
the entertainment, when they proposed to go home,
insinuating that the pleasure of their company was
wholly unexpected, and that he and his people had
very little corn—though *for forty swords* he thought
forty baskets might be collected.   In reply, Smith
asked if he had forgotten his own invitation thus
suddenly ; and then produced the messengers who
had carried it, and who happened to be near at hand.
The emperor affected to regard the affair as a mere
joke, and laughed heartily.   Smith then proposed
trade ; but Powhatan would take nothing but guns
and swords, and valued a basket of corn higher
than a basket of copper.   The captain was nettled,
and spoke his mind boldly and without reserve,
giving the emperor to understand withal, that necessity might force him to use disagreeable expedients
for relieving his own wants and the need of the
colony.

Powhatan listened to this declaration with coo
gravity, and replied with a córresponding frankness

"I will spare you what I can," said he, "and that within two days. But, Captain Smith, I have some doubts as to your object in this visit. I am informed that you wish to conquer more than to trade, and at all events you know my people must be afraid to come near you with their corn, so long as you go armed and with such a retinue. Lay aside your weapons, then. Here they are needless. We are all friends, all Powhatans." The information alluded to here was probably gathered from two or three Germans, who had deserted the colony and gone among the Indians.

A great contest of ingenuity now ensued between the Englishman and the savage—the latter apparently endeavoring to temporise only for the purpose of putting the former and his men off their guard. He especially insisted on the propriety of laying aside their arms. "Captain Smith," he continued, "I am old, and I know well the difference between peace and war. I wish to live quietly with you, and I wish the same for my successors. Now the rumors which reach me on all hands make me uneasy. What do you expect to gain by destroying us who provide you with food? And what can you get by war, if we escape you and hide our provisions in the woods? We are unarmed too, you see. Do you believe me such a fool as not to prefer eating good meat, sleeping quietly with my wives and children, laughing and making merry with you, having copper and hatchets and any thing else—as your friend—to flying from you as your enemy, lying cold in the woods, eating acorns and roots, and being so hunted by you meanwhile, that if but a twig break, my men will cry out there comes Captain Smith. Let us be friends, then. Do not invade us thus with such an armed force. Lay aside these arms."

The captain answered this speech, and several others to the same effect, until, either seeing or supposing that the emperor's object was hostile, he gave secret orders for hauling his boat ashore through the

10—3

ice, and landing those of his company who still remained aboard.   He also attempted to detain Powhatan with the delivery of divers rigmarole harangues;
but the latter was not to be so easily outwitted.   He
introduced two or three women to sustain a sharp
conversation with the enemy, and suddenly availed
himself of that opportunity to leave the house, with
all his attendants and luggage.   In a few minutes
Smith found himself surrounded with Indians ; and
thereupon, we are told, "with his pistoll, sword and
target, hee made such a passage among these naked
Diuils, that at his first shoot those next him tumbled
one over another."   The rest fled in all directions.

Powhatan was not yet discouraged.   His men
again flocked about Smith with civil explanations of
every thing which had happened ; and he himself
sent him a large and handsome bracelet by the hand
of one of his chief orators, with a speech full of
compliments and excuses.   Baskets were furnished
for carrying the corn which had been sold aboard
the boat ; and the Indians even offered their services
to guard the arms of the English, while *they* were
taking care of the provisions.   This favor was declined ; but as the English were still under the
necessity of waiting for the tide of the next morning,
no pains were spared to entertain them with feasts
and sports meanwhile.   Smith supposes that the
Sachem was all this time preparing his forces for
surprising them at supper.   He probably conjectured
right; and but for Pocahontas there is reason to believe
that this game would actually have succeeded.   The
kind-hearted princess came to Smith's quarters in the
woods, alone and in the evening, and earnestly advised him by all means to leave her father's territories
as soon as possible.   The latter was collecting all his
power, she said, to make an assault upon him, unless
those who were sent with his supper should themselves succeed in despatching him.

In less than an hour afterwards came eight or ten
lusty fellows, with great platters of venison and other

victuals, who were importunate that the English should *extinguish their matches,* the smoke of which they affected to think very disagreeable. The captain, without noticing this circumstance, made them taste every dish, and then sent some of them back to tell Powhatan that the English were ready to see him ; as for themselves, he understood their villany, but they should go free. Other messengers came in soon after, at intervals, to learn how matters went on. The night was spent without sleep on either side. Each party watched the movements of the other with vigilant eyes, while both were subtle and civil enough still to affect friendship. At high water, Smith went off with his company, leaving with the emperor, at his own request, an Englishman to kill game for him, and two or three of the Germans to assist him in building a house.

But the game was not yet over. He had no sooner set sail for Pamunkey, than the emperor despatched a deputation across the woods to Jamestown, to take advantage of his absence for buying up a quantity of ammunition and arms. On arriving, these messengers told Captain Winne, the temporary commander of the colony, " that their comming was for some extraordinary tooles and shift of apparell ; by which colourable excuse they obtained sixe or seuen more [of the colonists] to their confederacie, such expert cheeues, that presently furnished them with a great many swords, pike-heads, peeces, shot, powder and such like."* Indians enough were at hand to carry away the articles as soon as obtained ; and the next day, the deputation returned home unsuspected, after making an agreement for the services of such traitorous vagabonds as were willing to desert from the colony. One or two of those who had deserted already, had provided Powhatan with as many as three hundred hatchets, fifty swords, eight 'pieces and eight pikes.

---

* Smith's History, p. 213.

Meanwhile, Smith had arrived at Pamunkey, and here Opechancanough was entertaining him with all manner of feasting and mirth. On the day agreed upon between the parties for commencing trade, the captain, with fifteen of his men, went up a quarter of a mile from the river to the Sachem's house, the appointed rendezvous. He found no person there, excepting a lame man and a boy. The other houses in the village were entirely abandoned. Presently, however, came the Sachem, followed by many of his subjects, well armed with bows and arrows. Attempts were made to buy corn, but so unsuccessfully that Smith was provoked, and remonstrated as he had done with Powhatan. Upon this, the Sachem sold what provision was at hand, and promised to give better satisfaction the next day.

Then, accordingly, Smith made his appearance again. He found four or five men at the house with great baskets, but whether with any thing in them does not appear. Opechancanough himself came in soon after, and commenced a cheerful conversation, enlarging particularly upon the pains he had taken to keep his promise. Just at this moment one of Smith's company brought him word that the house was beset. The woods and fields all around him were thronged with more than seven hundred savages, armed and painted for battle.

The English, of whom there were only fifteen on shore, were generally much alarmed at this news, and could easily perceive that Opechancanough enjoyed their surprise. But Smith was now in his element. "My worthy countrymen," said he to his trembling comrades, "Had I no more to fear from my friends, than from these enemies, I should be willing to meet twice as many—would you but second me. But what course shall be taken? If we begin with them, and seize the king, we shall have more than our hands full to keep him and defend ourselves. If we kill them all, we must starve for want of their provisions. As for their fury, that is the

.east subject of apprehension. You know I have heretofore managed two or three hundreds of them alone. Now here are sixteen of us, to their seven hundred. If you dare stand but to fire your pieces, the very smoke will be enough for them. But at all events let us fight like men, and not die like sheep. First, however, let me propose some conditions to them, and so we shall have something to fight for." The occasion admitting of no argument, the company pledged themselves promptly to second him in whatever he attempted, or die.

The captain then advanced towards the Sachem, and addressed him. "Opechancanough," said he, "I perceive you are plotting to murder me, but I fear you not. As yet neither your men nor mine have done much harm. Now therefore take your arms— as you see here are mine—my body shall be as naked as yours—the island in the river is a fit place for a combat, and the conqueror of us two, shall be master of all. If you have not men enough about you, take time to muster more—as many as you will— only let every one bring his basket of corn, and against that I will stake the value in copper."

The Sachem replied very soothingly to this proposal. He was sorry to see any suspicion of unkindness ; and begged that the captain would do him the honor to accept a handsome present, (by way of peace-offering,) which was ready for him at the door of the house. The object of this suggestion was sufficiently obvious ; for besides the forty or fifty Indians con stituting the Sachem's body-guard within, "the bait,' as Smith calls it, at the door, (meaning the present) was guarded by about two hundred men, and thirty more were stationed behind a large tree which lay lengthwise athwart the passage-way with their arrows ready notched. It was now Smith's turn to make a movement. He seized the Sachem in the midst of his retinue, by his long locks, presenting a pistol ready-cocked at his bosom ; and in this position led him out trembling with terror, among the multitude

who surrounded the house. He immediately gave
up his vambrace, bow and arrows, and his frightened
subjects hastened to follow his example.

"I perceive, ye Pamunkies"—shouted the captain
at this moment, still holding on by the Sachem's
hair—"I perceive how eager ye are to kill me. My
own long suffering is the cause of your insolence.
Now shoot but one arrow to shed one drop of blood
for one of these men, or steal but the least of these
beads, and ye shall not hear the last of me so long
as a Pamunkey remains alive who will not deny the
name. I am not *now* in the mire of a swamp, ye
perceive. Shoot then, if ye dare. But at all haz-
ards ye shall load my boat with your corn, or I will
load her with your carcasses. Still, unless you give
me the first occasion, we may be friends, and your
king may go free. I have no wish to harm him or
you."

This speech had its effect. The savages laid aside
their arms, and brought in their commodities for
trade in such abundance, that the English at length
became absolutely weary of receiving them. Once
indeed, in the course of the day, some forty or fifty
stout fellows made a violent rush into the house
when Smith was asleep, and some two hundred
more followed close after them; but by Smith's
usual activity they were soon driven back, and then
the Sachem sent some of his ancients, or counsellors,
to excuse the intrusion. The rest of the day passed in
harmony, and towards night the captain began his
return-voyage down the river, leaving the Sachem
at liberty. Various attempts were made to surprise
him on the route, and he was at one time near being
poisoned to death in his food. On the other hand,
Smith was determined not to go home without his
revenge upon Powhatan. He returned by way of
Werowocomoco for the purpose of seizing him; but
he found, when he reached that village, that the
traitorous Germans had caused the emperor to abandon his new house, and carry off all his family and

provision. Those of the Powhatans who remained, treated the English so indifferently, that the latter had much ado to escape with their lives. They finally reached Jamestown after an absence of six weeks, with a cargo of four hundred and seventy-nine bushels of corn and two hundred pounds of deer-suet, that entire amount having been purchased for twenty-five pounds of copper and fifty pounds of iron and beads.

CHAPTER II.

Conduct of Powhatan after Smith's departure for England, and causes of it—Hostilities resumed—Peace finally effected by the capture of Pocahontas—Manner of gaining this point—Marriage of Pocahontas with John Rolfe—Death and character of Powhatan—His person, manner of living, talents, influence. His method and means of warfare—The discipline of his warriors—The manner in which he availed himself of the English arms and science—Causes of his hostility towards the colonists—His dignity—Shrewdness—Independence—Courtesy—Liberality—-Simplicity—-Affection for his relatives—A review of various opinions entertained of him by various historians.

FROM the date of the expedition of which the particulars have just been given, to the time of Smith's departure for England, a few months subsequent, the English and the Powhatans treated and traded with each other upon tolerably amicable terms. A principal cause of this harmony is to be looked for in several fortunate incidents which went to impress the savage simplicity of one party with an inordinate conception of the superiority of the other.

Soon after the return of the expedition, several articles were stolen at Jamestown by one of the Chickahominy Indians who traded there; and a pistol among the rest. The thief fled, but two of his brothers, suspected of being accessaries in the case, were apprehended. One of them was discharged, to go in search of the offender; and the other was imprisoned, with the understanding that unless the former should be successful in his search within twelve hours, *he* was to be hanged. But for his comfort during that interval, Smith furnished him with victuals, and charcoal for a fire In the evening, the man who had been discharged, returned with the pistol; but the poor fellow in the dungeon was meanwhile very nearly smothered with the smoke of his coal. Those who came to release him took him up for dead. "The other most lamentably bewayled his death, and broke forth into such bitter agonies that the President [Smith] to quiet him, told him that if he would steale no more, he would make him [his brother] alive again; but he little thought he could be recovered. Yet we doing our best with aqua Vita and Vinegar, it pleased God to restore him againe to life, but so drunke and affrighted that he seemed lunaticke, the which as much tormented and grieued the other, as before to see him dead. Of this maladie, vpon promise of their good behavour the President promised to recover him; and so caused him to be layd by a fire to sleepe, who in the morning having well slept had recovered his perfect senses, and then being dressed of his burning, and each a peece of copper given them, they went away so well contented *that this was spread among all the savages for a miracle*, that Captain Smith could make a man alive that was dead."[*]

Another of the incidents just alluded to is as follows. One of Powhatan's subjects, in his zeal to acquire knowledge and some other things, obtained possession of a large bag of gun-powder and the backe, as Smith calls it, of an armour. This ingenious artisan, on his return to Werowocomoco, determined to display these precious prizes to his wondering country-men, and at the same time to exhibit his own extraordinary skill in the management of them. He therefore began drying the powder upon the armour, as he had seen the soldiers do at Jamestown. Unluckily, he dried it too much. An explosion took place, which blew up the proprietor, together with one or two of the spectators who were peeping over his shoulders. Several others were badly scorched, and all horribly frightened; and for some time after powder fell into a general disuse with the savages, much to the benefit of the English.

---

[*] Smith's History, p. 226.

I.—D

These and other similar accidents, we are told, so affrighted Powhatan and his people, that they came in from every quarter with proffers of peace. Sev eral stolen articles were returned, the loss of which had never before been discovered; and whenever an Indian was convicted of theft, wherever he might be found, he was promptly sent in to Jamestown for his punishment. Not long afterwards we find that "so affraide was al those kings and the better sort of the people to displease vs [the colonists] that some of the baser sort that we haue extreamely hurt and punished for their villanies, would hire vs we should not tell it to their kings or countrymen, who would also punish them, and yet returne them to Iames-Toune to content the President for a testimony of their loues."

Still, the prowess and the name of Smith himself were the best preservatives of peace; and he had scarcely left the country for England when matters relapsed into their worst state. About thirty of the English were cut off by Powhatan's men at one time; and of a population of six hundred left in the colony at Smith's departure, there remained at the end of six months only sixty men, women and chi'dren. These were subsisted chiefly upon roots, herbs, acorns, walnuts, berries and now and then a little fish. The skins of horses, and even considerable quantities of starch, were used for food. Others went so far as to disinter and devour the body of an Indian who had been slain and buried. One man killed his wife, "powdered her," and had eaten a part of her before it was known. The poor wretch was hanged for his horrible deed of despair.

Peace was finally effected with Powhatan through the intervention, or rather by the mere medium of Pocahontas, in the following manner. Early in 1613,* two ships arrived at Jamestown with supplies

* This date is mentioned by all the Virginian historians; bu Prince, in his Annals, says that the voyage took place a yea. afterwards Belknap (Am. Biog.) is of the same opinion.

for the colony. These being insufficient, Captain Argall, who commanded one of them, was sent up the Potomac river to trade with the natives for corn. Here Argall formed a particular acquaintance with *Japazaws*, the chief sachem of the Potomacs or Patawomekes, and always a stanch friend of the English. He informed the captain, among other things, that Pocahontas was at this time in his territories, and not far distant, keeping herself in seclusion, and known only to a few trusty friends. What were the reasons which induced her thus to forsake her father's dominions for a foreigner's, does not appear. Stith supposes it was to withdraw herself from being a witness of the frequent butcheries of the English, whose folly and rashness, after Smith's departure, put it out of her power to save them. And very probably, as a later historian suggests,* she had already incurred the displeasure of the emperor by these repeated and futile though highly honorable attempts.

But whatever her motives might be, Argall had no sooner received intelligence of her situation, than he resolved on obtaining possession of her person, as a means—which he had no doubt the colony would thank him for—of effecting a peace with Powhatan. Japazaws seems to have been a well-meaning and honest fellow in general; but the temptation of a large new copper kettle, which Argall held out before him as the promised recompense for his aid and abettance in the case—the consideration of the praiseworthy object proposed to be accomplished by the measure—and last though not least of all, the captain's pledge that Pocahontas should not be harmed while in *his* custody, were sufficient to overcome his scruples. The next thing in order was to induce the princess—as this amiable and talented Indian female has generally been styled —to go on board Argall's boat. To that end, Japa-

---

*Burk's History of Virginia, Vol. I. p. 167

zaws, who had himself seen many of the English vessels before this, induced his wife to affect an extreme curiosity upon the subject, so intolerably importunate that he finally threatened to beat her. The good woman on the other hand actually accomplished a few tears. This happened in the presence of Pocahontas, and the scene was frequently repeated, until at last Japazaws, affecting to be subdued by the manifest affliction of his wife, reluctantly gave her permission to visit the vessel, provided that Pocahontas would have the politeness to go with her.

The princess, always complaisant, and unable to witness any longer the apparent distress of her kind friend and hostess, consented to go on board the ship. There they were civilly welcomed, and first entertained in the cabin. The captain then found an opportunity to decoy Pocahontas into the gun-room, on pretence of conferring there with Japazaws, but really because the kind-hearted Sachem, who had received ere this the brilliant wages of his sin, and began perhaps to relent, was unwilling to be known by the princess to have been concerned in the plot against her liberty. When Argall told her, in his presence, that she must go with him to the colony, and compound a peace between her father and the English, she wept indeed in the bitterness of her soul; as for Japazaws and his wife, they absolutely howled with inconsolable and inconceivable affliction. But the princess recovered her composure on finding herself treated with kindness; and while she turned her face towards the English colony, (which she had not seen since Smith's departure) with something even like cheerfulness at the prospect of doing good, her distressed guardian and his pliant spouse, with their copper kettle filled with toys, trudged merrily back to their own wigwam.

On Argall's arrival at Jamestown, a message was immediately despatched to Powhatan, "that his daughter Pocahontas he loued so dearly, he must ransom with our men, swords, peeces, tooles, &c.

hee trecherously had stolen."* This was not so complimentary or soothing as might have been imagined, it must be allowed (—the courtesy of Smith was no longer in the colony—) and this perhaps was the reason why, much as the unwelcome news of his daughter's captivity is said to have troubled him, he sent no answer to the message for the space of three months. Then, at the further persuasion of the council of Jamestown, he liberated and sent in seven of his English prisoners, with three rusty unserviceable muskets, an axe, a saw, and one canoe laden with corn. They were instructed to say that if Pocahontas should be given up, he would make satisfaction for all the injuries he had done, conclude a perpetual peace, and send in a bonus of five hundred bushels of corn. To this the council replied that his daughter, though they would use her well, could not be restored to him until all the English arms and captives in his possession should be delivered back to the owners. They did not believe, what he or some of his men had asserted, that these arms had been lost, or that the whites who remained with him were free volunteers in his service.

This ungracious message was no more conciliating than the former; nor was any thing more seen or heard of the emperor until the spring of 1614, when a party of one hundred and fifty colonists, well armed, went up his own river to Werowocomoco, taking Pocahontas with them. The Powhatans received them with scornful bravadoes, proudly demanding the purpose of this new invasion. The English answered, that they had brought the emperor's daughter, and that they expected the proper ransom for her, either peaceably or by force. The Powhatans rejoined, that if they came to fight, they were welcome, and should be treated as Captain Ratcliffe† had been. Upon this the English said they would

---

* Smith's History, Vol. II. p. 14.

† Massacred with the thirty colonists mentioned previously in this chapter. He was othe·wise called Sicklemore.

have a more civil answer at least, and forthwith com
menced making rapidly for the shore in their small
boats, the Indians having about the same time begun to let fly their arrows among them. They effected
a landing, and burned and destroyed every thing they
could find. The next day they sailed farther up the
river ; and meeting with a fresh party of Powhatans,
after some altercation and explanation, a truce was
concluded, and messengers were promised to be sent
off for the emperor. This was probably a mere
feint. It was also stated, that the English captives
or deserters had run off, for fear of being hanged by
their countrymen. As for the swords and pieces,
they were to be brought in the next day. But nothing was seen of them, and the English proceeded till
they came to a residence of Powhatan (called Matchot)
where were collected about four hundred of his
warriors, well armed. These men challenged the
English to land ; and when they did so, walked
boldly up and down among them ; demanded a conference with their captain ; and said, that unless
time should be allowed them to send and receive
directions from Powhatan, they would fight for
their own as well as they were able. Other bravadoes passed between the parties, but a truce was
finally agreed upon until noon of the next day.
Meanwhile, two of the brothers of Pocahontas—of
whom this is the first mention—came to see her.
They were delighted to find her in good health, and
promised to do every thing they could to effect her
redemption. Two of the English also set off to visit
Powhatan. They were not admitted to the emperor's presence—for what reason, it is not stated—
but Opechancanough treated them in the most hospitable manner. On their return, the whole party
descended the river to Jamestown.

One of the two messengers last named was John
Rolfe, styled by an old historian,* " an honest gentle-

---

* Ralph Hamer, whose relation is incorporated with some of
the oldest histories of other writers He was subsequently
one of the Council

man and of good behaviour;" but more especially
known by the event which we have now to notice—
his marriage with Pocahontas—between whom and
himself there had been an ardent attachment for
some time. The idea of this connexion pleased
Powhatan so much, that within ten days after Rolfe's
visit, he sent in one of his near relatives named
Opachiko, together with two of his sons, to see (as
says the authority just cited) the manner of the marriage; and to do in that behalf what they were requested for the confirmation thereof, as his deputies.
The ceremony took place about the first of April;
and from that time until the death of the emperor,
which happened in 1618, the most friendly relations were uniformly preserved with himself and
with his subjects.

There are too many memorable passages in the
history of this celebrated chieftain, and too many remarkable traits in his character, to be passed over
with a mere general notice. But, previous to any
other comment, it may be proper to mention certain
facts respecting him, which belong rather to the
curious than to the characteristic class. In the case
of all great men, as well as of many noted men who
are not great, there is a good deal of information
generally to be gathered, which may be interesting
without being strictly important. Powhatan was
both a great and a noted man, though a savage; and
the rude circumstances under which he proved himself the one, and made himself the other, should only
render him the more signally an object of popular
admiration and of philosophical regard.

In person, he is described, by one who saw him
frequently, as a tall well-proportioned man, with a
severe aspect; his head slightly gray; his beard thin
(as that of the Indians always is;) and "of a very
able and hardy body to endure any labor." As he
appeared to be about sixty years of age, when the
English first saw him, in 1607, he was probably about
seventy at his death. He troubled himself but little

with public affairs during his last years, leaving the charge of them chiefly to Opechancanough, as his viceroy, and taking his own pleasure in visiting the various parts of his dominions.

We have already had occasion to observe, that he had as many as three or four places of residence. Werowocomoco was abandoned for Orapakes, with the view of keeping at an agreeable distance from the colonists. The latter became a favorite resort. There, at the distance of a mile from the village, he had a house in which were deposited his royalties and his revenue—skins, copper, beads, red paint, bows and arrows, targets and clubs. Some of these things were reserved for the time of his burial; others were the resources of war. The house itself was more than one hundred feet in length—one historian says fifty or sixty yards—and as it seems to have been frequented only by the Indian priests, probably a sacred character attached to it in the minds of the multitude, which was one of the means of its security. Four rudely-graven images of wood were stationed at the four corners; one representing a dragon, the second a bear, the third a panther, and the fourth a gigantic man—all made evil-favoredly, as we are told, but according to the best workmanship of the natives.

The *state* which Powhatan adopted as emperor, appears in some degree from the preceding details of his history. He is said to have kept about his person from forty to fifty of the tallest men in his dominions; which might be the case in war, and upon occasions of parade and ceremony, more regularly than in peaceable and ordinary times. Every night, four sentinels were stationed at the four corners of his dwelling; and at each half-hour one of the body-guard made a signal to the four sentinels. Want of vigilance on their part was punished with the most exemplary strictness.

According to the universal custom of the North American natives, he kept as many wives as he thought proper; and is represented to have taken no little pleasure in their society. When the English saw him at home, reclining on his couch or platform, there was always one sitting at his head, and another at his feet; and when he sat, two of them seated themselves on either side of him. At his meals, one of them brought him water in a wooden platter to wash his hands, before and after eating; and another attended with a bunch of feathers for a towel. Some were the daughters, and had been the wives of distinguished rivals and enemies, conquered in battle. When he became weary of them, he transferred them as presents to his favorite warriors.

A general proof of the talents of Powhatan may be found in the station which he held, as well as the reputation he enjoyed far and wide among his countrymen. The Indian tribes are democracies. He who rules over them must acquire and sustain his influence by his absolute intellect and energy. Friends and family may assist, occasionally, in procuring rank; but they will not secure the permanent possession of it. Generally, therefore, the head-Sachem may be looked upon as comparatively a model of those qualities which his countrymen esteem suitable to that dignity. He must not only be a warrior, brave, hardy, patient, and indefatigable; but he must show talents for controlling the fortunes and commanding the respect of the community which he governs.

But in this case there is better evidence; and especially in the ultimate extent of Powhatan's government as compared with his hereditary dominions. These included but six tribes of the thirty which were finally subject to him, and all which must have become attached to his rule in consequence of the character maintained and the measures adopted by himself. Among others were the Chickahominies, a very warlike and proud people, numbering from two hundred to five hundred warriors, while the Powhat

10—4

ans proper, (the original nucleus, so to speak, of the emperor's dominion,) numbered less than a hundred. The fear which these savages entertained of him appears on many occasions, and particularly when they embraced an opportunity, in 1611, of exchanging his yoke for that of the English.   They were so desirous of this change—or in other words of procuring what they considered the protection of the new master against the power of the old—that they offered to adopt a national name indicating their subjection. A peace was accordingly concluded on condition—

I. That they should be forever called Tassautessus [Englishmen,] and be true subjects to King James and his deputies.

II. They were neither to kill nor detain any of the colonists, or their cattle, but to return them on all occasions.

III. They should stand ready to furnish three hundred warriors for the colony's service, against the Spaniards *or any other enemy.*

IV. They were not to enter the English settlements, but send word they were new Englishmen, (an obscure provision, meant to prevent confounding them with hostile tribes.)

V. Every fighting man, at the beginning of harvest, was to pay two bushels of corn as a tribute, receiving the same number of hatchets in return.

VI. The eight chief men were to see all this performed, on forfeit of being punished themselves Their salary was to be a red coat, a copper chain, the picture of King James, and the honor of being accounted *his* noblemen.

This treaty was concluded with a general assent, manifested by acclamation ; and then one of the old men began a speech, addressing himself first to those of his own age, then to the young, and lastly to the women and children, a multitude of whom were present.   He gave them to undersand how strictly these conditions must be observed, and how safe

they should t.ien be, on the other hand, "*from the
furie of Powhatan* or any enemie whatsoeuer," *
besides being furnished with arms to resist them.
The name of the emperor, it will be observed, is not
inserted in the articles of peace ; there was supposed
to be a hazard, probably, of its coming to his ears ;
and he had then himself just concluded an amicable
treaty.   " But all this," adds our historian, " was
rather for feare Powhatan and we being so linked
together, would bring them again to his subjection :
the which to preuent, they did rather chuse to be
protected by vs, than tormented by him, whom they
held a Tyrant."

We have seen, that of the whole Indian population
between the sea-coast and the Alleghany from east
to west, and between the borders of Carolina and
the river Patuxent in Maryland from south to north,
all who were not subject to Powhatan's dominions were leagued against him.   The former class
comprised the lowland tribes ; and the latter, the
mountaineers.   In the language of Stith, the Monacans and the Mannahoacks formed a confederacy
against the power and tyranny of Powhatan.   Another
writer says, that he also fought against the famous
Massawomekes ; a powerful and populous nation,
thought to be situated upon a great salt-water,
" which by all probability is either some part of
Cannada, some great lake, or some inlet of some sea
that falleth into the South Sea."   This is not a very
definite description, even for Smith to give ; but the
Massawomekes are generally understood to have been
no other, we believe, than the celebrated Five Nations
of New York.   At all events, they were exceedingly
troublesome to the northernmost tribes of Powhatan
—which might be a principal reason why they submitted the more willingly to him.   And thus, while
the greater part of his own empire was a conquered
one, he was environed by foreign enemies in every

---

* Authorities referred to in Smith's History, Vol. II.

direction, including the civilized colony on the sea-
coast.

As to his particular system of war and conquest,
we are not minutely informed. Like Indian warfare
in other sections and times, it is said to have consisted, in a great degree, of stratagem and surprisal
rather than force. In 1608, a rebellion which arose
among the Payuntatanks, was suppressed in the
following manner. They being near neighbors, a
number of his own tribe was sent into their villages,
who under some disguise or false pretence obtained
lodgings over night. The several houses were
meanwhile beset with ambuscades : and at an appointed signal, the two parties, within and without,
commenced an attack at the same moment. Twenty-
four Payuntatanks were slain, and their scalps carried
to Powhatan, who kept them some time suspended on
a line between two trees, as a trophy. The women and
children, as also the Werowance or Sachem, were
made prisoners, and afterwards slaves or servants.

Powhatan's warriors were regularly and thoroughly
disciplined. At one of his first interviews with the
English, a martial parade formed part of the entertainment. Two or three hundred Indians having
painted and disguised themselves in the fiercest manner possible, were divided into two companies, one
of which was temporarily styled Powhatans and the
other Monacans. Each company had its captain.
They stationed themselves at about a musket-shot
from each other. Fifteen men abreast formed the
front line of both, and the remainder ranked themselves in the rear with a distance of four or five
yards from rank to rank ; and not in file, but in the
opening between the files, so that the rear could
shoot as conveniently as the front. A parley now
took place, and a formal agreement was made that,
whoever should conquer, such warriors as survived
their defeat should have two days allowed them for
their own submission, while their wives and children
should at once become prize to the victor.

The parties advanced against each other -a sort
of sergeant commanding each flank, and a lieu-
tenant the rear: and the entire company came on
leaping and singing to warlike music, but every man
in his place. On the first flight of arrows, they
raised upon both sides a terrific clamor of shouts
and screeches. " When they had spent their arrows,
(writes the describer of this scene,) they joined togeth
er prettily, charging and retiring, every rank seconding
the other. As they got advantage, they caught their
enemies by the hair of the head, and down he came
that was taken. His enemy with his wooden sword
seemed to beat out his brains, and still they crept to the
rear to maintain the skirmish." The Monacan party
at length decreasing, the Powhatans charged them
in the form of a half moon. The former retreat, to
avoid being enclosed, and draw their pursuers upon
an ambuscade of fresh men. The Powhatans retire
in their turn, and the Monacans take this opportunity
of resuming their first ground. "All their actions,
voices and gestures, both in charging and retiring,
were so strained to the height of their qualitie and
nature, that the strangeness thereof made it seem very
delightful." The warlike music spoken of above was
a large deep platter of wood, covered with skin
drawn so tight as to answer the purpose of a drum.
They also used rattles made of small gourds or
pompion-shells; and all these—it may well be supposed—mingled with their voices, sometimes twenty
or thirty together, "made such a terrible noise, as
would rather affright than delight any man."
   It was probably by no little drilling of this descrip·
tion that Powhatan made soldiers of his subjects,
and it naturally enough mortified him, after taking
so much trouble with so much success, to see them
defeated so readily as they were by the English.
The chief cause, too, of this superiority, was a matter
of wonder. No Indian had ever before seen any
thing which resembled, in form or effect, the firearms of their strange enemy. For some time, there-

fore, their fear was attended with a superstitioi
against which no courage could prevail.   But Pow
hatan was not long in determining at all events to pui
himself on equal terms with the colonists, whatever
might be the hazard; and from that moment he
spared no efforts to effect his purpose. On Newport's
departure for England, he bargained away from him
twenty swords for twenty turkeys. He attempted the
same trade with Smith; and when the latter shrewdly declined it, his eagerness became such, we are told,
'that at last by ambuscadoes at our very gates they
[the Powhatans] would take them per force, surprise
vs at worke, or any way."*   Some of these troublesome fellows being seized and threatened, they
confessed that the emperor had ordered them to get
possession of the English arms, or at least some of
them, cost what it might.

He availed himself, with great ingenuity, of a disposition among some of the colonists to trade privately in these contraband articles ; and in that way
obtained large quantities of shot, powder and pike-
heads.   So, upon Smith's departure for the settlement, after his famous visit, in December, 1608, he
artfully requested the captain "to leaue him Edward
Brynton *to kille him foule,* and the Dutchmen *to finish his house.*"   This house, we have seen, was abandoned; and as for fowl, the idea of employing an
Englishman to hunt for his Powhatans was absurd.
He had no objection, however, to Brynton's gun oi
his martial services.   The Germans lie was probably
sure of already.   They proved traitors to the colony,
and soon after we find them diligently engaged in
arming and instructing the savages.   One of them
subsequently stated, that the emperor kept them at
work for him in duresse.   He himself sent answer
to Smith's demand for them, that they were at liberty to go if they chose—but as for carrying them fifty
miles on his back, he was not able.   The adroitness

---

* Smith's History., Vol. I.

with which he obtained arms at Jamestown, during Smith's absence, has already been the subject of comment.

The implicit obedience which he exacted of his own subjects, notwithstanding the apparently precarious tenure by which he held his command, is a striking indication of the extent of his mere personal influence. "When he listeth," says an old writer, "his will is a law, and must be obeyed: not onely as a King, but as halfe a God, they esteeme him. What he commandeth they dare not disobey in the least thing. At his feete they present whatsoever he commandeth, and at the least froune of his browe, their greatest spirits will tremble with feare." This sub ordination was sustained by measures which, for se verity and courage, would do no discredit to the most absolute despot of the Eastern world. On one occasion, certain offenders were burned to death in the midst of an immense heap of glowing coals, collected from many fires made for the purpose. A more merciful punishment was by braining the criminal with a club, as Smith was to have been sacrificed. The most horrible was fastening the poor wretch to a tree, breaking his joints one by one, and then whittling down the body with reeds and shells. Thrashing with cudgels was no trifle. Smith says he saw a man subjected to this discipline under the hands of two of his practised countrymen, till he fell prostrate and senseless; but he uttered no cry or complaint.

The extraordinary native shrewdness of Powhatan was abundantly manifested in the amusing advantages he obtained over Newport; his long and artful conversations with Smith, some of them sustained under the most embarrassing circumstances, merely to procure time; the promptness with which he rejected and defeated the proposal to make common cause against the Monacans—a bait, as he expressed it, too foolish to be taken; and, in fine, upon every occasion when the English undertook to negotiate or to argue with him.   He availed himself most essentially of the aid of the German deserters heretofore mentioned, but he had too much sagacity to trust them after they deserted *himself;* and so, when two of them fled to him a second time, with proposals for delivering his great rival, Captain Smith, into his hands, he only observed, that men who betrayed the captain would betray the emperor, and forthwith ordered the scoundrels to be brained upon the spot.*

Powhatan, like many others of his race, has been regarded with prejudice for the very reasons which entitle him to respect.   He was a troublesome enemy to the colonists.   His hostile influence extended for hundreds of miles around them; cutting off commerce with the natives in the first place, and making inveterate enemies of them in the next.   Powhatan, we are told, " still as he found means cut off their boats, and denied them trade ;"† and again, " as for corne, contribution and provision from the salvages, we had nothing but mortall wounds, with clubs and arrowes."   Here, too, we find the emperor availing himself of the disasters and despair of the colony, to procure swords, muskets and ammunition—so reckess had the colonists become through famine.

Still, it does not appear, that Powhatan adopted any policy but such as he believed indispensable to he welfare, not to say the existence, of his sovereign dominions.   His warfare was an Indian warfare, indeed.   But setting aside those circumstances of education and of situation which rendered this a matter both of pride and necessity, it may be safely said, that he but followed the example of those who should have known better.   Not only did he act *generally* in self-defence against what he deemed the usurpation of a foreign and unknown people, who had settled without permission upon his shores ; but he was galled and provoked by peculiar provocations

---

* Stith Book III.
† Authorities in Smith's History, Vol. II

in numerous instances. The mere liberty of taking possession of a part of his territory might have been overlooked. Probably it was so. In the earliest days of the settlement, when nothing could be easier for Powhatan than to extinguish it at a single assault, it is acknowledged that his people often visited the English and treated them with kindness.* Not long afterwards, indeed, they committed some trespasses, but meanwhile a party of the English had invaded the interior of the country. Considering the dissolute and unprincipled character of a large part of them, it is not improbable that still greater freedom was exercised with the Indians; such of course as the historians would be likely neither to record nor to know. And yet Smith himself has told enough—*of* himself—to make this point clear. In his very first expedition after corn, seeing, he says, "that by trade and courtesie nothing was to be had, *he made bold to try such conclusions as necessitie inforced.*" He let fly a volley of musketry, ran his boats ashore, skirmished with the natives, and forcibly obtained a supply of provisions. And thus —adds the scrupulous captain—

> "Thus God vnboundlesse by his power
> Made them so kinde would vs devour."

It was nothing to the emperor, or to his subjects, that Smith went beyond his authority in these matters. "The patient councill"—he writes in another connexion — "that nothing would moue to warre with the saluages, would gladly have wrangled with Captaine Smithe for his crueltie." He adds, that *his* proceedings—his *conclusions*, is his own language— had inspired the natives with such fear, that his very name was a terror. No wonder that he sometimes had peace and war twice in a day. No wonder that scarcely a week passed without some villany or other. Again, when the Chickahominies refused to trade, the President, "percieving [supposing] it was

---

* Ibid, Vol. I

Powhatan's policy to starve him," landed his com
pany forthwith, and made such a show of anger and
ammunition that the poor savages presently brought
in all their provisions.

So we are summarily informed in Mr. Hamer's
relation, that about Christmas (1611) "in regard of
the iniurie done vs by them of Apamatuk, Sır Thomas
Dale, without the losse of any *except some few Salvages,*" took possession of the territory and provision
of the tribe, made a settlement upon the former without ceremony, and called it New Bermudas! One
more illustration must suffice. It is a passage of
Smith's history relating to a detachment of vagabonds,
under the command of one West, who left Jamestown, and located themselves not far from Powhatan's
residence at the falls of the river. "But the worst
was, that the poore Salvages that daily brought in
their contributions to the President, that disorderly
company so tormented these poore soules, by stealing
their corne, robbing their gardens, beating them,
breaking their houses, and keeping some prisoners,
that they daily complained to Captaine Smith he had
brought them for Protectors worse enemies than the
Monacans themselves, which though till then for his
love they had endured, they desired pardon if hereafter they defended themselves—since he would not
correct them as they had long expected he would."
A most reasonable determination, civilly and candidly
expressed.

But, whatever may be said of the motives or method
of the warfare of Powhatan, it must be acknowledged
that his character appears to no disadvantage in
peace. We cannot but admire the Roman dignity
with which he rejected all offers of compromise, so
long as the English seemed disposed to take advantage of their own wrong in the violent seizure of
Pocahontas. They knew that this was his favorite
child, and they presumed on the strength of his attachment. But, much as her situation troubled him,
he would not sacrifice his honor s far as to nego-

tiate for her restoration on derogatory terms. He was afflicted, but he was still more incensed. When, however, he ascertained, by sending his sons to visit her, that she was well treated, and in good health, (though, we are somewhere told, "they had heard to the contrarie,") he began to think better of the offers of peace. Then came Rolfe "to acquaint him with the businesse," and kindly he was entertained, though not admitted to the presence of Powhatan. The young gentleman explained himself, however, to the emperor's brother; and the latter promised to intercede for him, as did also the two sons. Their explanations proved successful. The emperor was not only convinced that his daughter was entertained civilly by the English, but he was pleased with the honorable intentions and touched by the passionate and tender affection of Rolfe. No sooner, therefore, did the time appointed for the marriage come to his knowledge—and no doubt Rolfe had already had the politic courtesy to apply for his consent—than he despatched three members of his own family to confirm the ceremony. "And ever since," adds the historian, "we have had friendly trade and commerce, as well with Powhatan himselfe, as all his subjects." So jealous were he and they of injustice; and so susceptible were they, at the same time, of mild and magnanimous impressions.

We find characteristic anecdotes, to the same effect, in the curious account Mr. Hamer has left on record of a visit which he paid the emperor in 1614, soon after the conclusion of peace. After some conversation upon business matters, the visiter was invited to Powhatan's own residence, where was a guard of two hundred warriors, which, (as Mr. Hamer supposes,) always attended his person. Having offered that gentleman a pipe of tobacco, he immediately inquired after the health of Sir Thomas Dale, at that time President, and *then* of his own daughter and her husband; wishing to know especially how these two liked each other. Hamer answered, that

Sir Thomas was perfectly well; and as for Pocahontas, she was so contented, that she never would
return to her father's court again if she could. Powhatan laughed heartily at this reply, and soon after
asked the particular cause of Mr. Hamer's present
visit. On being told it was *private*, he ordered his
attendants to leave the house, excepting only the two
females—said to have been Indian queens—who always sat by him, and then bade Mr. Hamer proceed
with his message.

The latter began with saying, that he was the bearer
of sundry presents from Sir Thomas Dale, which
were delivered accordingly, much to the emperor's
satisfaction. He then added, that Sir Thomas, hearing of the fame of the emperor's youngest daughter,
was desirous of obtaining her hand in marriage. He
conceived, there could not be a finer bond of union
between the two people, than such a connexion;
and besides, her sister Pocahontas was exceedingly
anxious to see her at Jamestown. He hoped that
Powhatan would at least oblige himself so much, as
to suffer her to visit the colony when *he* should return.

Powhatan more than once came very near inter-
rupting the delivery of this message. But he controlled himself, and replied with great gravity to the
effect, that he gladly accepted the President's salutation of love and peace, which he certainly should
cherish so long as he lived; that he received with
many thanks the presents sent him as pledges thereof;
but that, as for his daughter, he had sold her, only a
few days before, to a great Werowance, living at the
distance of three days' journey, for three bushels of
Rawrenoke [Roanoke]. Hamer took the liberty to
rejoin, that a prince of his greatness might no doubt
recall his daughter, if he would—especially as she was
only twelve years of age—and that in such a case he
should receive for her from the President, three times
the worth of the Roanoke, in beads, copper and
hatchets.

To this Powhatan readily rejoined, that he loved his daughter as his life; and though he had many children, he delighted in her most of all. He could not live without seeing her, and *that* would be impossible if she went among the colonists, *for he had resolved upon no account to put himself in their power, or to visit them.* He therefore desired Mr. Hamer to say no more upon the subject; but to tell the President in his name. 1. That *he* desired no other assurance of the *President's* friendship than his word which was already pledged. He had himself, on the other hand, already given such assurance in the person of Pocahontas. *One was sufficient, he thought, at one time; when she died, he would substitute another in her stead.* But, meanwhile, he should consider it no brotherly part to bereave him of two children at once. 2. Though he gave *no* pledge, the President ought not to distrust him or his people. There had been already lives enough lost on both sides; and by his fault there should never be any more. He had grown old, and desired to die peaceably. He should hardly fight even for just cause; the country was wide enough, and he would rather retreat. "Thus much," he concluded, "I hope will satisfy my brother. And so here, as you are weary and sleepy, we will end." He then ordered a supper and good lodgings for his guest, and the latter took his leave for the night.

Early the next morning, Powhatan himself visited Mr. Hamer at his lodging-place, and invited him to return to his own wigwam. There he entertained him in his handsomest manner. The time passed pleasantly, and Mr. Hamer began to feel at home. By and by came in an Englishman, one who had been surprised in a skirmish three years before at Fort Henry, and detained ever since. He was so completely savage in his complexion and dress, that Hamer only recognised him by his voice. He now asked that gentleman to obtain leave for him to re turn with *him* to the colony; and the request was

accordingly made, and even pressed.   The emperor
was vexed at length.   "Mr. Hamer," said he, " you
have one of my daughters, and I am content.   But
you cannot see one of your men with me, but you
must have him away or break friendship.   But take
him, if you will.   In that case, however, you must go
home without guides [which were generally offered
the English on these occasions]: and if any evil
befalls you, thank yourselves."

Hamer replied that he would do so; but he would
not answer for the consequences, if any accident
should happen.   The emperor was incensed at this,
and left him; but he appeared again at supper time,
feasted his guest with his best fare, and conversed
cheerfully.   About midnight he roused Hamer from
a nap, to tell him he had concluded to let Parker
(the captive,) go with him in the morning.   But he
must remind Sir Thomas to send him, in consideration thereof, ten large pieces of copper, a shaving-
knife, a grindstone, a net, and sundry fish-hooks and
other small matters   For fear Hamer should forget
these particulars, he made him write a list of them
in what the historians call *a table-book*, which he
produced.   "However he got it,"[*] says the narrator,
" it was a faire one, and I desired hee would give it
me."   Powhatan evaded this modest request by saying that he kept it to show to strangers; but when
his guest left him in the morning, he furnished him
and his attendants with ample provision for his journey, gave each of them a buck's-skin, " as well
dressed as could be," and sent two more to his son-
in-law and his daughter.

There is much matter for reflection in this simple
narrative.   The sagacity of Powhatan in discerning
the true object of the visit, is worthy of the fearless
dignity with which he exposed it.   He gave little

---

[*] Probably of some English captive.   Smith wrote his famous letter to Jamestown, during his first captivity, on what he
calls the leaf of a table-book.

ced, it would seem to the pretext of marriage; and considering only the age of his daughter—especially as compared with the President's—there was reason enough why he should. His conjectures were undoubtedly correct, and he had some right to be offended at the jealousy which was still harbored by the colonists. Stith expressly states, that the policy of Sir Thomas was merely to obtain an additional pledge for the preservation of peace.*

The affection which Powhatan here manifests for his children, his hospitality even to one who took liberties upon the strength of it, his liberality, the resolution with which he maintained peace while he still evidently distrusted the English honor, his ready evasions and intelligent reasoning, his sensibility to insult which he nevertheless thought it beneath him to resent, are all easily to be perceived in this instance, and are well worthy to be regarded among other evidences of his temper and genius.

His self-command and his chivalrous courtesy, on every former occasion, would have done no dishonor, in another country and time, to the lion-hearted monarch of England himself. In this respect he was well matched with Smith; and it is not the least interesting point in the common history of the two, to observe the singular union of suavity and energy with which both effected their purposes. Immediately after delivering the celebrated reply which he sent to Newport's proposal by Smith, the historian adds that, "many other discourses they had, (yet both content to give each other content *in complimentall courtesies*) and so Captain Smith returned with his answer." In the same style, when Newport came himself—perceiving his purpose was to discover and invade the Monacans—we are told that he "refused to lend him either men or guides more than Nomantack, and so after some complimentall kindnesse on both sides," he presented the disappointed captain

---

* History, p. 133.

with seven or eight bushels of corn, and wished him a
pleasant journey to Jamestown.   He would not suffer
so brave a man as Smith to be even beheaded, without having first ordered two of his queens to serve
him with water and a bunch of feathers, and then
feasted him in what the victim himself considered
his best barbarous manner.   It is very evident there
was neither fear nor hypocrisy in any of these cases.

None of the noble traits we have mentioned lose
any of their charm from being connected, as they are,
with the utmost simplicity of barbarism.   The read
er of these times, therefore, may be allowed to smile
at the pertinacity with which this mighty warrior and
renowned monarch insisted upon Parker's being ransomed in fish-hooks ; and the solemn gravity with
which he divested himself of his mantle and old shoes
for the gratification and reward of Newport. The
presents sent to him by Sir Thomas Dale were two
pieces of copper, five strings of white and blue
beads, five wooden combs, ten fish-hooks, and a pair
of knives—not to mention the promise of a grindstone,
whenever he should send for it—clearly a much better bargain for his daughter, had he wished to dispose of her, than the two bushels of Roanoke.   The
Werowances and queens of conquered nations waited upon him at his meals, as humbly as certain kings
of the middle ages are said to have waited upon the
Pope ; but unlike his Holiness, Powhatan could make
his own robes, shoes, bows, arrows, and pots, besides
planting his corn for exercise, and hunting deer for
amusement.   The Indians generally subsisted on
fish in the spring, and lived light for some months
after; but " Powhatan, their great king, and some
others that are provident, rost their fish and flesh
vpon hurdles, and keepe it till scarce times."*

In fine, it would seem, that no candid person can
read the history of this famous Indian, with an at-

---

* Smith's account of the NATURAL INHABITANTS of
VIRGINIA.

tentive consideration of the circumstances under
which he was placed, without forming a high estimate of his character as a warrior, a statesman and a
patriot. His deficiencies were those of education and
not of genius. His faults were those of the people
whom he governed and of the period in which he
lived. His great talents, on the other hand, were his
own ; and these are acknowledged even by those
historians who still regard him with prejudice. Stith
calls him a prince of excellent sense and parts, and a
great master of all the savage arts of government and
policy. He adds, that he was penetrating, crafty, in-
sidious and cruel. "But as to the great and moral
arts of policy," he concludes, "such as truth, faith,
uprightness and magnanimity, they seemed to have
been but little heeded or regarded by him." Burk's
opinion appears to us more correct. In the cant of
civilisation, (says that excellent historian,) he will
doubtless be branded with the epithets of tyrant and
barbarian: But his title to greatness, though his
opportunities were fewer, is to the full as fair as that
of Tamerlane or Kowli Khan, and several others
whom history has immortalized ; while the proofs
of his tyranny are by no means so clear. Still, it
might have been as reasonable to say, that there are
no such proofs in being. The kind of martial law
which the emperor sometimes exercised over his
own subjects, was not only a matter of custom,
founded on the necessity which must always exist
among ignorant men ; but it was a matter of license,
which had grown into constitutional law, by common
consent. It has been justly observed, that there is no
possibility of a true despotism under an Indian
government. It is reason that governs,—nominally
at least—and the authority is only the more effectual
as the obedience is more voluntary.

10—5

CHAPTER III.

The family of Powhatan—His successor—Sequel of the his
tory of Pocahontas—Her acts of kindness to the colonists a
various times, and especially to Smith—His gratitude—Her
civilisation, and instruction in Christianity—Her visit tc
England in 1616—-Reception at Court—Interview with
Smith—His memorial respecting her to Queen Anne—Her
death and character—Her descendants.

THE family of Powhatan was numerous and influential. Two sons and two daughters have already
been mentioned. There were also three brothers
younger than himself; and upon them successively,
according to their several ages, custom seems to
have required that the government should devolve
after his own death. The eldest, OPITCHIPAN,* accordingly succeeded him, in form at least. But this
prince was an inactive and unambitious man—owing in some degree perhaps to his being decrepid;
and he was soon thrown into the shade by the superior energy and talent of Opechancanough, who
before many years engrossed in fact the whole power
of the government. Of the younger brother, KEKA-
TAUGH, scarcely any thing is known. He propably
died before any opportunity occurred of signalizing
himself in a public station. The sequel of the history
of OPECHANCANOUGH is well worthy of being dwelt
upon at some length: but previously, the order of
time requires us to devote a share of attention to the
fortunes of his celebrated niece, POCAHONTAS.
  This beautiful and amiable woman, whom John
Smith, in the excess of his admiration, styles " the

---

* By various writers called Itopatin, Itoyatin, Oetan, Opitchipan, Toyatan—a characteristic instance of the uncertainty
which attends the orthography of Indian proper names. One
cause is in the custom of changing the name upon great occa
sions. Opitchipan himself after his accession was called
Sasawpen; and Opechancanough, Mangopeeomen.

Numpareil of Virginia," has been distinguished in modern times, chiefly, by that single extraordinary act of courage and humanity to which the gallant historian was indebted for the preservation of his life. But this was by no means the only evidence of these noble qualities which history has preserved. Her name indeed is scarcely once mentioned by the most ancient chronicles of the colony, except in terms of high eulogy, and generally in connexion also with some substantial facts going strongly to justify the universal partiality with which her memory is regarded to these times.

In the earliest and most gloomy days of the settlement, immediately after Smith's return from his captivity, the liberal and thoughtful kindness of Pocahontas went very far to cheer the desponding hearts of the colonists, as well as to relieve their actual necessities. She came into Jamestown with her attendants once in every four or five days, for a long time ; and brought with her supplies of provisions, by which many lives are stated to have been saved. This will appear more fully from an ancient document which we shall hereafter transcribe at length.

When Smith was absent upon one of his Indian expeditions, emergencies occurred at Jamestown which rendered his presence extremely desirable. But not a man could be found who dared venture to carry a message to him from the council. He was known to be environed by enemies, and the hostility and power of Powhatan were at that period subjects of the most exaggerated apprehension. One Richard Wyffin at last undertook the hazardous enterprise. Encountering many dangers and difficulties, he reached the residence of Powhatan, a day or two after Smith had left it for Pamunkey. He found that great preparations for war were going on among the Powhatans ; and he soon became himself the object of suspicion. His life undoubtedly would have paid the forfeit of his rashness, had not Pocahontas, who knew his perilous situation even better than himself,

concealed him, and thwarted and embarassed the
search of the savages who pursued him, so that
by her means and extraordinary bribes and much
trouble in three days travell," as history says, " at
ength he found vs in the middest of these turmoyles,"
at Jamestown.)

Her conduct was the same after Smith's departure
for England. Of the thirty men who accompanied
Ratcliffe when he was massacred by the Indians, only
one escaped to the colony, and one was rescued by
Pocahontas. This was a boy named Henry Spilman,
who subsequently was restored to his friends,* and
from the knowledge of Indian languages which he
obtained during his residence with the Patowomekes
proved highly serviceable as an interpreter. Smith
himself was more than *once* under obligations to the
princess for his personal safety. We have alluded
to that occasion when he quartered, over night, near
he residence of her father. " Pocahontas, his dearest
ewell and daughter, in that darke night came through
the irksome woods, and told our Captaine great
cheare should be sent vs by and by ; but Powhatan
and all the power he could make, would after come
kill vs all, if they that brought it could not kill vs
with our owne weapons, when we were at supper.
Therefore if we would liue, she wished vs presently
to be gone. Such things as she delighted in, he
would haue giuen her ; but with the teares running
downe her cheekes, she said she durst not be seen to
haue any, for if Powhatan should know it, she were
but dead, and so she ran away by herself as she
came."† What an affecting instance of the most
delicate tenderness mingled with the loftiest courage.

It would have been strange indeed, if Smith, with
all his passionate chivalry, had been insensible of
these repeated kindnesses. Even Powhatan had

---

* He was destined, however, to die at last by the hands of the
savages, in 1623.

† Smith's History.

too good an opinion of him to suppose so, for he had the sagacity to rely upon his gratitude for political purposes. When some of the emperor's subjects were taken prisoners by Smith, (although peace was nominally existing,) and forced to confess that Powhatan had employed them to work mischief against the colony, the latter " sent messengers, *and his dearest daughter Pocahontas,*" with presents, to make apologies for the past, and promises for the future. Smith, on the other hand, (who understood as well as any one, the part of a gentleman,) after giving the prisoners such correction as he deemed necessary, treated them well for a day or two, and then delivered them to Pocahontas, " for whose sake onely he fayned to haue saued their liues, and gaue them libertie." The emperor was paid for this ingenuity in his own coin, when the colonists, in 1613, took the princess herself captive, relying on the well-known strength of his attachment to her, as the surest means of procuring peace.

Her subsequent history may be soon told. Rolfe had become ardently enamoured of her beauty, and he used the fortunate occasion of her stay in the colony—perhaps was active in bringing it on—to procure the intercession of the President in his behalf. Pocahontas cherished similar feelings towards himself, and when her brothers came to visit her she made one of them her confidant. Rolfe gained information of her sentiments, and thus was emboldened to prosecute his suit with a spirit worthy of the success which it met with. The parties married. In the course of a year or two, the young bride became quite an adept in the English language and manners, and was well instructed in the doctrines of Christianity. She was entitled by her new acquaintances the Lady *Rebecca.*

In 1616, she and her husband accompanied Sir Thomas Dale to England. King James, (that anointed pedant, as Stith calls him,) is said to have been offended with Rolfe for his presumption in marrying he daughter of a king—a crowned head, too, it will be recollected.—He might have thought, perhaps, following up his own principles, that the offspring of the marriage would be fairly entitled to succeed Powhatan in his dominion. But the affair passed off, with some little murmuring; and Pocahontas herself was received at Court, by both the King and Queen, with the most flattering marks of attention. Lord de la War, and his lady, and many other courtiers of rank, followed the royal example. The princess was gratified by the kindness shown to her; and those who entertained her, on the other hand, were unanimously of opinion, as Smith expresses himself, that they had seen many English ladies worse-favored, proportioned and behaviored.

The captain was at this time in England; and although upon the eve of leaving that country on a voyage to New England, he delayed his departure for the purpose of using every possible means in his power of introducing the princess to advantage. A memorial which he draughted with his own hand, and sent in to the Queen, is supposed to have had no little influence at Court. It is well worth transcribing, both as a curiosity of style, and as a document of authentic history. It reads thus:

"To the most high and vertuous Princess Queene Anne of Great Britain.

Most admired Queene,

The loue I beare my God, my King and Countrie hath so oft emboldened mee in the worst of extreme danger, that now honestie doth constraine mee presume thus farre beyond myselfe, to present your Maiestie this short discourse. If ingratitude be a deadly poyson to all honest vertues, I must be guiltie of that crime if I should omit any meanes to be thankful. So it is,

That some ten yeeres agoe, being in Virginia, and taken prisoner by the power of Powhatan their chiefe King, I received from this great Salvage exceeding great courtesie, especially from his sonne Nantaguans, the most manliest, comeliest, boldest spirit I euer saw in a salvage ; and his sister Pocahontas, the King's most deare and well-beloued daughter, being but a childe of twelue or thirteene yeeres of age, whose compassionate pitifull heart, of desperate estate, gaue mee much cause to respect her; I being the first christian this proud King and his grim attendants euer saw ; and thus inthralled in their barbarous power, I cannot say I felt the least occasion of want that was in the power of those my mortall foes to preuent, notwithstanding al their threats.

After some six weeks fatting among these Salvage Courtiers, at the minute of my execution, she hazarded the beating out of her owne braines to saue mine, but not onely that, but so preuailed with her father, that I was safely conducted to Iames-towne, where I found about eight and thirtie miserable poore and sicke creatures, to keepe possession of al those large territories of Virginia ; such was the weaknesse of this poore commonwealth, as had the salvages not fed us, we directly had starued.

And this reliefe, most Gracious Queene, was commonly brought vs by this Lady Pocahontas. Notwithstanding al these passages, when inconstant fortune, turned our peace to warre, this tender Virgin would still not spare to dare to visit vs, and by her our iarres haue been oft appeased, and our wants still supplyed. Were it the policie of her father thus to imploy her, or the ordinance of God thus to make her his instrument, or her extraordinarie affection to our nation, I know not. But of this I am sure; when her father, with the utmost of his policie and power, sought to surprise mee, hauing but eighteene with mee, the darke night could not affright her from comming through the irkesome woods, and with watered eies gaue me intilligence, with her

best aduice, to escape his furie; which had hee
knowne, he had surely slaine her.

Iames-toune, with her wild traine, she as freely
frequented as her father's habitation ; and during the
time of two or three yeeres, she next under God
was still the instrument to preserve this colonie from
death, famine and utter confusion, which if in those
times had once been disolued, Virginia might haue
line as it was at our first arrivall to this day.

Since then, this businesse hauing beene turned and
varied by many accidents from that I left it at, it is
most certaine, after a long and troublesome warre
after my departure, betwixt her father and our
colonie, at which time shee was not heard off, about
two yeeres after she her selfe was taken prisoner
Being so detained neere two yeeres longer, the colonie by that means was relieued, peace concluded
and at last reiecting her barbarous condition, shee
was maried to an English gentleman, with whom at
this present shee is in England ; the first Christian
euer of that nation, the first Virginian euer spake
English, or had a childe in marriage by an Englishman. A matter surely, if my meaning bee truly
considered and well vnderstood, worthy a Prince's
vnderstanding

Thus, most Gracious Lady, I haue related to your
Maiestie, what at your best leasure our approued
Histories will account you at large, and done in the
time of your Maiestie's life ; and howeuer this might
bee presented you from a more worthy pen, it
cannot from a more honest heart. As yet I neuer
begged any thing of the state, or any, and it is my
want of abilitie and her exceeding desert, your birth
meanes and authoritie, her birth, vertue, want and
simplicitie, doth make mee thus bold, humbly to
beseech your Maiestie to take this knowledge of her,
though it bee from one so vnworthy to be the reporter
as my selfe, her husband's estate not being able to
make her fit to attend your Maiestie.   The most and

least I can doe is to tell you this, because none so oft
hath tried it as my selfe; and the rather being of so
great a spirit, howeuer her stature.

If shee should not be well recieued, seeing this
kingdom may rightly haue a kingdom by her meanes,
her present loue to vs and christianitie might turne
to such scorne and furie, as to diuert al this good to
the worst of euill; where [whereas] finding so great
a Queene should doe her some honor more than she
can imagine, for being so kinde to your seruants and
subjects, would so rauish her with content, as en-
deare her dearest blood to effect that your Maiestie
and al the King's honest subjects most earnestly desire. And so I humbly kisse your gracious hands."

The final interview between the gallant and generous writer of this memorial and the princess who
was the subject of it, is an occasion too interesting
to be passed over without notice. She had been told
that Smith, whom she had not seen for many years,
was dead; but why this information was given her,
does not appear. Perhaps it was to make his appearance the more gratifying. Possibly, Master Rolfe,
in the heat of his passion, during the critical period
of courtship had deemed it advisable and justifiable
to answer, to this effect, the anxious inquiries she
would naturally make after Smith, especially during
her confinement at Jamestown. But whatever the
reason was, the shock of the first meeting had nearly
overwhelmed her. She was staying at Brentford,
after her visit to London, having retired thither to
avoid the noise and smoke of the metropolis, which
she was far from enjoying. Smith was announced,
and soon after made his appearance. She saluted
him--modestly, he says himself; and coolly, according to some other writers—and then turning away
from him, she covered her face, and seemed to be too
much discomposed for conversation.

Undoubtedly she was deeply affected with a multitude of conflicting emotions, not the least of which
was a just indignation on account of the imposition

which the English had practised upon her. For two
or three hours she was left to her own meditations
At the end of that time, after much entreaty, she was
prevailed upon to converse; and this point once
gained, the politeness and kindness of her visitant
and her own sweetness of disposition, soon renewed
her usual vivacity.

In the course of her remarks she called Smith
her Father. That appellation, as bestowed by a
King's daughter, was too much for the captain's
modesty, and he informed her to that effect. But
she could not understand his reasoning upon the
subject. "Ah!" she said—after recounting some
of the ancient courtesies which had passed between
them—" you did promise Powhatan that what was
yours should be his, and hee the like to you. You
called him Father, being in his land a stranger; and
by the same reason so must I doe you." Smith still
expressed himself unworthy of that distinction, and
she went on. " Were you not afraid to come into
my father's countrie, and caused fear in him and all
his people—but mee—and *fear* you I should here call
you father ? I tell you then I *will* ; and you must
call mee childe, and then I will bee foreuer and euer
your country-woman." She assured Smith, that she
had been made to believe he was dead, and that
Powhatan himself had shared in that delusion. To
ascertain the fact, however, to a certainty, that crafty
barbarian had directed an Indian, who attended her
to England, to make special inquiries. This was
Tomocomo, one of the emperor's chief counsellors,
and the husband of his daughter Matachanna—perhaps the same who had been demanded in mar
riage by Sir Thomas Dale, in 1614.

It is the last and saddest office of history to record
the death of this incomparable woman, in about the
two-and-twentieth year of her age. This event took
place at Gravesend, where she was preparing to
embark for Virginia, with her husband, and the
child mentioned in Smith's memorial. They were

to have gone out with Captain Argall, who sailed early in 1617; and the treasurer and council of the colony had made suitable accommodations for them on board the admiral-ship. But, in the language of Smith, it pleased God to take this young lady to his mercy. He adds, that she made not more sorrow for her unexpected death, than joy to the beholders to hear and see her make so religious and godly an end. Stith also records that she died, as she had long lived, a most sincere and pious Christian. The expression of a later historian is, that her death was a happy mixture of Indian fortitude and christian submission, affecting all those who saw her by the lively and edifying picture of piety and virtue, which marked her latter moments.*

The same philosophic writer, in his general observations upon the character of Pocahontas, has justly remarked, that, considering all concurrent circumstances, it is not surpassed by any in the whole range of history; and that for those qualities more especially which do honor to our nature—a humane and feeling heart, an ardor and unshaken constancy in her attachments—she stands almost without a rival. She gave evidence, indeed, of possessing in a high degree every attribute of mind and heart, which should be and has been the ornament and pride of civilized woman in all countries and times. Her unwearied kindness to the English was entirely disinterested; she knew that it must be so when she encountered danger and weariness, and every kind of opposition and difficulty, to bestow it, seasonably, on the objects of her noble benevolence. It was delicate, too, in the mode of bestowment. No favor was expected in return for it, and yet no sense of obligation was permitted to mar the pleasure which it gave. She asked nothing of Smith in recompense for whatever she had done, but the boon of being looked upon as his child. Of her character as a princess,

* Burk's Virginia, Vol. I.

evidence enough has already been furnished. Her dignity, her energy, her independence, and the dauntless courage which never deserted her for a moment, were worthy of Powhatan's daughter.

Indeed, it has been truly said that, well authenticated as is the history of Pocahontas, there is ground for apprehension that posterity will be disposed to regard her story as a romance. "It is not even improbable," says Burk, "that considering every thing relating to herself and Smith as a mere fiction, they may vent their spleen against the historian for impairing the interest of his plot by marrying the princess of Powhatan to a Mr. Rolfe, of whom nothing had been previously said, in defiance of all the expectations raised by the foregoing parts of the fable."

Young Rolfe, her only offspring was left at Plymouth, England, under the care of Sir Lewis Steukley, who undertook to direct his education—his tender years making it inexpedient to remove him to Virginia. As that gentleman was soon after completely beggared and disgraced by the part which he took in the proceedings against Sir Walter Raleigh, the tuition of Rolfe passed into the hands of his uncle, Henry Rolfe of London. He became in after years a man of eminence and fortune in Virginia, and inherited a considerable tract of land which had belonged to Powhatan. At his death he left an only daughter, who was married to Col. Robert Bolling. By him she had an only son, who was father to Col. John Bolling, (well known to many now living;) and several daughters married to Col. Richard Randolph, Col. John Fleming, Dr. William Gay, Mr. Thomas Eldridge and Mr. James Murray. This genealogy is taken from Stith; and he shows with sufficient minuteness, that this remnant of the imperial family of Virginia, which long survived in a single person had branched out into a very numerous progeny, even as early as 1747. The Hon. John Randolph of Roanoke is, if we mistake not, a lineal descendant of the princess in the sixth degree

CHAPTER IV.

Sequel of the history of Opechancanough—Renewal, by him and Opitchipan, of the treaty of peace—Finesse by which he extended his dominion over the Chickahominies—Preparations for War—Causes of it—Profound dissimulation under which his hostility was concealed—Indian custom of making Conjurers—Monœuvres against the English interest—The great massacre of 1622; circumstances and consequences of it—Particular occasion which led to it—Character and death of NEMATTANOW—Details of the war subsequent to the massacre—Truce broken by the English—New exertions of Opechancanough—Battle of Pamunkey—Peace of 1632 —Massacre of 1641—Capture of Opechancanough by the English—His death and character.

CAPTAIN Argall brought out from England, among other things, a variety of presents for Opechancanough, who seems now to have been, notwithstanding that Powhatan was still living, the chief object of the colony's apprehension and regard. He lamented, as the Indians did universally, the untimely fate of their favorite princess; but he also expressed himself satisfied with the care which had been taken of her son. Argall sent messengers to him immediately on his arrival at Jamestown; and the chieftain paid him a visit, and received his presents. Tomocomo, who returned with Argall, had conceived a dislike for Sir Thomas Dale, and he railed violently against him in particular, as he did against the English in general; but Opechancanough either was or affected to be convinced, that his anger and his accusations were equally groundless. On the death of Powhatan, in 1618, both himself and his royal brother Opitchipan renewed the ancient league of the emperor with the English; under the protection of which, we are told, every man peaceably followed his building and planting, without any remarkable accidents or interruption.*

---

* Stith.

A transaction which occurred in 1616, furnishes the best comment we can give upon the character of Opechancanough. It appears, that President Yeardly at that time undertook to relieve the necessities of the colony by collecting tribute of the Chickahominies. But, for some reason or other, that warlike people refused to pay it; and even sent him an answer to his demand, which he construed into an affront. He therefore called upon them, soon after, with a company of one hundred soldiers, well armed. Some threatening and bravado ensued on both sides, and a regular battle was the speedy consequence. The Indians were defeated, and as Yeardly was returning to Jamestown with his spoil, Opechancanough met him, and artfully effected an agreement with him, that he (Yeardly) would make no peace with the Chickahominies without *his* consent. He then went to that tribe, and pretended that he had, with great pains and solicitation, procured a peace for them. To requite this immense service, as it was now considered, they cheerfully proclaimed him King of their nation, and flocked from all quarters with presents of beads and copper. From this time he was content to be entitled the King of Chickahominy; and thus was subjected to him, with their own free consent, a brave and resolute people, who had successfully resisted, for many years, the power of every savage and civilized foe.

The English historians generally agree in representing Opechancanough as an inveterate enemy of the English from first to last. Such may have been the case; and he might have had what appeared to him reason and occasion enough for his hostility. The character of many of the colonists was but too well calculated to thwart the best intentions on the part of the government, however peaceable and just might be *their* theory of Indian intercourse. The discontent of Tomocomo might have its effect, too, and especially among the mass of his countrymen. The pledge of harmony which had existed in the person of Pocahontas was forgotten. But above all, Opechancanough was too shrewd a man not to percieve, in the alarming disproportion which was daily showing itself between the power of the English and the Indians of Virginia—independently of particular provocations—a sure indication of the necessity of a new system of defence.

Subsequent events confirm this conjecture. No better preparation for a war could have been made on the chieftain's part, than he effected in the submission of the Chickahominies. It is not unlikely that he himself instigated, through his satellites, the very insolence whereby they drew upon themselves that severe chastisement from the colony, which increased his own influence over them as much as it aggravated their hostility to the English. We find that, in 1618, they committed several outrages of a most flagrant character; and although Opechancanough, who was applied to for satisfaction, promised to send in the heads of the offenders, this was never done, and it may be questioned, whether he was not privy to, or perhaps the chief author and contriver of the whole affair. At all events, historians represent, that his regal authority over the tribe was thereby "firmly riveted and established."

Still, not only had the artful chieftain given no open cause of offence or evidence of hostility; but he absolutely succeeded, as we have seen, in completely quieting the suspicions of the colonists. In 1620, indeed, we find it recorded in the journal of Mr. Rolfe, that "*now Opechankanough will not come at vs that causes vs suspect his former promises.*" But this little uneasiness was wholly done away, on the arrival of Sir Francis Wyatt, the successor of Yeardly, in 1621. That gentleman immediately sent messengers to Opechancanough and Opitchipan, who both expressed great satisfaction at the accession of the new President, and cheerfully renewed their former leagues with the colony. The former also declared himself pleased with the idea of the English inhabit-

ıng the country He proposed, by way of amalga-
mating the two nations, that some of the white families should settle among his people, while some of
his should settle at Jamestown. A former promise
was confirmed, of sending a guide with the English
to certain mines represented to be situated above the
falls. Nay, so far was the deception carried, that
" Mr. Thorpe [the chief messenger] thought he
perceived more motions of religion in Opechancanough than could easily be imagined, in so great
ıgnorance and blindness. He acknowledged his own
religion not to be the right way ; and desired to be
instructed in the Christian faith. He confessed that
God loved the English better than them ; and he
thought the cause of God's anger was their custom
of conjuring their children, and *making them black
boys.*"*

---

* Allusion seems to be made here to a custom which is sufficıent-
ly singular to deserve some description. Smith calls it a yearly
sacrifice of children. A ceremony of the kind which was perform
ed near Jamestown may best be described in his own words.
" Fifteene of the properest young boyes, betweene ten and fifteene
yeeres of age, they paynted white. Hauing brought them forth,
the people spent the forenoone in dauncing and singing about them
with rattles. In the afternoone they put those children to the
roote of a tree. By them all the men stood in a guard, each hauing
a Bastinado in his hand, made of reeds bound together. This made
a lane betweene them all along, through which there were appointed fiue young men to fetch these children. So euery one of the
fiue went through the guard to fetch a childe, each after other by
turnes, the guard firecely beating them with their Bastinadoes,
and they patiently enduring and receiuing all, defending the children with their naked bodies from the vnmerciful blowes, that pay
them soundly, tho' the children escape. All this while, the women
weepe and cry out very passionately, prouiding mats, skinnes,
mosse and dry wood, as things fitting their childrens' funerals
After the children were thus passed the guard, the guard tore
down the trees, branches and boughs, with such violence that they
rent the body, and made wreaths for their heads, or bedecked
their hayre with the leaues. What els was done with the children
was not seene, but they were all cast on a heape in a valley as
dead, where they made a great feast for all the company. The
Werowance being demanded the meaning of this sacrifice, answer
ed, that the children were not all dead, but that the *Okee* or Dıvill
lid sucke the bloode from their left breast, who chanced to be his
oy lot, till they were dead ; but the rest were kept in the wilder-
nesse by the young men till nine months were expired, during
which time they must not converse with any, *and of these were*

It must have been about this time that Opechan-canough took the trouble to send some of his men to a sachem on the eastern shore, for a quantity of poison, peculiar to that region, and which he wished to use in his operations against the English.* This may have been the true object of the embassy ; and it may also have been but a cover for sounding the disposition of the eastern tribes towards the colony. Accordingly, it is recorded in the " Observations of Master Iohn Pory, secretarie of Virginia, in his travels," that Namenacus, the Sachem of Pawtuxent, made an application to the colony, in 1621, for the privilege of trading with them. The request was so far attended to, that the English promised to visit him within six weeks. Now it seems that their commerce with the Indians at this period was mostly carried on by the aid of one Thomas Salvage, an interpreter, and the same man whom Smith had left with Powhatan fourteen years before. The visit took place according to promise, and it was then ascertained that Opechancanough had employed one of his Indians to kill Savage. The pretence was, " because he brought the trade from him to the easterne shore." The truth probably was, that the chieftain was jealous of the English influence among the tribes of that region.

But the storm which had been gathering ever since the death of the emperor, was at length ready to burst upon the devoted colony. Opechancanough had completed every preparation which the nature of things permitted on his part ; and nothing remained, but to strike the great blow which he intended should utterly extinguish the English settlements forever. The twenty-second day of March, 1622—an era but too memorable in Virginian history—was selected for the time ; and a certain hour agreed

---

made their Priests and Coniurers." Master Pory says, in his Observations, that the Accomacks were a civil and tractable people : " nor doe they vse that deuil'ish custome *in making Black Boyes* "
  * Stith.

10—6

upon, to ensure a simultaneous assault in every di
rection.   The various tribes engaged in the conspiracy were drawn together, and stationed in the vicinity of the several places of massacre, with a celerity
and precision unparalleled in the annals of the conti
nent.   Although some of the detachments had to
march from great distances, and through a continued
forest, guided only by the stars and moon, no single
instance of disorder or mistake is known to have
happened.   One by one, they followed each other
in profound silence, treading as nearly as possible in
each other's steps, and adjusting the long grass and
branches which they displaced.*   They halted at
short distances from the settlements, and waited in
death-like stillness for the signal of attack.

   That was to be given by their fellow-savages,
who had chosen the same morning for visiting the
different plantations, in considerable numbers, for
the purpose of ascertaining their strength and precise situation, and at the same time preventing any
suspicion of the general design.   This, it should be
observed, had recently become too habitual a practice with the Indians, to excite suspicion of itself.
The peace was supposed to be inviolable.   The
savages were well known to be in no condition for
a war; and had shown no disposition for one.   The
English, therefore, while they supplied them generally with whatever they asked for, upon fair terms,
neglected to prepare themselves for defence.   They
were so secure, that a sword or a firelock was rarely
to be met with in a private dwelling.   Most of their
plantations were seated in a scattered and straggling
manner, as a water-privilege or a choice vein of rich
land invited them; and indeed it was generally
thought, the further from neighbors, the better.
The Indians were daily received into their houses,
fed at their tables, and lodged in their bedchambers;
and boats were even lent them previous to the twen

Burk.

ty-second, as they passed backwards and forwards for the very purpose of completing the plan of extirpation.

The hour being come, the savages, knowing exactly in what spot every Englishman was to be found, rose upon them at once. The work of death was commenced, and they spared neither sex nor age, man, woman nor child. Some entered the houses under color of trade. Others drew the owners abroad upon various pretences; while the rest fell suddenly on such as were occupied in their several labors. So quick was the execution, that few perceived the weapon or blow which despatched them. And thus, in one hour and almost at the same instant, fell three hundred and forty-seven men, women and children; most of them by their own arms, and all, (as Stith observes,) by the hands of a naked and timid people, who durst not stand the presenting of a staff in the manner of a firelock, in the hands of a woman.

Those who had sufficient warning to make resistance, saved their lives. Nathaniel Causie, an old soldier of Captain Smith's, though cruelly wounded, cleaved down one of his assailants with an axe; upon which the whole party who had surrounded him fled, and he escaped. At another place, two men held possession of a house against sixty Indians. At Warrasqueake, a Mr. Baldwin, whose wife was so badly wounded that she lay for dead, by repeatedly discharging his musket drove off the enemy, and saved both her and himself. Ralph Hamer, the historian, defended himself in his house, successfully, with spades, axes and brickbats. One small family, living near Martin's Hundred, where as many as seventy-three of the English were slain, not only escaped the massacre, but never heard any thing of it until two or three days afterwards. Jamestown and some of the neighboring places were saved by the disclosure of a Christian Indian named Chanco,

who wm confidentially informed of the design by
his brother, on the morning of the 22d.

Such was the evidence which Opechancanough
gave of his deep-rooted hatred of the English. And
yet, such was his profound dissimulation, that so late
as the middle of March, he treated a messenger sent
to him from the President with the utmost civility,
assuring him he held the peace so firm, that the sky
would fall sooner than it should be violated on his
part. Mr. Thorpe, an excellent man, who had taken
a peculiar interest in christianizing the Indians,
supposed that he had gained the especial favor of
Opechancanough by building him a very neat house
after the English fashion ; in which he took such
pleasure, as to lock and unlock his door a hundred
times a day.* He seemed also to be pleased with
the discourse and company of Mr. Thorpe, and expressed a desire to requite some of his kindness.
Nevertheless, the body of this unfortunate man was
found among the slain. Only two days before the
massacre, the Indians guided a party of the English
through the woods, and sent home one who had
lived among them to learn their language. On the
very morning of the fatal day, as also the evening
before, they came, as at other times, unarmed into
the houses of the English, with deer, turkeys, fish,
fruits and other things to sell ; and in some places
sat down to breakfast with the same persons whom
they rose up to tomahawk.

The particular occasion—as the historians consider
it—of the conspiracy, is too characteristic to be
omitted. There was a noted Indian, named NE-
MATTANOW, who was wont, out of vanity or some
unaccountable humor, to dress himself up with
feathers, in a most barbarously fantastic manner.
This habit obtained for him among the English the
name of *Jack-of-the-feather*. He was renowned
among his countrymen both for courage and cun-

---

* Stith.

ning, and was esteemed the greatest war-captain of those times. But, what was most remarkable, although he had been in many skirmishes and engagements with the English, he had always escaped without a wound. From this accident, seconded by his own ambition and craft, he obtained at length the reputacion of being invulnerable and immortal.

Early in 1622, Nemattanow came to the house of one Morgan, who kept and sold a variety of well-selected commodities for the use of the Indians. Smitten with a strong desire to obtain some of them, Nemattanow persuaded Morgan to accompany him to Pamunkey, on the assurance of an advantageous traffic at that place. On the way, he is supposed to have murdered the trader. Within two or three days, he returned again to the house of his victim, where were only two stout young men, servants of Morgan, at home. They, observing that he wore their master's cap on his head, inquired after him; and Jack told them frankly he was dead.

Confirmed in their previous suspicions by this declaration, they seized him, and endeavored to carry him before Mr. Thorpe, who lived at a neighboring settlement. But their prisoner troubled them so much by his resistance, and withal provoked them so intolerably by his bravadoes, that they finally shot him down, and put him into a boat, in order to convey him the remaining seven or eight miles of the way. But the Indian soon grew faint; and finding himself surprised by the pangs of death, he requested his captors to stop. In his last moments he most earnestly besought of them two great favors; first, never to make it known that he was killed by a bullet; and secondly, to bury him among the English, that the certain knowledge and monument of his mortality might still be concealed from the sight of his countrymen. So strong was the ruling passion in death.

Opechancanough was so far from being a particular friend of Nemattenow that he had given the

President to understand, by a messenger, sometime
before the transaction just related, that he should
consider it a favor in *him*, if he would take measures
to have Jack despatched. The popularity of the
war-captain was the only reason why he forbore to
take such measures himself. Nevertheless, with a
consummate wiliness he availed himself of this
same popularity, on the death of his rival—as Jack
seems to have been—the better to inflame and exas-
perate the Indians against the whites. He affected
to be excessively grieved at his death, and for sometime was unusually loud in his declarations of resentment and his threats of revenge. A messenger came
from the President, to ascertain what was intended
by these demonstrations of hostility, and again all
was quiet as before ; nothing could induce the Sachem to violate the vast regard which he had always
entertained for the English. About the same time he
gave them liberty, by negotiation, to seat themselves
any where on the shores of the rivers, within his
dominions, where the natives had no villages. The
treaty he had already made for the discovery of
mines, as well as for mutual friendship and defence,
was at his request engraven on a brass plate, and
fastened to one of the largest oaks growing upon his
territories, that it might be had always in remembrance.*

For several years after the massacre, a war was
waged between the colonists and the savages, so inveterate and ferocious as to transmit a mutual abhorrence and prejudice to the posterity of both. The
former obtained at this period the name of the LONG-
KNIVES, by which they were distinguished to a very
late day in the hieroglyphic language of the natives.
Every precaution and preparation was taken and
made upon both sides, in view of a desperate conflict.
Orders were issued by the government, from time to
time, directing a general vigilance and caution against

---

* Belknap's Am. Biog. p. 64, Vol. II.

the enemy who now engrossed all thought; and especially prohibiting the waste of arms and ammunition. The remnants of the settlements were drawn together into a narrower compass. Of eighty plantations all were abandoned but six, which lay contiguous at the lower part of James river; and three or four others, of which the owners or overseers, refusing to obey public orders, intrenched themselves, and mounted cannon for their own separate defence.*

A considerable space of territory between the Virginians and the savage tribes, was wasted with fire, for the sole purpose of laying bare the stealthy approaches of the enemy, who, under cover of the long grass and underwood, and the gigantic shield of the oak and cypress, had heretofore been able to advance unperceived, and rise up in attack almost from under the very feet of the English. But even a boundary of fire could not always restrain the fury, nor elude the skill, of the Indians. Wisely content with short and sudden incursions, for plunder and revenge rather than conquest, they frequently succeeded in carrying off the corn and cattle of the colonists, and sometimes their persons into captivity They were themselves, on the other hand, hunted like beasts of prey. No prisoners were made; no quarter was given.

From the time of the massacre, Opechancanough seems no longer to have taken the least trouble to conceal his hostility. He returned a haughty answer to the first demand made upon him for the redemption of the English captives; and trampled under foot the picture of the English monarch, which was sent to him as a compliment. Late in 1622, when Captain Croshaw was trading on the Potomac, with the only tribe which was now willing to carry on commerce, he had scarcely landed from his vessel, when a messenger arrived from Opechancanough to Japazaws,

---

* Purchas V. 1792.

(king of the Patawomekes,) bearing two baskets of beads as a royal present, and soliciting the king to murder his new visitants on the spot. He was assured, that whether he did *his* part or not, before the end of two moons, there should not be an Englishman left in the whole country. Japazaws first disclosed the message to his guest; and then, after thinking and talking of it two days, made answer that the English were his friends, and Opitchipan (the Powhatan emperor) his brother; and therefore there should be no more blood shed between them by his means. The beads were returned by the messenger.

After this, the colonists had their season of success; and more Indians are said to have been slain during the autumn and winter of 1622—3, than had ever before fallen by the hands of the English, since the settlement of Jamestown.* But the course adopted by the civilized party sufficiently indicates the desperate state of their affairs. They availed themselves of a stratagem worse than barbarous in its principle, however circumstances might be supposed in this case to justify it. A peace was offered to the enemy and accepted; but just as the corn which the latter were thus induced to plant, was beginning to grow ripe, the English fell upon them in all directions at a given hour of an appointed day, killed many, and destroyed a vast quantity of provisions. Several of the greatest war-captains were among the slain; and for sometime Opechancanough himself was reported to be one. This rumor alone, so long as believed, was equal to a victory; "for against *him*," says the historian, "was this stratagem chiefly laid."

Such language furnishes evidence enough of the apprehension which his movements and reputation had excited. But he gave more substantial reasons for the respect which he still wrested from his enemy by his prowess. A battle took place at his own village of Pamunkey, in 1625, in which the main

---

* Stith.

body of the savages numbered eight hundred bowmen, independently of detachments from remote
tribes; and though the English, led on by Governor
Wyatt in person, succeeded in driving the enemy
from the field, they were unable to pursue them even
as far as Matapony. That town was their principal
depot and rallying point, and the acknowledged
inability to reach it, though but four miles distant,
proves that the battle was by no means decisive. It
appears from this affair, too, that all the efforts of
the English, during an inveterate war of three years,
had not driven the tribes even from the neighborhood
of their own settlements. What was more discour-
aging, Opechancanough was not to be deceived a
second time by the arts of diplomacy. In 1628, the
governor's proclamation, which announced the ap-
pointment of commissioners to negotiate with the
enemy, declared expressly an intention to repeat the
stratagem of 1622; * but the plan failed of success,
and the Pamunkies and Chickahominies—most immediately under the influence of Opechancanough
—were more troublesome at this period than ever
before.

Four years afterwards, the same tribes made an
irruption so furious and alarming, that every twentieth man was despatched, under the command of the
governor, to *parley* with them—a term in the records
which shows forcibly, as Burk observes, the respect
this brave people had inspired. But Opechancanough was still implacable; and when, in the course
of 1632, a peace was at last formally concluded, so
little dependence was placed on that circumstance,
that even while the commissioners on both sides
were adjusting the preliminaries, a proclamation
was issued, forbidding the colonists either to parley
or trade with the Indians.

This truce or treaty was understood to be on both
sides a temporary expedient; but the chieftain was

---

* Ancient Records of Virginia.

I.—H

the first to take advantage of it. During nine years
he remained quietly making his preparations for the
conflict which his sagacity told him must some day
or other be renewed. The hour at length arrived.
The colony was involved in dissensions. Insurrec-
tions had taken place. The governor was unpopu-
lar, and the people were unprepared and heedless.
Opechancanough lost not a moment in concerting
measures for effecting at a single blow the bloody,
but in his bosom noble design, which had already
engrossed the solicitude and labor of so large a part
of his life.

He was now advanced in years, but his orders were
conveyed with electric rapidity to the remotest tribes
of the great confederacy associated under his influence. With the five nearest his own location, and
most completely under his control, he resolved to
make the principal onset in person. The more distant stations were assigned to the leading chiefs of
the several nations ; and thus the system of a war
that raged from the mouth of the Chesapeake to the
heads of all the great rivers, which flow into it, was
so simple as to render confusion impossible. The
whole force was let loose upon the entire line of the
English settlements at nearly the same instant of
time. Five hundred persons perished in the massacre.* Many others were carried into captivity.
The habitations, corn, household utensils, instruments of farming, every thing essential to comfort,
and almost every thing necessary to life, was con-
sumed by fire. But for circumstances in the situa
tion of the settlements, over which Opechancanough
had no control, and which he could not guard against,
the fate of Virginia had been decided by this single
blow.

As it was, every other labor and thought were
suspended in the terrors of an Indian war. The
loom was abandoned. The plough was left in its

---

* Beverly's History, p. 49.

furrow. All who were able to bear arms were embodied as a militia for the defence of the colony; and a chosen body, comprising every twentieth man, marched into the enemy's country under Governor Berkeley's personal command. The operations of the war, which raged thenceforth without any intermission until the death of Opechancanough—and that alone was expected to end it—are detailed by no historian. The early Virginian records which remain in manuscript are altogether silent respecting this period; and the meagre relation of Beverly is the only chronicle which has survived the ravages of time. This circumstance of itself sufficiently indicates the confusion and dismay of the era.

Opechancanough, whose last scene now rapidly approaches, had become so decrepid by age, as to be unable to walk, though his spirit, rising above the ruins of his body, directed, from the litter upon which his Indians carried him, the onset and the retreat of his warriors. The wreck of his constitution was at length completed by the extreme fatigues encountered in this difficult and laborious service. His flesh became macerated; his sinews lost their elasticity; and his eyelids were so heavy that he could not see, unless they were lifted up by his faithful attendants. In this forlorn condition he was closely pursued by Berkeley with a squadron of horse, and at length surprised and taken. He entered Jamestown, for the first time in his life, as the most conspicuous figure in the conqueror's triumph.

To the honor of the English, they treated their distinguished captive with the tenderness which his infirmities demanded, and the respect which his appearance and talents inspired. They saw the object of their terror bending under the load of years, and shattered by the hardships of war; and they generously resolved to bury the remembrance of their injuries in his present melancholy reverse of fortune. His own deportment was suitable to his former glory, and to the principles of an Indian hero

He disdained to utter complaint or to manifest uneasiness. He believed that tortures were prepar ing for him ; but instead of any consequent reduc tion in his haughtiness, his language and demeanoi bespoke the most absolute defiance and contempt.

But generally he shrouded himself in reserve ; and as if desirous of showing his enemies that there was nothing in their presence even to rouse his curiosity, and much less to excite his apprehensions, he but rarely permitted his eyelids to be lifted up. He continued in this state several days, attended by his affectionate Indian servants, who had begged permission to wait upon him. But his long life of near an hundred years* was drawing to its close. He was basely shot through the back by one of the soldiers appointed to guard him, from no other provocation than the recollection of his ancient hostility.

To the last moment his courage remained unbroken. The nearer death approached, the more care he seemed to use in concealing his dejection, and preserving the dignity and serenity of his aspect. Only a few minutes before he expired, he heard an unusual bustle in the room where he was confined. Having ordered his attendants to raise his eyelids, he discovered a number of persons crowding round him, for the purpose of gratifying an unseasonable curiosity. The dying chief felt the indignity, but disdaining to notice the intruders he raised himself as well as he could, and with a voice and air of authority, demanded that the *governor* should be immediately brought in. When the latter made his appearance, the chieftain scornfully told him, that " had it been *his* fortune to have taken *Sir William*

---

* So write some historians, but as he is understood to have been younger than Powhatan, the estimate is possibly too large by ten or twenty years. It is said that Berkeley had proposed taking him to England, as a living argument to counteract the representations made in that country as to the unhealthiness of the Virginian climate.

Berkeley prisoner, *he should not have exposed him as a show to his people.*"*

Such was the death of Opechancanough. His character is too well explained by his life to require any additional comment. His own countrymen were more extensively and more completely under his influence than they had been under that of Powhatan himself. This is the more remarkable from the fact that Opitchipan, whose age and family at least entitled him to some deference, retained the nominal authority of emperor so long as he lived. Beverley says, that Opechancanough was not esteemed by the Indians to be in any way related to Powhatan; and that they represented him as the prince of a foreign nation residing at a great distance somewhere in the Southwest. He might be an emigrant or an exile from the empire of Mexico, or from some of the tribes between that region and Virginia. The same historian describes him as a man of large stature, noble presence and extraordinary parts. Stith calls him a politic and haughty prince. Burk entitles him the HANNIBAL of VIRGINIA.

He was perhaps the most inveterate and troublesome enemy which any of the American colonies have ever met with among his race. The general causes which made him so, independently of his inherent talents and principles, are to be looked for in the situation of the tribes under his command, and especially in the relations existing between them and the colonists. He saw, that either the white or the red man must sooner or later establish an exclusive superiority; and he very reasonably decided upon doing all in his own power to determine the issue in favor of his country and himself. But more particu lar provocations were not wanting. Even after the peace of 1636, great as the anxiety was for its preservation, "the subtle Indians," says Beverley, "resented *the encroachments on them by Hervey's grants.*" A

---

* Beverley.

late historian expresses himself in warmer terms.　It was not enough, he writes, that they had abandoned to their invaders the delightful regions on the sea-shore, where their fathers had been placed by the bounty of heaven—where their days had rolled on in an enchanting round of innocence and gayety—where they had possessed abundance without labor, and independence without government.　The little that remained to them was attempted to be wrested from them by the insatiable avarice and rapacity of their enemies.*

---

* Burk, Vol. II.

CHAPTER V.

Biography of other Virginian chieftains—OPITCHIPAN—
Some particulars respecting TOMOCOMO—His visit to
England, interview with Captain Smith, and return to
America—JAPAZAWS, chief sachem of the Patowomekes—
His friendship for the English—Ill treatment which he re-
ceived from them—TOTOPOTOMOI, successor of Opechan-
canough—His services—His death in 1656—Notices of
several native chiefs of North Carolina—GRANGANIMO,
who dies in 1585—MENATENON, king of the Chowanocks
—ENSENORE, father of Granganimo; and WINGINA, his
brother—Plot of the latter against the Hatteras colony—
His death—Comment on the Carolinian Biography.

THE characters we have heretofore noticed are far
the most prominent in the Indian history of Virginia.
Indeed, they are almost the only ones which have
been preserved with distinctness enough to excite
much interest in them as individuals. Still, there
are several which ought not to be wholly passed
by ; and the want of a vivid light and coloring in
some of them, may perhaps be compensated, at
least, by the appearance of milder qualities than are
predominant in the portraitures we have hitherto
sketched.

The extant information respecting certain members
of the Powhatan family, whose history has not been
concluded, may soon be detailed. Opitchipan is not
mentioned subsequently to the great battle of Pamunkey, in 1625, when for the first time he appears
to have placed himself at the head of his countrymen,
in opposition to the English. As the name of
Opechancanough in not even alluded to in the records
of that period, it may be presumed he was accidentally absent. *Generally*, he seems to have been out
of favor with his reigning brother, and to have con-
tended against his influence, such as it was, in all
his designs hostile to the colony. Opitchipan d'isap-

proved of the great massacre of 1622 ; and early in the ensuing season we find him sending in Chanco, the Christian convert who disclosed the conspiracy in that case, with a message to Governor Wyatt, that if *he* would send ten or twelve men, he would give up all the English prisoners in his possession— (which, as we have seen, Opechancanough had refused to do.) He even promised to deliver up his implacable brother—if brother he was—bound hand and foot. "Captain Tucker," says Stith, "was accordingly sent upon this service, *but without the desired success.* However, Opitchipan sent back *Mrs. Boyce*, naked and unapparelled, in manner and fashion like one of their Indians." So insignificant, even with these savages, was the power of mere family rank, as opposed to the authority of reputation and talent.

One of the chief counsellors and priests of Powhatan, and the husband of his daughter Matachanna, was TOMOCOMO, who went to England with Pocahontas, and returned with Captain Argall. Smith, who calls him Vttamatomakkin, says he was held by his countrymen to be "a very understanding fellow." The same inference might be made from the commission which Powhatan gave him, on the occasion just alluded to, to take the number of the people in England, and to bring him an exact and minute account of their strength and resources. Tomocomo set about that business with equal simplicity and zeal. Immediately on his arrival at Plymouth, he procured a long stick, whereupon to cut a notch with his knife for every man he should see. But he soon became weary of his task, and threw his stick away. When the emperor inquired, on his return, how many people there were, he could only compare them to the stars in the sky, the leaves on the trees, and the sands on the sea-shore.

Mr. Purchas, (compiler of the famous collection of voyages,) was informed by President Dale, with whom Tomocomo went out from Virginia, that Opechancanough, and not Powhatan, had given him

his instructions; and that the object of them was
not so much to ascertain the population, as to form
an estimate of the amount of corn raised, and oɪ
forest trees growing in England. Nomantack and
the other savages who had previously visited that
country, being ignorant, and having seen little of the
British empire except London, had reported a very
large calculation of the men and houses, while they
said almost nothing about the trees and corn. It
was therefore a general opinion among the Indians,
that the English had settled in Virginia only for the
purpose of getting supplies of these two articles;
and in confirmation, they observed their continual
eagerness after corn, and the great quantities of cedar,
clapboards, and wainscoting, which they annually
exported to England. Tomocomo readily undeceived
his countrymen upon this point. Landing in the
west of England in summer, and travelling thence
to London, he of course saw evidences of great agri-
cultural and rural plenty and wealth; and was soon
obliged to abandon the account he had undertaken
to keep—his arithmetic failing him on the first day.

In the British metropolis, he met accidentally with
Captain Smith; and the two immediately renewed
their ancient acquaintance. Tomocomo told the captain, that Powhatan had given orders to request of
him—if indeed he was not dead, as reported—the
favor of showing Tomocomo the English God, and
also their King, Queen and prince, of whom they
had formerly conversed so often together. "As to
God," as Stith expresses it, " Captain Smith excused
and explained the matter the best he could." As to
the king, he told Tomocomo he had already seen
him, which was true. But the Indian denied it; and
it was not without some trouble that Smith, by mentioning certain circumstances, convinced him of the
fact. The Indian then assumed a most melancholy
look, "Ah!" said he, "you presented Powhatan a
white dog which he fed as himself. Now, I am certainly better than a white dog; but your king has

10—7

given me nothing." Such an arch sense, adds the historian, had this savage of the ' stingy' treatment he had received at court. Nothing is known of Tomo-como after his return to America.

The most constant friend and ally of the Virginian English, for twenty years from the settlement of Jamestown, was JAPAZAWS, the Sachem—or, as the old writers call him, the king—of the Potomacs or Patowomekes. He was a person of great influence and authority on the whole length of the river which bears to this day the name of his tribe; being in fact a kind of petty emperor there, and always affecting to treat Powhatan and the other emperors rather as brethren than superiors. He had two hundred bowmen in his own village, at the date of the great massacre. The entire population which was more or less subject to him, appears, though somewhat indistinctly, from Smith's account of his first inter-view with the Sachem and his people, in 1608.

" The 16th of Iune," he writes, " we fell with the riuer Patowomek. Feare being gone and our men recouered, we were al content to take some paines to know the name of that seuen-mile broad riuer. For thirtie miles sayle we could see no inhabitants. Then we were conducted by two Salvages vp a little bayed creeke towards Onawmanaient, where al the woodes were layd with ambuscadoes to the number of *three or foure thousand* Salvages, so strangely paynted, grimed and disguised, shouting, yelling and crying as so many spirits from hell could not haue showed more terrible. Many brauadoes they made, but to appease their furie, our captaine prepared with as seeming a willingness as they to encounter them. But the grazing of our bullets vpon the water (many being shot on purpose they might see them) with the ecco of the woodes, so amazed them, as downe went their bowes and arrowes; and (exchanging hostages) Iames Watkins was sent six myles vp the woodes to *their King's* habitation. We were kindly vsed of those Salvage of v' em we vnderstood they

were commanded to betray us by the direction of
Powhatan." After this, he was supplied with plenty
of excellent provisions by the subjects of Japazaws,
and furnished by that sachem himself with guides to
conduct his party up some of the streams. Finally,
he "kindly requited this kinde king and al his kinde
people."

Thus auspiciously commenced a valuable acquaintance; and it is eminently worthy of observa
tion, with what fidelity of friendship the English
were repaid for the courtesy shown to this intelligent
barbarian, and for the justice done to his subjects.
Ever afterwards, they sustained the English cause,
and supplied the English necessities, when all the
rest of their countrymen were willing neither to
treat nor trade upon any terms. When Argall arrived, in 1614, for example, "he was sent to the
riuer Patawomeake," (as Master Hamer calls it,)
"to trade for corne, the Salvages about vs hauing
small quarter, but friends and foes as they found
aduantage and opportunitie." Then, Argall "hauing entred into a great acquaintance with Japazaws,
an old friend of Captaine Smith's, and so to all our
nation, ever since hee discouevered the countrie,"
the negotiation ensued which resulted, as we have
heretofore shown, in getting possession of the person
of Pocahontas, and thereby ultimately effecting a
general peace.

The warmth of the Sachem's gratitude perhaps
caused him to lay too little stress on the hospitality
due to a princess and a guest—if guest she was—but
the struggle which attended the bargain, and the
sorrow which followed it, both show that Japazaws
was not without principle or feeling. The argument
which probably turned the balance in his mind, respected the prospect of a treaty to be brought about
by means of Pocahontas, in which she and Powhatan had much more interest than himse'f. The
bright copper kettle was a subordinate consideration,
though not a slight one. We have seen, that the

Powhatan Sachems were willing to barter almost
their birthright for a pound or two of blue beads.
At all events, Japazaws must have credit for the delicate arrangement by which the princess was first
notified of her forlorn condition. *"Iapazaws treading
oft on the Captaine's foot,* to remember he had done
his part, the captaine, when he saw his time, persuaded Pocahontas to the gun-roome, faining to have
some conference with Iapazaws, *which was only that
shee should not percieue hee was any way guiltie of her
captiuitie."*

In 1619, Iapazous — so called by master John
Rolfe—came to Jamestown, for the first time, to
desire that two ships might be sent to trade in his
river, corn being more abundant than for a long
time before. Parties were sent, accordingly ; but,
for some reasons, not explained, they met with in
different success in the commerce, and so concluded
to take eight hundred bushels of corn by force.
That Japazaws was not much in fault, would appear
from the circumstance that he had no part in the
great conspiracy of 1622 ; immediately after which
we find, that Captain Croshaw went up the Potomac,
" where he intended to stay and trade for himself by
reason of the long acquaintance he had with *this
King*, that, so earnestly entreated him now to be his
friend, his countenancer his captaine and director
against the Pazaticans, the Nacotchtanks and Moya-
ons, his mortall enemies."*

Croshaw gladly availed himself of this invitation,
first for the sake of conducting his commerce to
advantage, and secondly, for the purpose of " keeping
the king as an opposite to Opechancanough." It
was soon afterwards, that the chieftain last named sent
his messengers to Japazaws, with presents of beads,
and proposals of alliance against the English—both
which were rejected. Then we are told, that " Captaine Hamer arriuing with a ship and a pinnace a

---

* Smith's History, Vol. II.

Patawomeke, was kindly entertained both by him [Croshaw] and the king." The two were living snugly together at this time ; using common efforts for supplying the colony—or at least the captain—on the one hand, and for suppressing the king's enemies, as named above, on the other. Their union was at length interrupted by the machinations of an exile Sachem, who had taken refuge at Potomac from the discontent of his own subjects. Angry with Japazaws for not assisting him in the recovery of his dominion, he forged an artful story about Japazaws and his tribe having recently leagued with Opechancanough.

That story he told to one Isaac Madison, who had just been sent to Potomac by Governor Wyatt, with a reenforcement of thirty men, and a commission expressly charging him to assist the Patowo mekes against their enemies, and to protect them and their corn to his utmost power. To give his falsehood the air of probability, this savage Iago cunningly commented upon certain circumstances which had recently occurred. Madison was at length so much alarmed, that sending for Japazaws to his own strong-house (which Japazaws himself had assisted him in fortifying,) he locked in the Sachem, his son, and their four attendants, set over them a guard of soldiers, and then made a violent and bloody assault upon the neighboring village of the Indians. The king remonstrated, but in vain. He denied all the charges brought against him, to no purpose. Madison then led him and the other five prisoners to his ship, promising to set them at liberty as soon as his men were safely aboard. The king meanwhile prevented his subjects from annoying the English on the way. But, contrary to all good faith, the captives were carried to Jamestown, and detained there till the following October, when they were taken home by Captain Hamer and ransomed with a quantity of corn. Madison was prosecuted afterwards for his infamous conduct, but never punished. The Patowomekes must of course have been estranged oy it from the English interest, though there is no evidence of their ever opposing them in arms. Japazaws kept himself aloof, and is no more mentioned in history.

The death of Opechancanough was a signal for the dissolution of the famous confederacy which it had required the whole genius of that chieftain and his predecessor to form and maintain. The tribes relapsed into their former state of separate government ; and no formidable leader ever again roused them to union. The nominal successor of Opechancanough was TOTOPOTOMOI, whom we do not find even mentioned until after a lapse of ten years from his accession. The ancient records of Virginia show, that in 1651, an Act of Assembly was passed, assigning and securing to Totopotomoi such lands on York river as he should choose ; and commissioners were appointed to conduct him and his attendants in safety to Jamestown, and from that place home again, after the adjustment of the treaty. The termination of his reign and life was as follows. Five years subsequent to the date last mentioned, and after an interval of profound peace with the Indians which had continued for fifteen years, information was suddenly received at Jamestown, that a body of inland or mountain savages, called Rechahecrians, to the number of six or seven hundred, had seated themselves near the falls of James river, with the apparent intention of forming a regular settlement. The motives of this singular movement have never been explained. It is only known, that it gave no little alarm to the colonists ; and that active preparations were made for driving the new enemy back to their own territories. A campaign ensued, and a battle was fought; and in this battle fell the king of the Powhatans, gallantly fighting in aid of the English, at the head of one hundred warriors. Victory declared for the Rechahecrians, but a peace was soon after negotiated with them on terms satisfactory to both parties.

Totopotomoi has at least his name immortalized
by the author of Hudibras, who introduced him (to
make out a rhyme,) in his noted allusion to a certain
scandal upon the New England colonists.

> A precious brother having slain.
> In time of peace, an Indian,
>   *   *   *   *   *
> The mighty TOTTIPOTIMOY
> Sent to our elders an envoy,
> Complaining sorely of the breach
> Of league, held forth by brother Patch.
>   *   *   *
> For which he craved the saints to render
> Into his hands, or hang, the offender.
> But they, maturely having weighed,
> They had no more but him of the trade—
> A man that served them in a double
> Capacity, to preach and cobble—
> Resolved to spare him ; yet to do
> The Indian *Hogan Mogan* too
> Impartial Justice, in his stead did
> Hang an old weaver that was bed-rid.

We may certainly be amused with the wit of the
satirist in this case, without insisting upon a strict
proof of his statements.

Such is the meagre biography of the last of the
Virginian chieftains. We shall close this chapter
with some particulars respecting two or three of the
principal Indians known, at an earlier date, to the
first colonists of Carolina. One of these was WIN-
GINA, the king of a considerable tract of territory
called Wingandacoa, bordering upon Albemarle
Sound. Another was GRANGANIMO, the brother of
Wingina. Not much information is extant concerning either of these persons ; but the little which is
known derives an additional interest both from the
style of the ancient writers of that period, and from
the circumstance that the foreign settlements which

ed to this partial acquaintance were among the very
first upon the continent.

On the 27th of April, 1584, Philip Amidas and
Arthur Barlow sailed from the west of England, as
commanders of two barks, fitted out by Sir Walter
Raleigh, for the purpose of exploring a vast tract
of country granted to him by a patent from Queen
Elizabeth, of the March previous.   Taking the
usual route by way of the Canaries and West Indies,
they approached the coast of the Southern States,
(now so called,) on the second of July, (enjoying for
a day or two " a most delicate sweete smell " from
the shore.)   After sailing one hundred and twenty
miles north, they entered the first harbor they met
with, returned thanks to God for their safe arrival,
went to view the neighboring land, and then took
possession of it, formally, " for the Queene's most excellent majestic."   " Which done," writes our ancient
chronicler, "they found their first landing-place sandy
and low, but so full of grapes that the very surge of
the sea sometimes overflowed them ; of which they
found such plenty in all places, on the sand, the
greene soyle and hils, as in the plaines, as well on
euery little shrub as also climbing towardes the tops
of high cedars, that they did thinke in the world
were not the like abundance."

This beautiful spot was the island of Wococon,
supposed to be the same now called Ocracock.   The
newly arrived adventurers wandered over every part
of it with mingled feelings of amazement and delight.   Goodly woods covered the green bosom of
its quiet valleys.   There, we are told, were the highest and reddest cedars of the world, " bettering them
of Azores or Libanus.   There, were Pynes, Cypres,
Saxefras, the Lentisk that beareth mastick, and many
other of excellent smelle and qualitie.   Then there
were deere and conies, and fowl in such incredible
abundance, that the discharge of a musket would

---

* See the Collections of Hackluyt.

raise a flock of them from under the very feet of the travellers, with a noise, 'as if an army of men had shouted altogether.' "

On the third day, three of the natives appeared in a canoe, one of whom went fearlessly aboard an English bark. The crew could hold no conversation with him; but they gave him a shirt, a hat, wine and meat. These he liked exceedingly; and so having satisfied his curiosity with gazing, he paddled off to the distance of half a mile. He there loaded his boat with fish in a short time, then landed on a point near by, divided his booty into two heaps—" pointing one heap to the ship, and the other to the pinnace"—and then departed. This pacific interview was followed with happy consequences. The next day Granganimo appeared, with forty or fifty of his people. He came to the point with his train, and seated himself upon a mat. A party of the English went ashore, well armed; but instead of showing any indications of suspicion or fear, he made signs to them to be seated at his side—stroking their heads and breasts, as also his own, no doubt in testimony of his good will. He then made a long speech to his new visitants—probably of welcome—and they presented divers gewgaws to him in return, which he politely accepted. He was so much regarded by his attendants, that none of them would sit or even speak in his presence, with the exception of four. To them the English gave other presents; but they were immediately put into Granganimo's hands, who signified, with an air of dignity, that every thing of this nature must be at his own disposal.

At the next interview, the English entertained him with a display of many commodities calculated to dazzle and surprise him. But none of them struck his fancy like a large bright pewter dish plate, and a copper kettle, for the former of which he gave twenty deer-skins,* and for the latter fifty

---

* Then valued at a crown each. The anecdote reminds one of JAPAZAWS.

L.—I

He made a hole in the plate, and hung it about his
neck for a breastplate.   Much other "truck" passed
between the parties, in such good humor and good
faith, that in the course of a day or two a meeting
took place on board one of the vessels, and the
Sachem ate, drank and made merry with the English, like one of their own number.   Not long afterwards, he brought his wife and children, who are
described as slender, but well-favored and very modest.   The wife wore, as her husband did, a band of
white coral on her forehead, and in her ears brace-
lets of pearl,* "hanging down to her middle, of the
size of large peas."   Her female followers had pen-
dants of copper; and the noblemen—as those who
seemed to be leading characters among the males
are entitled—had five or six in each ear.   All were
dressed alike in skins.   The women wore their hair
long on both sides of the head; the men, only on
one.

The next step in the acquaintance, and a very
natural one, was that great numbers of people began
to come in from various parts of the neighboring
coast, bringing skins, coral and different kinds of
dyes for sale; none of which, however, any of them
but the noblemen ("them that wore red copper on
their heads, as *he* did,") would undertake to barter
in presence of Granganimo himself.   The character
of the Sachem showed itself more and more to advantage at every interview.   With a very considerate
and civil regard for the comfort of the English, he
never paid them a visit without previously signifying the number of boats he should bring with him,
by fires kindled upon the shore; so that his strength
might be exactly estimated.   He invariably kept,
with perfect punctuality, every promise which he
made in the course of traffic, as he also regularly
sent to the vessels, daily, a gratuitous fresh supply

---

* So called by the early writers on various occasions. Probably they were shells, or rock-crystal, or something of that
kind.

ot provisions—generally a brace of bucks, conies, rabbits, and fish ; and sometimes melons, walnuts, cucumbers, pears and other roots and fruits. Finally, he invited the English to visit him at his own residence, on the north end of an island called Roanoke, distant about twenty miles from the harbor first made by the colonists.

The invitation was promptly accepted by a party of eight of the English. They found Granganimo's village to consist of nine houses, built of cedar, and fortified with sharp palisades, "and the entrance like a turnpik." The Sachem himself was absent when they arrived ; but his wife came out eagerly to meet them. Some of her people she commanded to draw their boat ashore, that it might not suffer from the sea's dashing; others to carry the English on their backs through the surf, and put away their oars under cover. Meanwhile she conducted her guests into a house containing five apartments. As they were wet with rain, she had a large fire kindled in an inner apartment, washed their feet and their clothes, and then served up a bountiful dinner in another room. "She set on the bord standing along the house somewhat like frumentie, sodden venison and rosted fish ; and in like manner mellons raw, boyled rootes, and fruites of diuers kindes."

She manifested the utmost anxiety for the comfort of her guests. While they were eating, two or three Indians happened to enter, with bows and arrows, upon which the English started up and laid hold of their arms. She perceived their distrust, but instead of being offended, caused the weapons of the intruders to be snapped asunder, and themselves to be beaten. Still the company did not feel perfectly at home, and towards evening they retired to their boat. This grieved her not a little ; but she sent them a supper. When she saw them jealously pushing off some rods from the shore for a safe anchorage, she sent them mats to shelter them from the rain, and directed a guard of her people to watch during the night upon the shore. On the whole, it has been justly observed, that there is scarcely in all history a picture of un-affected and generous hospitality more striking than this.

Wingina, meanwhile, lay at his chief town, ill of wounds he had recently received in battle; and the English saw nothing of him. Nor was any thing more seen of Granganimo, until April of the next year, when Sir Richard Grenville brought out a col-ony of one hundred and eight persons, whom he left on the Carolinian shore at Hatteras. Granganimo then came on board his ship in his usually friendly and fearless manner. But it was his last visit. He died during the year 1585.

This event produced a great alteration of affairs in the colony. They were settled on Roanoke, an island at the mouth of Albemarle Sound, and that situation made it quite convenient for them to visit the coast and the country in various directions, which they were instructed to do. They explored, there-fore, in the course of their expeditions, as far south as beyond Pamlico river; and as far north as the territory of the Chesapeaks, on the bay of their own name. They also went up Albemarle Sound and Chowan river, one hundred and thirty miles, to a nation of Indians called Chowanocks, living above the junction of the Nottaway and the Meherrin.

We mention these particulars for the sake of in-troducing MENATENON, the king of the tribe last named. His province is described as the largest on the whole length of the river; and the town of Chowanock, it is said, could bring seven hundred bowmen into the field. Menatenon was lame—owing probably to a wound in battle—but writes an old chronicler "he had more understanding than all the rest." He amused the colonists, and especially their governor, Mr. Lane, with a story about a copper mine and a pearl fishery, somewhere along the coast. He also gave a strange account of the head of the river Moratuc, (now called the Roanoke,) where lived a king (he affirmed,) whose country bordered on the sea, and who took such an abundance of pearls from it, that not only his skins and his noblemen's, but his beds and his houses were garnished with that ornament. Mr. Lane expressed a wish to see a specimen of them ; but Menatenon readily replied, that the king of that rich country *reserved them expressly for trading with white men.**

The source of the Moratuc was described as springing out of a vast rock, standing so near the sea, that in storms the surges beat over it. As for the copper, *that* he said was generally collected in great bowls, covered with skin, at a place particularly described, and yielded two parts of metal for three of ore. There might be a shadow of foundation for some of these relations ; but the chief object of Menatenon—who was a captive among the colonists at the time of his making them—must have been to render himself an important man in their eyes, and perhaps to lead them into some hazardous enterprise. Hearing them talk much about mines and pearls, and the South Sea—which were all hobbies with the credulous adventurers of that period—he adapted his discourse accordingly, and his eager hearers were simple enough to believe every thing he asserted.†

They even undertook the proposed expedition in search of the copper mine and the South Sea ; and had actually advanced nearly two hundred miles up

---

* " This King was at Chowanock two yeares agoe to trade with *blacke pearle*, his worst sort whereof I had a rope, *but they were naught;* but that king he, [Menatenon] sayth hath store of *white*, and had trafficke with white men, for wnom he reserved them."

† " The Mangoaks haue such plentie of it, they beautifie their houses with great plates thereof: this the salvages report; and young Shiko, *the King Chawonocks sonne my prisoner,* that had been prisoner among the Mangoaks, &c.   *   *   *

Menatenon also confirmed all this, and promised me guides to this mettall country, &c.

the country, before famine and fatigue, and the
hostility of innumerable savages compelled them to
turn about. It seems that Wingina had heard of
this expedition — perhaps from Menatenon — and
like that cunning though crippled Sachem, he did
all in his power to make it both specious in prospect
and fatal in result. After having said every thing
to excite the curiosity and avarice of the colonists,
till he saw them determined to go, he sent word to
the different powerful tribes living on their proposed
route, that the English were coming *against them;*
and that the sooner they suppressed this new enemy,
the better. Hence it was, that the party several
times came very near being cut off by the savages;
and hence, instead of being plentifully supplied with
choice provisions, as expected, they were glad to
live several days upon two dogs ' boiled down with
saxefras leaves.'

Fortunately for the colony, several circumstances
concurred in the period of distress which succeeded
this enterprise, to prevent Wingina from making
open war upon them. One was the influence of
his father, ENSENORE, the best friend, next to Granganimo, whom the English had ever found among
the natives. But the safe return of the expedition
made a stronger impression upon the mind of Wingina. Rumors had been circulated that the party
were all starved or slain ; and then he had "begun
to blaspheme our God that would suffer it, and not
defend vs, so that old Ensenore had no more credit
for vs ; for he began by al the deuises he could to
inuade vs."* But the return of the expedition after
having defeated all enemies—"asswaged a little his
deuises, and brought Ensenore in respect againe
that our God was good, and wee their friends, and
our foes should perish, &c."

The last observation suggests another circumstance

---

* See the journal of Governor Lane, as preserved in the old
collections.

which went to restrain the enmity of the chieftain.
This was a mortal epidemic, of unknown character,
which prevailed exclusively among the Indians, and
carried off great numbers. The colonists had the
art to make these simple beings regard it as a punishment for the hostility hitherto manifested towards the
English. Wingina himself, who lived in the immediate vicinity of the colony, was exceedingly overcome by his superstition. Twice he was very sick,
and came near dying. He then dismissed the priests
who usually attended him, and sent for some of the
English to pray for him, and to be—as Master Heriot
expresses it, in his "Observations" upon this voyage—
" a meenes to our God that hee might liue with him
after death." He supposed that he had offended the
Deity of the English by his blasphemy. They were
themselves in great repute, of course. " This maruei-
lous accident in all the country wrought so strange
opinion of vs that they could not tell, whether to
thinke vs Gods or men." Of the two, they considered
the former most probable, for the whites having no
women among them, the inference in their minds
was, that instead of being born of women, they were
men of an old generation many years past, and risen
again from immortality.* All which, we are told, so
changed the heart of PEMISSAPAN (—a name assumed
by Wingina since the death of Granganimo—) that,
at Ensenore's suggestion, when the English were
reduced to extremities for want of food, he sent in
his subjects to make fish-weirs for them, and to plant
the fields they had hitherto thought of abandoning.

But in April, 1586, Ensenore died ; and as Wingina
had now completely recovered his health, and most
of the enemies which the colony had among the
tribes took this opportunity of renewing their machinations, he relapsed into his former hostility. Ar-
rangements were made for collecting seven or eight
hundred Indians, under pretence of solemnizing the

---

* Heriot

funeral of Ensenore. Half of them were to lie in ambush for those of the colonists who daily straggled along the coast in pursuit of crabs, fish and other provisions. The other detachment was to assault the settlement of Roanoke, at a signal by fire in the night. Even the particular houses were allotted to be burned by particular persons or parties. Twenty were charged to beset the dwelling of Governor Lane, and fire the reeds which covered it; this would bring *him* out, naked and unarmed, and then they could despatch him without danger. The same order was made for Mr. Heriot's, and various other habitations, which were to be fired at the same instant. In the meantime, as it was of great consequence to reduce the strength of the colony by dispersing it, Wingina provided for breaking up the weirs, and strictly pro-hibited all trade in provisions. He kept himself aloof also with a similar view.

The plan was well concerted, and not without suc-cess. The Governor was soon obliged to send off twenty of the colonists to a part of the coast called Croatan, merely that they might collect the means of their own sustenance. Ten more were sent to Hatte-ras for the same purpose ; and other small companies scattered themselves about on the seacoast, to gather oysters and roots. But the ingenuity of the civilized party, driven to desperation, finally prevailed against the chieftain's naked shrewdness. The Governor sent him word he was going to Croatan, to meet an English squadron which had touched there with supplies, covering the object of this fabrication by also requesting the services of a few Indians to fish and hunt for the colony. Desirous of gaining time, Wingina promptly replied, that he would himself visit Mr. Lane in eight days. No doubt he expected to complete his conspiracy in this interval.

But the Governor was not so to be deceived. He resolved, on the contrary, to pay the Sachem a visit the next day after receiving his answer. Previous to that, however, he proposed to surprise the Indians at

Wingina's old settlement on the island (Roanoke) and to take their canoes from them. But they, too, were on the alert, so entirely had Wingina prepared them for emergencies. "For when I sent to take the canows," says Mr. Lane in his Journal, "they met one going from the shore, overthrew her, and cut off two Salvages' heads ; wherevpon the cry arose, being by their spies perceived ; *for they kept as good watch ouer vs as we ouer them.*" A skirmish ensued, and the Indians fled into the woods. The next morning, the Governor crossed over to a place on the main called Dassamonpeak, and sent Wingina word he was going to Croatan, and having certain complaints to make to him respecting his subjects, would be happy to call upon him by the way. On the faith of this proposal, the chieftain, with several of his principal men, met the Governor's party on their route. But no conversation took place. The Governor gave an appointed watchword to his men on approaching, and they fired upon the Indians. Wingina was shot through with a pistol-bullet, and fell. Recovering his feet immediately, he fled, and was near escaping his pursuers, when an Irish boy shot him a second time. He was soon overtaken, and then beheaded on the spot.

We do not feel disposed to dismiss these biographies of the Carolinian Sachems, short and slight as they are, without offering such comment as they most obviously suggest. It appears singular, at first sight, that so striking a difference of feeling towards the English should be manifested by the two brothers. Perhaps there was fault on both sides. Master Heriot admits, that some of the colony, "towards the latter end showed themselves too furious, in slaying some of the people in some Townes, vpon causes that on our part might haue been borne with more mildnesse." We have seen with how little ceremony the Governor proceeded to take summary measures. He was driven to extremities, indeed, but that in itself was no fault of the Indians—they were not under obligation to supply him, though it appears that they some-times did, gratuitously.

Perhaps a remark should be made respecting a provocation which occurred when the colony was first left by Grenville. The English went about ranging the coast from tribe to tribe, and from town to town—which very circumstance, besides being probably accompanied by other trespasses, and at all events wholly unlicensed by the natives, could hardly be looked upon as either friendly or just. Then, " at Aquascosack the Indians stole a silver cup, *wherefore we burnt the towne, and spoyled their corne,* and so returned to our fleet at Tocokon."* This was certainly no way to make friends, and those who are familiar with the Carolinian history subsequent to Wingina's death, will remember that the injury was by no means forgotten. Finally, setting aside the attempt to justify either party, it will be noticed, by such as may take the pains to look into the annals of this period, that the greater part of the information which the Govern or received of the Sachem's motives and movements came through the medium of that shrewd cripple, Menatenon, and his son Shiko. Whatever the facts might be, then, the evidence was clearly inadequate if not wholly inadmissible.

---

* Relation of Lane

CHAPTER VI.*

Synopsis of the New England Indians at the date of the
Plymouth Settlement—The Pokanoket confederacy—The
Wampanoag tribe—Their first head-Sachem, known to the
English—MASSASOIT—The first interview between him and
the whites—His visit to Plymouth, in 1621—Treaty of peace
and friendship—Embassy sent to him at Sowams, by the Eng-
ish—Anecdotes respecting it—He is suspected of treachery
or hostility, in 1622—His sickness in 1623—A second deputa·
tion visits him—Ceremonies and results of the visit—His intercourse with other tribes—Conveyances of land to the English—His death and character—Anecdotes.

THE clearest, if not the completest classification
of the New England Indians, at the date of the settlement of Plymouth, includes five principal con-
federacies, each occupying their own territory, and
governed by their own chiefs. The Pequots inhabited the eastern part of Connecticut. East of them
were the Narraghansetts, within whose limits Rhode
Island, and various smaller islands in the vicinity,
were comprised. The Pawtucket tribes were situated chiefly in the southern section of New Hampshire,
the Massachusetts tribes around the bay of their own
name ; and between these upon, the north and the
Narraghansetts upon the south, the Pokanokets
claimed a tract of what is now Bristol county, (Rhode
Island) bounded laterally by Taunton and Pawtucket rivers for some distance, together with large parts
of Plymouth and Barnstable.

This confederacy exercised some dominion over

---

* Not to subject ourselves to the charge of plagiarism, it
may be proper to remark here, that several passages in the
following notices of the Pokanoket Sachems have been taken
almost unaltered from an article on *Indian Biography*, published heretofore in the North American Review, and written by
the author of this work. The same is true of a part of the
subsequent notice of Tecumseh and his brother

the Indians of Nantucket and Martha's Vineyard,
and over several of the nearest Massachusetts and
Nipmuck tribes;—the latter name designating an
interior territory, now mostly within the boundaries
of Worcester county.   Of the Pokanokets, there
were nine separate cantons or tribes, each governed
by its own petty sagamore or squaw, but all subject
to one grand-sachem, who was also the particular
chief of the Wampanoag canton, living about
Montaup.*

The first knowledge we have of the Wampanoags,
and of the individuals who ruled over them and
the other Pokanokets, is furnished in the collections
of Purchas, on the authority of a Captain Dermer
the Master Thomas Dirmire spoken of by John
Smith in his *New England Trialls,* as "an vnderstanding and industrious gentleman, who was also with
him amongst the Frenchmen."   Dermer was sent
out from England in 1619, by Sir F. Gorges, on account of the President and Council of New England,
in a ship of two hundred tons.   He had a Pokanoket
Indian with him, named SQUANTO, one of about
twenty who had been kidnapped on the coast by
Captain Hunt, in 1614, and sold as slaves at Malaga
for twenty pounds a man.†   Squanto and a few
others of the captives were either rescued or redeem
ed, by the benevolent interposition of some of the

---

* This celebrated eminence (frequently called, by corruption
of the Indian name, Mount-Hope) is a mile or two east of the
village of Bristol.   It is very steep on all sides, and ter-
minates in a large rock, having the appearance to a distant
spectator, of an immense dome.

† It is gratifying to learn from Smith that Hunt was punished, though not according to the baseness of his infamous
crime.   " He betraied foure and twentie of these poore Saluages aboord his ship, and most dishonestly and inhumanely
for their kinde usage of me and all our men, carried them with
him to Maligo, and there for a little priuate gaine sold those
silly Saluages for Rials of eight; *but this vilde act kept him
ever after from any more imploiement to these parts.*"-
Generale Historie of New England, published in 1632

monks upon that island. "When I arrived," says
Dermer in his letter to Purchas, "at my savage's
native country, finding all dead, I travelled along a
day's journey to a place called Nummastaquyt, where,
finding inhabitants, I despatched a messenger a day's
journey further west, to Pacanokit, which border-
eth on the sea; whence came to see me *two kings*
attended with a guard of fifty armed men, who being
well satisfied with that my savage and I discoursed
unto them, (being desirous of novelty) gave me content in whatsoever I demanded. Here I redeemed
a Frenchman, and afterwards another at Massta-
chusitt, who three years since escaped shipwreck at
the northeast of Cape Cod." One of these two kings,
—as the sachems were frequently entitled by the
early writers,—must have been MASSASOIT, so well
known afterwards to the Plymouth settlers; and
probably the second was his brother Quadepinah.
The "native country" of Squanto was the vicinity
of Plymouth, where the Indians are understood to
have been kidnapped. Thousands of them, there,
as well as elsewhere along the whole coast of New
England, had been swept off by a terrible pestilence.

The first appearance of Massasoit,* after the settlement of Plymouth, was upon the 22d of March,
1621, a week previous to which some information
concerning him had been gathered from an Indian
named Samoset, who entered the village with great
boldness, and greeted the inhabitants with a "welcome." On the second occasion, he came in with
four others,—having engaged to introduce some of
the Wampanoags, to traffic in furs,—among whom
was Squanto, at that time probably the sole remain-

---

* We have given the most simple orthography of this word.
It is frequently written Massasoyt, Massasoiet, Massasowat,
&c. Mr. Belknap says, (American Biography,) that contemporary pronunciation made it a word of four syllables, with
the accent on the second,—Mas-sass-o-it. The sachem subsequently assumed another name, which has undergone still
more various modifications,—Oosamequin, Woosamequin, and
Ausamequin, are some of them.

ing native of Plymouth.   This party brought a few
fish and skins to sell, and informed the English that
the great sachem, with his brother and his whole
force, were near at hand.   Massasoit soon appeared
upon the neighboring hill, with sixty men.   As they
seemed unwilling to approach nearer, Squanto was
despatched to ascertain their designs ; and they gave
him to understand, that they wished some one
should be sent to hold a parley.

Edward Winslow was appointed to this office,
and he immediately carried presents to the sachem,
which were willingly accepted.   He addressed him
also in a speech of some length, which the Indians
listened to with the decorous gravity characteristic
of the race, ill-explained as it was by the interpreter.
The purport of the speech was, that King James
saluted the sachem, his brother, with the words of
peace and love ; that he accepted him as his friend
and ally ; and that the Governor desired to see him,
and to trade and treat with him upon friendly terms.
Massasoit appears to have made no special reply to
this harangue, for the sufficient reason, probably,
that he did not precisely comprehend the drift of
it.   He paid more attention to the sword and armor
of Winslow while he spoke ; and when he had ceased speaking, signified his disposition to commence
the proposed trade forthwith by buying *them*.   They
were not, however, for sale ; and so, leaving Winslow in the custody of his brother, he crossed a brook
between him and the English, taking with him
twenty of the Wampanoags, who were directed to
leave their bows and arrows behind them.   Beyond
the brook he was met by Captain Standish and
another gentleman, with an escort of six armed men,
who exchanged salutations with him, and attended
him to one of the best houses in the village.*   Here,

---

* A stone arch has in modern times been thrown over this
brook, to point out the precise spot of the meeting.   The hill
where the chieftain first appeared was by the settlers of his
time called " Strawberry-Hill."

a green rug was spread upon the floor, and three or four cushions piled on it for his accommodation. The Governor then entered the house, followed by several soldiers, and preceded by a flourish of a drum and trumpet,—a measure probably recommended by Standish, and which answered the purpose of delighting and astounding the Wampanoags, even beyond expectation. It was a deference paid to their sovereign, which pleased as well as surprised them. The sachem and the Governor now kissed each other, and after the interchange of certain other civilities, sat down together, and regaled themselves with what Neal calls an entertainment. It consisted, it seems, chiefly of "strong waters, a thing the savages love very well; and the sachem took such a large draught of it at once, as made him sweat all the while he staid." A treaty was concluded upon this occasion, the terms of which were as follows.

1. That neither he, nor any of his (Massasoit's) should injure or do hurt to any of their people.

2. That if any of his did any hurt to any of theirs, he should send the offender, that they might punish him.

3. That if any thing were taken away from any of theirs, he should cause it to be restored, and they should do the like to his.

4. That if any did unjustly war against him, they would aid him; and if any did war against them, he should aid them.

5. That he should send to his neighbor confederates, to inform them of this, that they might not wrong them, but might be likewise comprised in these conditions of peace.

6. That when his came to them upon any occasion, they should leave their arms behind them.

7. That so doing, their Sovereign Lord, King James, would esteem him as his friend and ally.

"All which," says Morton,—and some other annalists agree with him,—"he liked very well, and withal, at the same time, acknowledged himself content to become the subject of our Sovereign Lord the King aforesaid, his heirs and successors ; and gave unto him all the lands adjacent, to him and his heirs forever." This acknowledgement of the sovereignty of the King, if it really made a part of the agreement, certainly deserved a place as a distinct article ; being by far more important than all the others. The grant of land,—and this grant constituted the entire title of the Plymouth settlers, as against the natives,— is confirmed by subsequent transactions, and especially by the acts of Massasoit. But his submission to the authority of King James, as a subject to a sovereign, is more doubtful ; nor does it by any means accord with the seventh express article. That the treaty itself also was not preserved precisely as it was probably understood, may be inferred from the variations of it given by Mourt in his Relation. According to *his* sixth article, for example, a just reciprocity is maintained, by providing that the English should leave their *pieces* behind them in their interviews with the Indians. This distinction between alliance and subjection,—at least in the mind of one of the parties,—seems to have been too much overlooked.

Such, however, was the first treaty made with the Indians of New England,—a passage in its history of great interest. It was made upon peaceable and honorable terms. The Indians came in voluntarily to make it ; and though they received as a consideration for the immense territory granted at the time, only a pair of knives, and a copper chain with a jewel in it for the grand sachem ; and a knife, a jewel to hang in his ear, a pot of strong water, a good quantity of biscuit, and some butter for Quadepinah,*—yet were all parties satisfied with the substance as they were gratified by the ceremonies of

---

* So minutely is the transaction described in *The Journal of a Plantation at Plymouth*, preserved by Purchas, and re-published among the Historical Collections of Massachusetts There is reason to think that Winslow was the author

the agreement. It is pleasing to learn from history, that this simple negotiation was remembered and adhered to on both sides for the unparalleled term of half a century ; nor was Massasoit, or any of the Wampanoags during his lifetime, convicted by the harshest revilers of his race, of having violated, or attempted to violate, any of its plain, just, and deliberate provisions.

The two parties seem to have regarded each other on this occasion with a curiosity of equal interest and minuteness ; for while the sachem was inspecting the armor of Winslow, and his Wampanoags exerting themselves to blow the trumpet in imitation of their hosts,* the English by-standers, on the other hand, were making their own observations. The writer of the *Journal of a Plantation settled at Plymouth,* describes Massasoit as " a very lusty man, in his best years, an able body, grave of countenance, and spare of speech." In his attire, he is said to have differed little from the rest of his followers, ex cepting that he wore a large chain of white bone-beads about his neck, which was, probably, one of the royal *insignia ;* and that he had suspended from it behind, a little bag of tobacco, which he *drank,* says the writer, " and gave us to drink." His appearance otherwise does not seem to have been particularly elegant ; his face being painted of a sad red, like murrey, and both head and face so oiled that he " looked greasily." His only weapon was a long knife, swinging at his bosom by a string. His attendants were probably arrayed for this great occasion with peculiar attention to etiquette ; some of them being painted black, others red, yellow, or white ; some wearing crosses and " other antick works ;" and several of them dressed in furs or skins of various descriptions. Being tall, strong men also, and the first natives whom most of the Colonists had ever

---

* " He marvelled much at our trumpet, and some of his men would sound it as well as we could."—*Journal.*

J.—K

seen near at hand, they must have made to them a somewhat imposing, as well as interesting spectacle.

Leaving a few of their number among the whites, as hostages, the Wampanoags retired to the woods about half a mile distant and spent the night; and Winslow acted as *their* hostage. The English were not yet prepared, it would seem, to put faith in the professions of savages; for they kept strict watch all night, besides retaining the security just named. Their guests, on the contrary, enjoyed themselves quietly in the woods; and there were some of their wives and children with them, who must have come upon this courteous visit from a distance of forty miles. The sachem sent several of his people the next morning, to signify his wish that some of his new friends would honor *him* with their presence. Standish and one Alderton* " went venturously " among them, and were cordially, if not royally welcomed with an entertainment of tobacco and ground-nuts. "We cannot yet conceive," continues our still unsatisfied informant, "but that he is willing to have peace with us ; for they have seen our people sometimes alone two or three in the woods at work and fowling, when they offered them no harm, as they might easily have done." They remained at their encampment till late in the forenoon ; the Governor requiting the sachem's liberality, meanwhile, by send ing an express messenger for his large kettle, and filling it with dry peas. " This pleased them well ; and so they went their way ;"—the one party as much relieved, no doubt, as the other was gratified.†

---

* From whom the outer point of Boston harbor is said to have been named.

† Such was the earliest visit, of ceremony or business at least, which the natives of New England paid to the Colonists. The account given of it, though *ex parte*, as all such descriptions must be, is honorable to the former in the highest degree. They show that many, if not most of the savages, who were fairly dealt with, were at first as sensible and as prone to kindness as could have been wished. They went unarmed

We meet with Massasoit again in July 1621 ; an embassy being then sent to him at his own residence, Montaup or Sowams. This embassy consisted of Edward Winslow and Stephen Hopkins ; and the objects of it were, says Mourt,* "that *forasmuch as his subjects came often and without fear upon all occasions amongst us,*" so the English went now to visit him, carrying with them a coat from the Governor to his friend the sachem, as a token of good will, and desire to live peaceably. It was farther intimated, though with great delicacy, that whereas his people came frequently and in great numbers to Plymouth, wives, children, and all, and were always welcome,—yet being but strangers in the land, and not confident how their corn might prosper, they could no longer give them such entertainment as they had done, and still wished to do. If Massasoit himself, however, would visit them, or any special friend of his, he should be welcome. A request was then made, that the Pokanokets, who had furs, should be permitted to dispose of them to the Colonists. The Governor wished him also to exchange some corn for seed with the Plymouth people.

The remaining article in this message is more illustrative of the relations understood to exist and to be desirable between the parties. On the first arrival of the Colonists at Cape Cod, it seems they had found corn buried there in the ground. Seeing no inhabitants in the neighborhood, " but some graves of the dead newly buried," they took the corn, with the intention of making full satisfaction for it whenever it became practicable. The owners of it were

---

among the settlers without fear, disposed to be honest and friendly at all events, and as hospitable as their means permitted. It will appear in the sequel, that they continued so for a long course of years, as they also continued faithful to their express obligations.

* See MOURT'S RELATION, part of which is also preserved in the COLLECTIONS. The name of the publisher only seems to be attached to it.

supposed to have fled through fear. It was now proposed, that these men should be informed by Massasoit,—if they could be found,—that the English were
ready to pay them with an equal quantity of corn,
English meal, or "any other commodities they had
to pleasure them withal;" and full satisfaction was
offered for any trouble which the sachem might do
them the favor to take. This proposal was equally
politic and just.

The visiters met with a generous, though humble
hospitality, which reminds one of the first reception
of Columbus by the West-Indian islanders. They
reached Namaschet about three o'clock in the afternoon; and there, we are told, the inhabitants entertained them with joy, in the best manner they were
able; giving them sweet bread* and fish, with a less
acceptable accompaniment of boiled musty acorns.
Various civilities were exchanged after this primitive
and savory repast,—as ancient, by the way, as the
early Greeks,—and some time was passed very pleasantly in shooting a crow at a considerable distance,
to the vast astonishment and amusement of the
Indians. They were then directed to a place about
eight miles distant, (Middleborough) where, says the
Journalist, they should find "more store and better
victuals." They were welcomed, on their arrival,
by a party who were catching great numbers of fine
bass in Taunton river, and who gave them a supper
and a breakfast in the morning, besides the privilege
of lodging in the woods near by over night.

Attended by six of their hosts the next day, they
were assisted in passing the river; and here they
met with the first indications of ill-will, in the persons of two old Indians upon the opposite bank.
These two, espying them as they entered the river,
ran swiftly and stealthily among the high grass to

---

* Called *mazium*, and made of Indian corn, no doubt.
Gookin says, that a meal which they made of parched maize
was so sweet, so hearty, and so *toothsome*, that an Indian
would travel many days with no other food

meet them ; and then, with loud voices and drawn
bows, demanded of the strangers who they were ;
" but seeing we were friends," it is added, " they
welcomed us with such food as they had, and we
bestowed a small bracelet of beads on them." The
remarks which follow this, upon the conduct of the
six attendants, we cannot forbear citing at large,
irrelevant to our main purpose as they are. " When
we came to a small brook," says our accurate writer,
" where no bridge was, two of them desired to carry
us through of their own accords ; also fearing we
were, or would be weary, offered to carry our pieces ;
also if we would lay off any of our clothes, [it being
excessively hot,] we should have them carried ; and
as the one of them had found more special kindness
from one of the messengers, and the other savage
from the other, so they showed their thankfulness
accordingly, in affording us help and furtherance in
the journey."

After one more entertainment on the way, our
travellers reached Sowams. Massasoit was not at
home, but arrived soon after, and was saluted by his
visiters with a discharge of musketry. He welcomed
them kindly after the Indian manner, took them into
his lodge, and seated them by himself. They then
delivered their message and presents, the latter comprising a horseman's coat of red cotton, embroidered
with fine lace. The sachem mounted this superb
article without delay, and hung the chain, which
they also gave him, about his neck, evidently enjoying the unspeakable admiration of the Wampanoags,
who gazed upon him at a distance. He now answered the message, clause after clause ; and particularly
signified his desire to continue in peace and friendship with his neighbors. He gathered his men
around him in fine, and harangued them ; they occasionally confirming what he said by their customary ejaculations. Was not he, Massasoit, commander of the country about them ? Was not such a
town within his dominions—and were not the peo-

ple of it his subjects—and should they not bring
their skins to him, if he wished it?

Thus he proceeded to name about thirty of his
small settlements, his attentive auditors responding
to each question. The matter being regularly settled, he lighted tobacco for his guests, and conversed
with them about their own country and King, mar-
velling, above all, that his Majesty should live without a squaw. As it grew late, and he offered no
more substantial entertainment than this,—no doubt
for the sound reason, that he had nothing to offer,
—his guests intimated a wish to retire for the night.
He forthwith accommodated them, with himself and
his wife, they at one end and his visiters at the other,
of a bed consisting of a plank platform, raised a foot
or two from the ground and covered with a thin
mat. Two of his chief men, probably by way of
compliment, were also stationed upon the same
premises; and this body-guard performed their
pressing duty of escort so effectually, that no other
circumstances were necessary to make the honored
guests " worse weary of their lodging than they had,
been of their journey."

On the following day, many of the petty chiefs,
with their subjects, came in from the adjacent country, and various sports and games were got up for
the entertainment of the English. At noon, they
partook, with the sachem and about forty others,
of a meal of boiled fish *shot* by himself, (probably
with arrows.) They continued with him until the
next morning, when they departed, leaving Massasoit
"both grieved and ashamed" that he could not better entertain him. Very importunate he was, adds
the journalist, to have them stay with him longer;
but as they had eaten but one meal for two days
and a night, with the exception of a partridge, which
one of them killed; and what with their location at
night, the " savages' barbarous singing of themselves
to sleep," musquitoes without doors, and other tri-
fling inconveniences within, could not sleep at all:

they begged to be excused,—on the score of conscience, Sunday being near at hand,—not to mention that they were growing light-headed, and could hardly expect, if they stayed much longer, to be able to reach home.

Massasoit's friendship was again tested in March, 1622, when an Indian, known to be under Squanto's influence,[*] came running in among a party of colonists, with his face gashed, and the blood fresh upon it, calling out to them to flee for their lives, and then looking behind him as if pursued. On coming up, he told them that the Indians, under Massasoit, were congregating at a certain place for an attack upon the Colony; that he had received his wounds in consequence of opposing their designs; and had barely escaped from them with his life. The report occasioned no little alarm; although the correctness of it was flatly denied by Hobamock, a Pokanoket Indian resident at Plymouth, who recommended that a messenger should be sent secretly to Sowams, for the purpose of ascertaining the truth. This was done, and the messenger, finding every thing in its usually quiet state, informed Massasoit of the reports circulated against him. He was excessively incens

---

[*] Which, it may be here observed, was quite considerable. Squanto was ambitious and meddlesome, though not malicious —well-disposed and serviceable to the English, but a little too anxious to have credit for that fact among his countrymen. He amused himself with telling them that the whites kept the plague barrelled up in their cellars, that they intended war upon various tribes, &c. for the sake of being employed, sometimes hired, to act as mediator; and of course he always succeeded in settling the difficulty. Squanto died in November, 1622, on an expedition fitted out by Governor Bradford for obtaining corn among the Indians. His last request was, that the governor would pray for him that he might go to the Englishman's God in Heaven. He bequeathed his little property to his English friends. So perished the last aboriginal of the Plymouth soil. He sometimes played 'Jack upon both sides,' as Hubbard says, but his death was justly conside ed a public loss.

ed against Squanto, but sent his thanks to the Gov
ernor for the opinion of his fidelity, which he understood him to retain ; and directed the messenger
to assure him, that he should instantly apprize him
of any conspiracy which might at any future time
take place.

That the declarations of Massasoit, upon this occasion, were far from being mere words of compulsion
or of courtesy, is abundantly proved by his conduct
during the next season, 1623.   Early in the spring of
that year, news came to Plymouth, that he was very
sick at Sowams ; and it was determined to send Mr.
Winslow to visit him once more, in token of the
friendship of the colonists.   That gentleman immediately commenced his journey, being provided with
a few cordials, and attended by " one Master John
Hampden, a London gentleman, who then wintered
with him, and desired much to see the country,"—
no doubt the same character so eminently distinguished afterwards in the politics of England.

They heard, at various places on their route, that
the sachem was already dead ; and their guide,
Hobamock, indulged himself all the way in the most
unbounded grief.   They found him still living, however, on their arrival ; and the multitude of depend-
ents and friends who thronged his lodge, made way
as fast as possible for their admittance and accommodation.   He appeared to be reduced to the last
extremities.   Six or eight women were employed
in chafing his cold limbs, and the residue of the
numerous company were exerting themselves to the
utmost, meanwhile, in making what Winslow rather
uncharitably calls " such a hellish noise as distem-
pered those that were well."*   He had the good sense

---

* Probably an Indian Powah was leader of the chorus.
Of these barbarian quacks, Roger Williams says, that " the
poore people commonly dye under their hands," for the very
good reason that they " administer nothing, but howle, and
roar, and hollow over them, and begin the song to the rest of
the people about them, who all joyne (like a quire) in praver to

to wait for the conclusion of the ceremony ; and the exhausted performers being then satisfied they nad done all that in them lay for the benefit of the patient, one of them apprised him of the arrival of the English.

"*Who* have come?" muttered the sachem, still conscious, though his sight was wholly gone. They told him Winsnow had come, (as they generally substituted *n* for the English *l.*) "Let me speak with nim then," he replied, " Let me speak one word to nim." Winslow went forward to the matted plat form where he lay, and grasped the feeble hand which the sachem, informed of his approach, held out for him. " Art thou Winsnow ?" he whispered the question again, (in his own language,) " Art thou Winsnow ?" Being readily answered in the affirma tive, he appeared satisfied of the fact. But "O Winsnow," he added mournfully, " I shall never see thee again !"

Hobamock was now called, and desired to assure the sachem of the Governor's kind remembrance of him in his present situation, and to inform him of the articles they had brought with them for his use. He immediately signified his wish to taste of these ; and they were given him accordingly, to the great delight of the people around him. Winslow then proceeded to use measures for his relief, and they wrought a great change in him within half an hour. He recovered his sight gradually, and began to converse, requesting his good friend Winslow, among other things, to kill him a fowl, and make him some English pottage, such as he had seen at Plymouth. This was done for him, and such other care taken as restored his strength and appetite wonderfully within the day or two of Winslow's stay.

His expressions of gratitude, as well as those of his delighted attendants, were constant, as they were

---

the gods for them." *Key to the Indian Language,* chapter xxxi.

10—9

evidently warm from the heart. Finally, as his
guests were about to leave him, he called Hobamock
to his side, and revealed to him a plot against the
colonists, recently formed, as he understood, among
certain of the Massachusetts tribes, and in which he
had himself been invited to join. He also recom
mended certain summary measures for the suppression of the plot, and concluded with charging Hobamock* to communicate the intelligence to Winslow
on the way to Plymouth. It may be added here,
that these measures were subsequently executed by
Standish, and were successful. The conspiracy itself
was occasioned by the notorious and outrageous
profligacy of the banditti of " Master Weston," at
Weymouth.

The leading particulars in the residue of Massasoit's life, may soon be detailed. In 1632, he was
assaulted at Sowams, by a party of Narraghansetts,
and obliged to take refuge in an English house. His
situation was soon ascertained at Plymouth, and an
armed force being promptly despatched to his suc-
cor, under his old friend Standish, the Narraghansetts retired. About the year 1639, he probably
associated his eldest son, Moanam or Wamsutta, with
him in the government; for they came together into
open court at Plymouth, it is said, on the 28th of
September of that year, and desired that the ancient
treaty of 1621 might remain inviolable. They also
entered into some new engagements, chiefly going to
secure to the Colony a pre-emptive claim to the
Pokanoket lands. " And the whole court," add the
records, " in the name of the whole government for
each town respectively, did then likewise ratify and
confirm the aforesaid ancient league and confede
racy."

---

* The date of this Indian's death is not known. He is said
to have once been a war-captain among the Massachusetts
tribes. Hubbard describes him as a ' proper lusty young man,
and of good account among the Indians of those parts for his val
or.' He was useful, like Squanto, without being troublesome

From this time, the names of the father and son are sometimes found united, and sometimes not so, in instruments by which land was conveyed to the English. In 1649, the former sold the territory of Bridgewater in his own name. " Witnes these presents"—are the words of the deed—" that I Ousamequin Sachim of the contrie of Pocanauket, haue given, granted enfeofed and sould unto Myles Standish of Duxborough Samuel Nash and Constant Southworth of Duxborough aforesaid in the behalfe of all ye townsmen of Duxborough aforesaid a tract of land usually called Saughtucket extending in length and the breadth thereof, as followeth, that is to say— [here follow the boundaries of what is now *Bridgewater*]—the wch tract the said Ousamequin hath given granted enfeofed and sould unto ye said Myles [Standish] Samuel Nash and Constant Southworth in the behalfe of all ye townsmen of Duxborough as aforesaid wth all the emunities priveleges and profitts whatsoever belonging to the said tract of land wth all and singular all woods underwoods lands meadowes Riuers brooks Rivulets &c. to have and to hould to the said Myles Standish Samuel Nash and Constant Southworth in behalfe of all the townsmen of the towne of Duxborough to them and their heyers forever. In witnes whereof I the said Ousamequin have here unto sett my hand this 23 of March 1649

The m^k of ⌇ Ousamequin.

In consideration of the aforesaid bargain and sale wee the said Myles Standish Samuel Nash and Constant Southworth, doe bind ourselves to pay unto ye said Ousamequin for and in consideration of ye said tract of land as followeth

7	Coats a y^d and half in a coat	Myles Standish
9	Hatchets	
8	Howes	Samuel Nash
20	Knives	
4	Moose skins	Constant Southworth."
10	Y^ds and half of cotton	

The original document of which we have here given a literal and exact copy has been preserved tc this day. It is in the handwriting of Captain Standish.

The precise date of Massasoit's death is unknown. In 1653, his name appears in a deed by which he conveyed part of the territory of Swansey to English grantees. Hubbard supposes that he died about three years subsequent to this; but as late as 1661, he is noticed in the Records of the United Colonies, as will appear more particularly in the life of his eldest son. Two or three years afterwards, conveyances were made of the Pokanoket lands in which he appears to have had no voice; and it may be fairly inferred that he died in that interval. He must have been near eighty years of age.

Such are the passages which history has preserved concerning the earliest and best friend of the Pilgrims. Few and simple as they are, they give glimpses of a character that, under other circumstances, might have placed Massasoit among the illustrious of his age. He was a mere savage; ignorant of even reading and writing, after an intercourse of near fifty years with the colonists; and distinguished from the mass of savages around him, as we have seen, by no other outward emblem than a barbarous ornament of bones. It must be observed, too, as to them, that the authority which they conferred upon him, or rather upon his ancestors, was their free gift, and was liable at any moment to be retracted, wholly or in part, either by the general voice or by the defection or violence of individuals. The intrinsic dignity and energy of his character alone, therefore, must have sustained the dominion of the sachem, with no essential distinction of wealth, retinue, cultivation, or situation in any respect, between him and the meanest of the Wampanoags. The naked qualities of his intellect and his heart must have gained their loyalty, controlled their extravagant passions to his own purposes, and won upon their personal confidence and affection.

That he did this appears from the fact, so singular in Indian history, that among all the Pokanoket tribes, there was scarcely an instance of even an individual broil or quarrel with the English during his long life. Some of these tribes, living nearer the Colony than any other Indians, and going into it daily in such numbers, that Massasoit was finally requested to restrain them from " pestering " their friends by their mere multitude,—these shrewd beings must have perceived, as well as Massasoit himself did, that the colonists were as miserably fearful as they were feeble and few. Some of them, too,—the sachem Corbitant, for example,—were notoriously hostile, and perhaps had certain supposed reasons for being so. Yet *that* cunning and ambitious savage extricated himself from the only overt act of rebellion he is known to have attempted, by " soliciting the good offices of Massasoit," we are told, " to reconcile him to the English." And such was the influence of the chief sachem, not only over him, but over the Massachusetts sachems, that nine of the principal of them soon after came into Plymouth from great distances, for the purpose of signifying their humble respect for the authority of the English.

That Massasoit was beloved as well as respected by his subjects and neighbors, far and wide, appears from the great multitude of anxious friends who thronged about him during his sickness. Some of them, as Winslow ascertained, had come more than one hundred miles for the purpose of seeing him ; and they all watched *his* operations in that case, with as intense anxiety as if the prostrate patient had been the father or the brother of each. And meagre as is the justice which history does the sachem, it still furnishes some evidence, not to be mistaken, that he had won this regard from them by his kindness. There is a passage of affecting simplicity in Winslow's Relation, going to show that he did not forget their minutest interests, even in his own almost unconscious helplessness. " That morning," it is

said, "he caused me to spend in going from one to
another among those that were sick in the town
[Sowams]; requesting me to treat them as I had
him, and to give to each of them some of the same
I gave him, *saying they were good folk.*"

But these noble traits of the character of Massasoit are still more abundantly illustrated by the whole
tenor of his intercourse with the whites. Of his
mere sense of his positive obligations to them, including his fidelity to the famous treaty of 1621,
nothing more need be said, excepting that the annals
of the continent furnish scarcely one parallel even to
that case. But he went much farther than this.
He not only visited the Colony in the first instance
of his own free will and accord, but he entered into
the negotiations cheerfully and deliberately ; and in
the face of their manifest fear and suspicion.   Hence-
forth the results of it were regarded, not with the
mere honesty of an ally, but with the warm interest
of a friend. It was probably at his secret and delicate
suggestion,—and it could scarcely have been without
his permission, at all events,—that his own subjects
took up their residence among the colonists, with the
view of guiding, piloting, interpreting for them, and
teaching them their own useful knowledge. Winslow speaks of his *appointing another* to fill the place
of Squanto at Plymouth, while the latter should be
sent about among the Pokanokets, under *his* orders,
" to procure truck [in furs] for the English.

The vast grant of territory which he made in the
first instance has been spoken of. It was made with
the simple observation, that his claim to it was the
sole claim in existence. It was also without consideration ; the generous sachem, as Roger Williams
says of the Narraghansetts in a similar case, " being
shy and jealous of selling the lands to any, and choosing rather to make a gift of them to such as they
affected." Such is the only jealousy which Massasoit can be said ever to have entertained of the
English. Nor do we find any evidence that he

repented of his liberality, or considered it the incau
tious extravagance of a moment of flattered complai
sance. We do find, however, that he invariably
watched over the interest of the grantees, with more
strictness than he would probably have watched over
his own. He laid claim, in one instance, to a tract
for which Mr. Williams had negotiated with the
Narraghansetts, — that gentleman being ignorant
perhaps, of an existing controversy between the two
tribes. "It is mine," said the sachem, "It is mine
and *therefore theirs,*" — plainly implying that the
ground in question was comprised within the original
transfer. Whether this claim was just, or whether
it was insisted upon, does not appear; but there is
indication enough, both of the opinion and feeling
of Massasoit.

An anecdote of him, recorded by Governor Winthrop, under the title of a "pleasant passage," is still
more striking. His old friend *Winsnow,* it seems,
made a trading voyage to Connecticut, during the
summer of 1634. On his return, he left his vessel
upon the Narraghansett coast, for some reason or
other, and commenced his journey for Plymouth
across the woods. Finding himself at a loss, probably,
as to his route, he made his way to Sowams, and
called upon his ancient acquaintance, the sachem.
The latter gave him his usual kind welcome, and,
upon his leaving him, offered to conduct him home,
—a pedestrian journey of two days. He had just
despatched one of his Wampanoags to Plymouth,
with instructions to inform the friends of Winslow,
that *he* was dead, and to persuade them of this melancholy fact, by specifying such particulars as their
own ingenuity might suggest. All this was done
accordingly; and the tidings occasioned, as might
be expected, a very unpleasant excitement throughout the Colony. In the midst of it, however, on the
next day, the sachem entered the village, attended
by Winslow, and with more than his usual compla-
cency in his honest and cheerful countenance He

was asked why such a report had been circulated
the day previous. "That Winsnow might be the
more welcome," answered he, "and that you might
be the more happy,—it is my custom." He had
come thus far to enjoy this surprise personally; and
he returned homeward, more gratified by it, without
doubt, than he would have been by the most fortunate foray among the Narraghansetts.

It is intimated by some writers, rather more frequently than is either just or generous, that the sachem's fear of the tribe just named lay at the foundation of his friendship. It might have been nearer
the apparent truth, considering all that is known of
Massasoit, to say, that his interest happened to coin-
cide with his inclination. At all events, it was in
the power of any other of the sachems or kings
throughout the country, to place and sustain themselves upon the same footing with the colonists, had
they been prompted either by as much good feeling
or good sense. On the contrary, the Massachusetts
were plotting and threatening on one hand, as we
have seen,—not without provocation, it must be allowed,—while the Narraghansett sachem, upon the
other, had sent in his compliments as early as 1622,
in the shape of a bundle of arrows, tied up with a
rattlesnake's skin.

Nor should we forget the wretched feebleness of
the Colony at the period of their first acquaintance
with Massasoit. Indeed, the instant measures which
he took for their relief and protection, look more
like the promptings of compassion, than of either
hope or fear. A month previous to his appearance
among them, they were reduced to such a pitiable
condition by sickness, that only six or seven men
of their whole number were able to do business in
the open air; and probably their entire fighting
force, could they have been mustered together, would
scarcely have equalled that little detachment which
Massasoit brought with him into the village, delicate-
ly leaving twice as many, with the arms of all, be-

hind him; as he afterwards exchanged six hostages
for one. No wonder that the colonists " could not
yet conceive but that he was willing to have peace
with them."

But the motives of the sachem are still further
manifested by the sense of his own dignity, which,
peaceable as he generally was; he showed promptly
upon all suitable occasions. Both the informal grant
and the formal deeds we have mentioned, indicate
that he understood himself to be the master of his
ancestral territory as much in right as in fact. There
is nothing in his whole history, which does more
honor to his intelligence or his sensibility, than his
conduct occasioned by the falsehoods circulated
among the colonists against him by Squanto. His
first impulse, as we have seen, was to be offended
with the guilty intriguant; the second, to thank the
Governor for appealing to himself in this case, and
to assure him that he would at any time " send word
and give warning when any such business was towards." On further inquiry, he ascertained that
Squanto was taking even more liberties with his
reputation than he had been aware of. He went
forthwith to Plymouth, and made his appeal personally to the Governor. The latter pacified him as
well as he could, and he returned home. But a very
short time elapsed before a message came from him,
entreating the Governor to consent to the death of
the renegade who still abused him. The Governor
confessed in reply, that Squanto deserved death, but
desired that he might be spared on account of his
indispensable services. Massasoit was not yet satis
fied. The former messenger was again sent, " with
divers others," says Winslow in his Relation, "*de
manding* him, [Squanto] as being one of Massasoit's
subjects, whom by our first articles of peace we
could not retain ; yet because he would not willingly
do it [insist upon his rights] without the Governor's
approbation, he offered him many beaver-skins for
his consent thereto." The deputation had brought

these skins, accordingly, as also the sachem's own
knife, for the execution of the criminal. Squanto
now surrendered himself to the Governor, as an
Indian always resigns himself to his fate upon similar occasions; but the Governor still contrived a
pretext for sparing him. The deputies were "mad
with rage and impatient of delay," as may be supposed, and departed in great heat.

The conduct of the sachem in this case was mani
festly more correct than that of his ally. He understood as well as the Governor did, the spirit of the
articles in the treaty, which provided, that an offender upon either side should be given up to punishment upon demand; and he was careful to make
that demand personally, explicitly and respectfully.
The Governor, on the other hand, as well as the
culprit himself, acknowledged the justice of it, but
manœuvred to avoid compliance. The true reason
is no doubt given by Winslow. It is also given in
the language of John Smith. "With much adoe,"
says the honest Captain, "we appeased the angry
king and the rest of the saluages, and freely forgaue
TUSQUANTUM, *because he speaking our language we
could not be well without him.*" The king was angry,
then, as he well might be; and the Governor took
the trouble, he was both bound and interested to
take, to appease him. It is not to be wondered at,
perhaps, that the particulars of this transaction are
so little dwelt upon by the writers of that period.
Winslow barely states,—speaking, in another connexion, of the Indians being evidently aware of the
weakness of the Colony,—that, what was worse,
" now also Massasoit seemed to frown upon us, and
neither came nor sent to us as formerly." This passage is no less significant than brief; but not more
so than a subsequent dry observation respecting
Squanto, " whose peace, before this time, (the fall
of the same year) *was wrought* with Massasoit."

Such were the life and character of Massasoit. It
is to be regretted, that so few particulars are pre-

served of the former, and that so little justice, consequently, can be done to the latter. But so far as
his history goes, it certainly makes him one of the
most remarkable men of his race. There is no nobler instance in all history, of national fidelity, (for
which he mainly must have the credit,) or of individual friendship. This instinct of a generous nature
in the first instance, being confirmed by a course of
conduct generally alike creditable to the feelings and
shrewdness of the Colonists, finally settled itself in
the mind of Massasoit as ineradicably as his affection
for his own subjects. " I know now," said he to Winslow, on his first recovery from the severe sickness
we have mentioned, "I *know* that the English love
me,—I love them,—I shall never forget them."

But putting even the most unnatural construction
upon the professions and the conduct of the sachem,
the relation he commenced and for forty-five years
sustained with the English, must be allowed to show
at least a consummate sagacity. He certainly succeeded during all this time, not only in shielding his
tribes from their just or unjust hostility, but in gaining their respect to such a singular degree, that the
writings of no single author within our recollection
furnish one word to his disparagement. Even Hubbard speaks of him with something like regard ;
notwithstanding the obnoxious trait in his character
indicated in the following passage. " It is very remarkable," he says, " that this Woosamequin, how
much soever he affected the English, was never in
the least degree well affected to their religion." It
is added furthermore, that in his last treaty with the
whites at Swanzey,—referring to a sale of land which
we have mentioned,—he exerted himself to bind
them solemnly "never to draw away any of his
people from their old pagan superstition and devilish
idolatry to the Christian religion."* This he insisted

---

* In that rare tract (published in London, 1651.) entitled
" The Light appearing more and more towards the perfect

on, until they threatened to break off the negotiation on account of his pertinacity, and he then gave up the point.

Massasoit did not distinguish himself as a warrior; nor is he known to have been once engaged in any open hostilities, even with the inimical and powerful tribes who environed his territory. This is another unique trait in his character; and considering the general attachment of all Indians to a belligerent life, their almost exclusive deference for warlike qualities, the number and scattered location of the Pokanoket tribes, and especially the character of their ancient neighbors, this very fact is alone sufficient to distinguish the genius of Massasoit. All the native nations of New England, but his, were involved in dissensions and wars with each other and with the whites; and they all shared sooner or after the fate which he avoided. The restless ringleaders who plotted mischief among the Massachusetts, were summarily knocked upon the head by Miles Standish, while hundreds of the residue fled, and miserably perished in their own swamps. The Pequots,—a nation who could muster three thousand bowmen but a short time previous,—were nearly exterminated in 1637; and the savages of Maine, meanwhile, the Mohawks of New York, the Narraghansetts and the Mohegans were fighting and reducing each others' strength, as if their only object had been, by ultimately extirpating themselves, to prepare a way in the wilderness for the new comers.

Day" &c. and written by the Rev. Thomas Mayhew, it is stated, that some of the Christian Indians of Martha's Vineyard had a conversation with " Vzzamequin a great Sachem or Governor on the maine Land (coming amongst them) about the wayes of God "—he enquiring what earthly good things came along with them, and what they had gained by their piety, &c. This was previous to 1650.

CHAPTER VII.

Massasoit succeeded by his son ALEXANDER—The occasion of that name being given by the English — History of Alexander previous to his father's death—Covenant made with Plymouth in 1639—Measures taken in pursuance of it, in 1661—Anecdote illustrating the character of Alexander —Notice of the charges made against him—Examination of the transaction which led to his death—Accession of PHILIP—Renewal of the treaty by him—Interruption of harmony—Supposed causes of it—Measures taken in consequence—Philip's submission—Letter to the Plymouth Governor—Second submission in 1671—Remarks on the causes of PHILIP'S WAR.

MASSASOIT was succeeded in the Pokanoket government by his eldest son Moanam or Wamsutta, known to the English chiefly by the name of ALEXANDER; which appellation he received at the same time when that of PHILIP was conferred on his younger brother. The two young men came together, on that occasion, into open court at Plymouth, and, professing great regard for the English, requested that names should be given them. Their father not being mentioned as having attended them at the observance of the ceremony, has probably occasioned the suggestion of his death. It would be a sufficient explanation of his absence, however, that he was now an old man, and that the distance of Sowams from Plymouth was more than forty miles. It is easy to imagine, that the solicitude he had always manifested to sustain a good understanding with his Plymouth friends, might lead him to recommend this pacific and conciliatory measure, as a suitable preparation for his own decease, and perhaps as the absolute termination of his reign.

There is some reason to believe, indeed, that Alexander had a share in the Pokanoket sovereignty many years previous to the date of the ceremony

just mentioned. The Plymouth records show, that
on the 25th of September, 1639, the father came
into court, bringing Moanam with him. He desired
that the old treaty of 1621 might remain inviolable,
"and the said Woosamequin or Massasoit, and Moanam or Wamsutta," did also promise that he nor they
shall or will needlessly and unjustly raise any quarrels, or do any wrongs to other natives, to provoke
them to war against him ; and that he or they shall
not give, sell or convey, any of his or their lands
territories or possessions whatsoever, to any person
or persons, without the privity and consent of the
Government of Plymouth aforesaid ; "and the whole
court in the name of the whole government, for each
town respectively, did then likewise ratify and confirm the aforesaid ancient league and confederacy ;
and did also further promise to the said Woosamequin and Moanam his son, and his successors, that
they shall and will from time to time defend them,
when occasion shall require, against all such as shall
rise up against them to wrong or oppress them un
justly."

Agreeably to the terms of this covenant, the Rec
ords of the Colonies for 1661 set forth, that a message
was that year sent by the United Commissioners to
Uncas, chief Sachem of the Molegans.* The
complainants in that case were the General Court of
Massachusetts ; and the charge alleged against Uncas was a violent " Invading of Wesamequin and the
Indians of Quabakutt *whoe are and longe haue bine
Subjects to the English.*" The dominion here assumed, is probably intended to apply only to the Quabakutt Indians, and not to Massasoit. Uncas, in his
answer, professed that he was ignorant they were
subjects of Massachusetts, " and *further* says they
were none of Wesamequin's men but belonging to
Onopequin his deadly enemie." &c.

He then alleges "that Wesamequin his son and

---

* See the message and reply at large in the LIFE of Uncas

diuers of his men *had fought against him diuers times.*" The last paragraph of the answer—which was given in by Major Mason in behalf of Uncas—is as follows :

" Alexander allis [*alias*] Wamsutta Sachem of Sowamsett being now att Plymouth hee challenged Quabauke Indians to belong to him and further said that hee did war Warr against Vncas this summer on that account."

It is very clear at least that Alexander maintained, fearlessly and frankly, what he believed to be his rights ; nor does it appear, that the exercise of his sovereignty in this manner was objected to by the party which had the best, if not only right to object. He manifested the same independence in regard to the efforts of the English missionaries ; so that Hubbard concludes he had " neither affection for the Englishmen's persons, nor yet for their religion."

This is licentious reasoning, at the best ; for not a tittle of evidence exists in the case, so far as we are aware, which goes to rebut the just inference to be drawn from the circumstance that no difficulty or controversy occurred between Alexander and his allies from his accession to his death—with a single exception. The excepted case, which comes in order now to be considered, is one of the more importance, that its immediate effect was to terminate at once the reign and life of the chieftain.

In connexion with the remark last cited from Hubbard, that historian barely observes, that the Governor and Council were informed of the fact. Mather states, with no more particularity, that the sachem solicited the Narraghansetts to rebel with him ; upon *the good proof whereof*, the Plymouth Government adopted certain summary measures. From other sources we find, that this proof was communicated by letters from Boston, where it was probably founded upon rumors gathered from straggling Indians. At all events, no conclusive testimony appears in the case ; and it may be plausibly surmised, therefore, that none was ever received, the writers just cited not being remarkably prone to omit matters of this kind. The rumor might originate from circumstances really suspicious ; but were this true, and far more, if it were both false and malicious, like the charges against Massasoit, we may well question both the justice and the policy of the steps taken by the Plymouth Government.

"They presently sent for him, to bring him to the court," says Hubbard,—a very remarkable proceeding, related with a corresponding brevity. The business was intrusted, it also appears, to a gentleman who was neither afraid of danger, nor yet willing to delay in a matter of this moment. We are then told that this gentleman, Mr. Winslow, forthwith taking eight or ten stout men with him, well armed, set out for Sowams ; that he fortunately met with Alexander, at a few miles' distance, in a wigwam with eighty of his followers ; that they seized upon the arms of the party, which had been left without the wigwam, and then went in and summoned the sachem to attend them to Plymouth. He obeyed, reluctantly, being threatened that "if he *stirred* or refused to go, he was a dead man." Such was his spirit, however, adds Hubbard, that the very surprisal of him threw him into a fever. Upon this, he requested liberty to return home, and the favor was granted to him on certain conditions ; but he died upon the way.

This account agrees with Mather's. "The Government sent that valiant and excellent commander," says the Reverend Doctor, "to fetch him down before them. The major-general used such expedition and resolution in this affair, that, assisted with no more than ten men, he seized upon Alexander at a hunting-house, notwithstanding his numerous attendants about him ; and when the raging sachem saw a pistol at his breast, with a threatening of death to him if he did not quietly yield himself up to go down to Plymouth, he yielded, though not very quietly, thereunto." Mather attributes his death, furthermore, to the " inward fury of his own guilty and haughty mind." Now, even if the sachem were not compelled to travel faster or further than was decent in his unfortunate situation, as one of our authorities is careful to argue ; and granting to the other, that he was treated (on the march) with no other than that humanity and civility, *which was essential to the Major-General,** it is abundantly clear, we conceive, that a more hot-blooded or high-handed measure could hardly have been executed by the adventurous John Smith himself. The son of Massasoit, and the ruler of a nation who had been forty years in alliance and warm friendship with the Colonists,—throughout all their feebleness, and in spite of all jealousies and provocations,—was assaulted in his own territory and among his own subjects, insulted, threatened, and finally forced to obey a summons of his ancient ally to appear before *his* court for his trial. It does not appear that he was even apprised of the occasion which required his attendance. And what is worse than all the rest, the whole proceeding was founded, so far as we can ascertain, upon no better testimony than accusations gathered from stragglers at Boston, and then communicated " by letters " to Plymouth. It must be admitted, that a different coloring is put upon the affair by the Rev. Mr. Cotton, whose relation may be found among the excellent notes appended to Mr. Davis's recent edition of Morton. He states, that the sachem readily consented to attend Winslow ; and that he was barely examined before certain justices at Eastham, and dismissed. This account, however, does not much mitigate the essential circumstances of the case ; and it admits the fact, that the sachem died within two or three days after being carried home on the shoulders of his men,

---

* Among other civilities, he was offered the use of a horse on the journey, and declined that favor on the ground that some of his women, in the company, were obliged to walk ; a fine trait of savage politeness.

10—10

although the English party seem to have found him
in perfect health.

Such was the ignominious death of Alexander,
and under such circumstances did the government
devolve upon his brother Metacom,—or Philip, as
he is generally called.   That Prince seems to have
assumed the Pokanoket government, favored by a
more than usual popularity ; for the event was cele
brated by the rejoicing and revelry of multitudes of
his subjects, sachems and others, gathered together
from the remotest limits of his territory.   One of his
earliest measures, was to appear with his uncle before the Plymouth Court, following the example of
his father and brother.   He expressed an earnest
wisn for the continuance of peace and amity ; and
pledged himself,—as the Court did also upon the
other hand,—to use all suitable measures for effecting
that desirable purpose.   For several years after this,
the intercourse between the two parties went on,
ostensibly, as it had done in former times, though
probably not without some distrust upon both sides.

The first public interruption of this harmony occurred in 1671, during which season Philip was
heard to complain, openly, of certain encroachments
by the English upon his hunting-grounds.   About
the same time, rumors were circulated that his subjects
frequently assembled at various places in un-
wonted numbers; and were repairing their guns,
and sharpening their hatchets.   The Plymouth Government were alarmed.   They sent messengers to
communicate with the Massachusetts Government,
and at the same time other messengers to Philip, not
"to fetch him before the Court," as in the case of his
brother, but to ascertain his intentions.

He seems to have paid a dignified regard to this
measure.   On the 10th of April, a message was received from him, inviting the officers of the Plymouth
Government to a conference.   It was received by
the latter at Taunton, where also were several gentlemen, despatched by the Massachusetts Government,

with instructions to mediate between the contending parties. Governor Prince, of Plymouth, sent word back to Philip,—who was tarrying meanwhile at what is now called Three-mile-river, about four miles from Taunton green,—that he was heartily disposed to treat with him, and expected that the sachem would come forward for that purpose ; and his personal safety was guaranteed in case he should do so. Philip so far complied with the request, as to advance a considerable distance nearer the village. He then stationed himself at a place called Crossman's mill, placed sentinels on a hill in his rear, and again despatched messengers to the Governor, desiring an interview. This, the town's-people, who could scarcely be restrained from falling forthwith upon the Indian party, would not permit. At last, the Massachusetts Commissioners, volunteering to take the supposed hazard upon themselves, went to Philip, and persuaded him to consent to a conference. This was on condition that his men should accompany him ; and that the business should be done at the meeting-house, one side of which was to be reserved for the Wampanoags, and the other for the English.

The council took place agreeably to these arrangments, in the old meeting-house of Taunton. The English stood upon one side, solemn and stern in countenance, as they were formal in garb ; and opposite to them, a line of Indian warriors, armed and arrayed for battle, their long black hair hanging about their necks, and their eyes gleaming covertly with a flame of suspicion and defiance, scarcely to be suppressed. Philip alone was their orator. He denied that he entertained any hostile design ; and promptly explained his preparations for war, as intended for defence against the Narraghansetts. The Commissioners rejoined, however, with such arguments and evidence as satisfied themselves and completely surprised him. At least, he affected to admit all that was alleged against him ; and though he refused to give compensation for past aggressions, he

and some of his counsellors subscribed an acknowledgement drawn up by the English in the words
following :

"Taunton, April 10th, 1671.

Whereas my father, and my brother and myself
have formerly submitted ourselves unto the king's
majesty of England, and to this colony of New
Plymouth, by solemn covenant under our hand ; but
I having of late, through my indiscretion and the
naughtiness of my heart, violated and broken this
my covenant with my friends, by taking up arms
with an evil intent against them, and that ground-
lessly ; I being now deeply sensible of my unfaithful-
ness and folly, do desire at this time solemnly to renew
my covenant with my ancient friends, and my father's
friends above mentioned, and do desire that this
may testify to the world against me if ever I shall
again in my faithfulness towards them (whom I have
now and at all times found kind toward me) or any
other of the English colonies.   And as a pledge of
my true intentions for the future to be faithful and
friendly, I do freely engage to resign up to the
Government of New Plymouth all my English arms,
to be kept by them for their security so long as they
shall see reason.   For the true performance of the
promises, 1 have hereunto set my hand, together
with the rest of my counsel.

In presence of	The mark P of PHILIP,
WILLIAM DAVIS,	The mark V of TAVOSER,
WILLIAM HUDSON,	The mark M of Capt. WISPOKE,
THOMAS BRATTLE.	The mark T of WOONCHAPONCHUNK.
	The mark 8 of NIMROD."

From the tenor of this submission, it has been
generally supposed that the Sachem was frightened
into it.   Hence Hubbard relates, that "one of his
captains, of far better courage and resolution than
himself, when he saw his cowardly temper and disposition, flung down his arms, called him white-
livered cur, *or to that purpose*, and from that time
turned to the English," &c.   This might be true,

though it is well known, that Mr. Hubbard's authority in regard to every thing touching the character of Philip is to be regarded with many allowances for his intemperate prejudice. He hesitates not, almost as often as he finds occasion to mention his name, to pay him the passing compliment of ' caitiff,' ' hell-hound,' ' fiend,' ' arch-rebel,' and various similar designations of respect and affection.

But there is no doubt that the acknowledgement was at least a mere artifice to gain time. Apparently it had no effect in reference to the impending hostilities, other than to hasten them by aggravating the ill-will of the Indians. It does not appear that their arms were given up, even so far as stipulated in the submission. The following reply of Philip to some communication respecting them may be deemed exposition of his side of the question. The precise date is undetermined.

" SACHEM PHILIP, his answer to the letter brought to him from the GOVERNOR of NEW PLYMOUTH.

First. Declaring his thankfulness to the Governor for his great respects and kindness manifested in the letter.

Secondly. Manifesting his readiness to lay down their arms, and send his people about their usual business and employments, as also his great desire of concluding of peace with neighboring English.

Thirdly. *Inasmuch as great fears and jealousies hath been raised in their minds by several persons, which now they better understand the falsity of such reports, as hath formerly been conveyed unto them,* Philip doth humbly request the Governor will please favorably to excuse and aquit them from any payment of damage, *or surrendering their arms,* they not apprehending themselves blameworthy in those late rumors.

Fourthly. They are not at present free to promise to appear at court, hoping there will be no necessity of it, in case their freedom for peace and readiness to lay down arms may be accepted ; as also suggestions of great danger that will befall them, in case they appear, with harsh threats to the Sachem, that may be considered.

Per me,   SAMUEL GORTEN *Junior*."

Whether Philip was at this time preparing for war cannot be decided: but he was evidently as yet unprepared. He went to Boston, therefore, during the month of August (1671). He knew the Massachusetts government to be more friendly to him than the Plymouth ; and although letters had arrived that very day from the latter place, announcing an intention of declaring war upon him forthwith, the Sachem succeeded in persuading the Massachusetts authorities of his entire innocence. They sent a proposal to Plymouth for a new council, to settle all difficulties. This being declined, they gave their opinion decidedly against war. Staggered by this declaration, the government of the old colony consented to try the effect of another mediation. A conference of all parties soon after took place at Plymouth : and the following articles of accommodation were agreed upon.

"1. We, PHILIP and my Council and my subjects, do acknowledge ourselves subject to his Majesty the King of England, and the government of New Plymouth, and to their laws.

2. I am willing and do promise to pay unto the government of Plymouth one hundred pounds in such things as I have ; but I would intreat the favor that I might have three years to pay it in, forasmuch as I cannot do it at present.

3. I do promise to send unto the governor, or whom he shall appoint, five wolves' heads, if I can get them ; or as many as I can procure, until they come to five wolves yearly.

4. If any difference fall between the English and myself and people, then I do promise to repair to the governor of Plymouth, to rectify the difference amongst us.

5. I do promise not to make war with any, but with the Governor's approbation of Plymouth.

6. I promise not to dispose of any of the lands that I have at present, but by the approbation of the governor of Plymouth.

For the true performance of the premises, I the said Sachem; Philip of Paukamakett,* do hereby bind myself, and such of my council as are present, ourselves, our heirs, our successors, faithfully, and do promise; in witness thereof, we have hereunto subscribed our hands, the day and year above written.

[In the presence of the Court, divers magistrates, &c.]	The mark P of PHILIP.
	The mark [of UNCOMPAEN.
	The mark † of WOCOKON.
	The mark 7 of SAMKAMA."

This negotiation was a new stratagem: † and the success of it answered the purpose of Philip completely; for although he does not appear to have killed one wolf, or paid one cent, even " in such things as he had," nothing occurred for three years, to rouse the suspicions of the Colonies.   There can scarcely be a doubt, that during all this time,—if not for a longer time previous,—the sachem was matur-

---

* *Alias* Pokanokit.   Other variations of this ill-fated word, are

PACKANOKIK and PUCKANOKICK, by	PURCHAS.
POCANAKET.	MORTON.
POCKANOCKETT.	MORTON'S CONTINUATOR
PACANOKIK.	PRINCE.
POKANOCKETT.	HUTCHINSON.
PAWKUNNAWKUTT.	GOOKIN.
PUCKANOKIK.	WINSLOW'S RELATION
POKANACKET.	HUBBARD.

† Mather remarks upon the passage thus: " When the **Duke** of Archette, at his being made governor of Antwerp castle, took an oath to keep it faithfully for King Philip of Spain, the officer that gave him his oath used these odd words. *If you perform what you promise, God help you; if you do it not, the Devil take your body and soul!* and all the 'standers-by cried *Amen!*'   But when the Indian King Philip took his oath, nobody used *these words* unto him; neverthe- less you shall see anon whether *these words* were not expres sive enough of what became of him!"

ing one of the grandest plans ever conceived by any savage ;—that of utterly exterminating the English of the northern provinces. This, he was well aware, could only be done by means commensurate with the danger and difficulty of the enterprise. The Colonies were no longer the feeble and timid allies, known fifty years before to his father. They had grown in numbers and in strength ; and still more in experience and spirit. Nothing less, than a general union of the New England tribes, who lived among and around them all, would furnish a safe guarantee for the complete success of such a war as was now meditated.

To that great preparation, then, the whole energies of Philip must be devoted. It was as difficult, he well knew, as it was desirable. The ruler of one small confederacy,—already suspected, and constantly under the close scrutiny of his powerful neighbors, —he must unite and interest in one common object, a multitude of scattered nations who had met and known each other, until this time, only in jealousy, envy, revenge, and in many cases hereditary and inveterate war ; and among whose councils no similar plan, for any purpose whatever, had ever been conceived of. How far Philip surmounted these obstacles, will be seen. The great train of events we are approaching, are so interesting both as a passage of general history, and still more, as they implicate and illustrate the character of Philip, that it may be proper to take some notice of the causes which gave rise to them. It is well known, that his English contemporaries looked upon him, very generally, with feelings far from benevolent. It was natural under the circumstances that they should do so ; but it is no more necessary, than it is philosophical or just, on the other hand, to confide implicitly either in their opinions or their statements. Philip and his Wampanoags are unlucky enough, like the lion in the fable, to have no painter.

It should be observed here, that Philip like his

elder brother, unquestionably considered himself an ally and not a subject of the English ;—at least, until his nominal submission in 1671. Even the same authorities who record this submission, speak of his *renewing* his ancient covenant, (as indeed the instrument itself shows.) A distinct article recognises Massasoit as an independent sovereign. Philip, then, held the same relation to the English, that his father and brother had done for the fifty years, during which the two parties had treated and associated upon equal and intimate terms. He was bound by the same engagements, and possessed of the same rights ; and it only remains to be seen, if due regard was paid to these circumstances upon either side.

Now, we look upon the assault of Alexander, in 1662, in the first place, as not only a sufficient cause of suspicion and resentment, but of war ; and that, upon the best construction which can be put upon the most favorable of the *ex-parte* relations that appear upon record. By the old treaty itself, which Alexander also took the gratuitous trouble to *renew,* —and without any reference to courtesy or humanity or to national fidelity, or to personal friendship, existing up to this date,—the English were bound generally to treat him as an allied sovereign, and especially to make a preliminary demand of satisfaction, in all cases of complaint. We have seen that the charge brought against him in 1662,—vague and unsupported as it was,—was not so much as explained to the sachem, previously to his being taken from his own territory by an armed force, and carried before an English Justice of the Peace. In no other instance does the Plymouth Colony seem to have exercised an authority of this nature, even over the meanest subjects of the sachem. "Inasmuch as complaint is made, that many Indians pass into divers places of this jurisdiction," say the records of the Colony for 1660, " it is enacted that no strange or foreign Indians be permitted to become residents, and 'that *notice be given to the several sagamores to prevent the same.*' "

A remark might be made upon the policy of laws
like these, so far as the Pokanokets were concerned;
as also of the acts of 1652, and 1653, which prohibi-
ted the sale of casks, barques, boats and horses, to
the Indians, besides providing a punishment for such
of them, resident in the Colony, as should violate the
Christian sabbath, or discharge their guns in the
night-time.   But these regulations the Government
had an undoubted right to make, as Massasoit and
Philip had possessed a right,—which, however, they
were complaisant enough to relinquish,—of selling
their own lands to purchasers of their own choosing.

Such was the state of things previous to the sub
mission of 1671.   With regard to this, it is quite
clear that, even if Philip was made to *understand* the
instrument which it is well known he could not *read*,
he could look upon it only as an insult, imposed upon
him under circumstances amounting to duress.   Independently of any force, too, he must have thought
himself justified, by the manifest disposition and the
summary measures of the English, in availing him
self of any stratagem to lull suspicion and to gain
time.   He might or might not, at this period or before, have meditated acting offensively against them,
in revenge of the indignity suffered by his brother
and his nation ; but it was certainly both prudent
and patriotic in him, to put himself on the defensive.
He had a right, it appears to us, both to drill his own
people in martial exercises, and to make alliances
with his Indian neighbors.

It might have been a safe policy in the Plymouth
Government, to have considered these things, in regard at least to what they might call the jealous and
barbarous prejudices of the Indians, before proceeding
to extremities with either Alexander or Philip.   On
the contrary, while they enacted laws, and encouraged accusations, and took the execution of the penalty
of them into their own hands, they used no means to
conciliate Philip, but sending for him to appear before " the Plymouth Court."   Whether they were

cautious in all other respects after this time to avoid
offence, it is not to be expected that history should
enable us to determine. We find, however, that certain of the Colonists, in 1673, took upon them to negotiate treaties for land with private subjects of Philip ; and there is no reason to doubt, that they entered
and kept possession accordingly. As the sachems
are known to have been as tenacious of their territory
in claim, as they were liberal of it in disposal, it may
well be conceived that this first instance of a similar
nature upon record, should occasion Philip no little
dissatisfaction. In imitation of the English courtesy
he might have despatched Nimrod, Tobias, Woonk
aponcpunt, or some other of his "valiant and excellent" majors-generals to "fetch down" the offending
grantees to Sowams. He seems to have taken no
express notice of the affair. But that he understood
his territorial rights, is apparent from the singular
communication which follows. It is preserved in the
Collections of the Massachusetts Historical Society,
(volume second of the first series,) as precisely copied
from the original, which is still preserved at Plymouth.

"King Philip desire to let you understand that he
could not come to the Court, for Tom, his interpreter,
has a pain in his back, that he could not travel so far,
and Philip sister is very sik.

"Philip would intreat that favor of you, and aney
of the magistrats if *aney English or Engians speak
about aney land, he pray you to give them no answer at
all.* This last summer he made that promis with
you, that he would not sell no land in seven years
time, *for that he would have no English trouble him
before that time,* he has not forgot that you promis
him.

"He will come as soon as possible as he can to
speak with you, and so I rest, you very loving friend,
Philip, dwelling at mount hope nek."*

* Since the text was written, our opinion has been confirmed
by meeting with the following significant query in a petition

This unique letter is addressed " To the much
honered Governor, Mr. Thomas Prince, dwelling at
Plymouth." As Philip himself could neither read
nor write, the honor of the orthography and construction must be attributed to the infirm interpreter. But
the sentiments are worthy of the sachem himself, and
they certainly manifest a mingled civility and independence which do him great credit. No date is
affixed to the letter. If it do not refer to the transaction just mentioned, it was probably prompted by
some other of the same description. The interest
which the sachem felt in cases of this kind, is apparent from one of his own conveyances, made in 1668.
It was of a tract included within the present limits
of Rochester, upon the sea-shore. He drafted an
accurate plan of it with his own hand, (still preserved
upon the records of the Old Colony) and forwarded
it to the Court, with the following explanation.

" This may inform the honorable Court," we read,
" that I, Philip, am willing to sell the land within this
draught, but the Indians that are upon it may live
upon it still ; but the land that is mine that is sold,
and Watashpoo is of the same mind. I have put
down all the principal names of the land we are now
willing should be sold." Watashpoo was probably
one of the occupants, chiefly interested in the case.
The letter ends thus ; " Know all Men by these Presents, That Philip has given power unto Watashpoo,
and Sampson, and their brethren, to hold and make
sale of said land to whom they will," &c. This letter
must have been sent in compliance with some request from his Plymouth friends. It is dated at
Pocanauket ; subscribed by the capital P, which was

---

cf Mr. Gookin and Mr. Elliot to the Massachusetts Government
in 1684, for the rescinding of certain purchases made of the
Indians which they considered fraudulent:—" *Was not a
principal cause of the late war about encroachments on
Philip's lands at Mount Hope ?*" No remarks of ours can
add to the force of a suggestion from such a source.

tue sachem's mark ; and attested, and no doubt written, by his secretary, John Sassamon.

Sassamon is distinguished in history as having been the immediate occasion of the first open hostilities. He was born in some family of praying Indians, an·ı after receiving a tolerable education at Cambridge and other places, was employed as a school-master at Natick. The composition above cited rather supports Hubbard's remark, that he was a " cunning and plausible Indian, well skilled in the English language." This writer says, that he left the English on account of some misdemeanor. Mather states, that " apostatizing from the profession of Christianity, he lived like a heathen, in the quality of secretary tc King Philip." He adds, that he afterwards deserted the sachem, and gave such notable evidences of repentance, as to be employed in preaching among the Indians at Natick, under the eye of his old instructer, the venerable Eliot.

This was another of the provocations which must have annoyed Philip. Hubbard states expressly, that Sassamon was importunately urged to forsake him ; and it appears from other sources, that there had previously been such an entire confidence between the two, that the Secretary was intrusted with all the secrets of his master. The provocation went still farther. Sassamon, either having or pretending to have some occasion to go among the Pokanokets frequently, availed himself of this opportunity to scrutinize their movements, and to report them as he thought proper to the English. In consequence of this, Philip and some of his subjects were ' examined,' we are told, but nothing definite was learned from them. Soon after, Sassamon disappeared ; and as he had expressed some well-founded fears of meeting with a violent death in the course of these manœuvres, his friends were alarmed. They commenced a search, and finally found his dead body in Assawomset pond, (in Middleborough) where a hole in the ice, through which he

O

had been thrust, was still open, and his hat and gun
left near by, as if he had drowned himself. "Furthermore," says Mather, " upon the jealousies of the
spirits of men that he might have met with some
foul play, a jury was empanelled, unto whom it appeared that his neck was broken, *which is one Indian
way of murdering.*"

The next step of the Plymouth Government was
to seize upon three Pokanoket Indians, on the testimony of a fourth, "*found*," says Hubbard, " *by a
strange providence.*" This man swore that he had
seen the murder committed from a hill near the
pond. It must be inferred that he swore to the identity
of the prisoners, for it appears they were convicted
from "his undeniable testimony and other circumstances,"* and forthwith hanged. Whatever may be
said of the *legal*, the *moral* probability certainly is,
that they were guilty. They were probably appointed
to execute the judgment of Philip upon Sassamon,
one of them being Tobias, a man of some distinction
At all events, Philip must have thought himself justified in taking this summary measure with a vaga-
bond who was mean enough to avail himself, as
Sassamon did, of being tolerated in *his* territory after
having betrayed his confidence, and apparently for
the very purpose of following up his own treason.

---

* The Colonists were but too ready, throughout these transactions, to believe any thing and every thing which supported a
charge against Philip. One of the undeniable circumstances
is, probably, stated by Mather. The dead body bled afresh,
says the Doctor, on the approach of Tobias, " yea, upon the
repetition of the experiment, it still happened so," albeit he
had been deceased and interred for a considerable while before.

CHAPTER VIII.

Preparations for war between Philip and the Colonies—Great excitement of the times—Deposition of Hugh Cole—Immediate occasion of hostilities—Commencement of them, June 24th, 1675—Summary sketch of the war—Consequences to the parties engaged—Exertions, adventures and escapes of King Philip—His death—Anecdotes respecting him—Observations on his character—His courage, dignity, kindness, independence, shrewdness, and self-command—Fate of his family—Defence of his conduct.

WHATEVER had previously been the disposition or determination of Philip, it is universally agreed, that subsequent to the transaction mentioned at the close of the last chapter, he took but little pains either to conceal his own hostility or to check that of his subjects. It would be incredible that he should. He well remembered what had happened to his brother in much more peaceable times ; and, as several historians intimate, he must actually have apprehended 'the danger his own head was in next.' A passage in one of his letters heretofore cited, is to the same purpose—" as also suggestions of great danger in case they [his subjects] there [at Plymouth] appear ; *with harsh threats to the sachem, that may be considered."*

Every preparation was now made for the impending crisis on either side. The following ancient document, taken from the records of Plymouth, shows that the agitation of all the parties concerned had already arrived to a high pitch. It is the deposition of one Hugh Cole, taken in court previous to Sassamon's death, and attested by Nathaniel Morton as secretary :*

" Hugh Cole, aged forty-three, or thereabouts, being deposed, saith ;—That in February last past before the date hereof, he went to Shewamett, and

---

* Vide 6th. Vol. Man. His. Coll. 1st Series

two Englishmen more with him: and that their
business was *to persuade the Indians to go to Plymouth*,
to answer a complaint made by Hezekiah Luther
The Indians (saith he) seeing us, came out of the
house towards us, being many of them, at the least
twenty or thirty, with staves in their hand ; and
when the Indians saw there were but three of us,
they laid down their staves again.   Then we asked
the Indians what they did with those staves in their
hands ?   They answered, that they looked for Englishmen to come from Plymouth, to seek Indians, to
carry them to Plymouth.   But they said they were
not willing to go.   And some time after, in the same
morning, Philip, the chief sachem, sent for me to
come to him ; and I went to Mount Hope to him ;
and when I came to Mount Hope, I saw most of
the Indians that I knew of Shewamett Indians, there
at Mount Hope, and they were generally employed
in making of bows and arrows, and half pikes, and
fixing up of guns.   And I saw many Indians of
several places repair towards Mount Hope.   And
some days after I came from Mount Hope, I, with
several others, saw one of Captain Willett's rangers,
coming on post on horseback, who told us, that king
Philip was marched up the neck with about three
score men ; and Zacary Eddy, on his report, went to
see if he could find them ; and he found them towards
the upper part of the neck, in several companies.
One Caleb Eddy further saith, that he saw many
there in arms ; and I was informed by John Padduck,
that he saw two several guns, loaded with bullets or
slugs.   And I further testify, that those Indians that
I saw come towards Mount Hope, as aforesaid, came
better armed than I usually have seen them.   Further
saith not."

The Pokanokets mustered at Mount Hope, early
in the spring of 1675, from all quarters, and the
whole country was in agitation.   The ungovernable
fury of some of these fierce warriors was the immediate occasion of the war which ensued.   They had

not the power which Philip himself had, of enduring provocation with the reservation of revenge; and they were by no means so well aware, on the other hand, of the advantages to be gained by such a course. At length, a party of them expressed their feelings so intolerably—soon after the execution of their three countrymen—that an Englishman at Swanzey discharged his musket at one of them, and wounded him. This affair took place June 24, 1675, a day memorable in American history as the commencement of PHILIP'S WAR. "Now," says a reverend historian of those times, "war was begun by a fierce nation of Indians upon an honest, harmless Christian generation of English, who might very truly have said unto the aggressors, as it was said of old unto the Ammonites, '*I have not sinned against thee, but thou doest me wrong to war against me.*'" Such no doubt was the persuasion of a large majority of the cotemporary countrymen of the learned divine.

Hostilities were now promptly undertaken. A letter was sent to Philip, in the month of June, which, of course, did no good; applications were also made to the Massachusetts Government for immediate assistance; forces were raised and stationed throughout the Colony; and matters very soon after proceeded to a length which made compromise or conciliation impossible. We do not intend to give for the present the well-known particulars of this celebrated war. It is sufficient to observe, that it was carried on for more than a year with a violence, and amid an excitement unparalleled, perhaps, in the history of the country; and that it terminated with the death of Philip, late in the season of 1676.

The result of it was decisive, as the sachem was well aware that it would be, of the fate of the New England Indians. The Pokanokets were nearly exterminated. The Narraghansetts lost about one thousand of their number in the celebrated swamp-fight at Sunke-Squaw. All the Indians on the

Connecticut river, and most of the Nipmucks who
survived, fled to Canada, (where they were subsequently of great service to the French) and a few
hundreds took refuge in New York. The English
detachment of Captain Church alone, are estimated
to have killed about seven hundred between June
and October of 1676. Large numbers of those who
were captured were sent out of the country, and sold
as slaves.

But the triumph of the conqueror was dearly
bought. The whole fighting force of the four Colonies seems to have been almost constantly in requi-
sition. Between one and two thousand men were
engaged at the swamp-fight alone,—an immense
force for a population of scarcely forty thousand
English throughout New England. Thirteen towns
were entirely destroyed by the enemy ; six hundred
dwelling-houses burned ; and about the same number
of Englishmen killed, so that almost every family
lost a relative. The mere expense of the war must
have been very great ; for the Commissioners of the
United Colonies afterwards estimated the disburse-
ments of the Old Colony alone, at more than one
hundred thousand pounds.

Such was the war of King Philip—sustained and
managed, upon his side, by his own single-handed
energy and talent alone. Not that the sixty Wampanoags of the sachem's own house-hold, as it were,
or even the various tribes of the Pokanoket country,
were his sole supporters ; but that all the other tribes,
which supported him, did it in consequence of his
influence, and were induced to unite and operate
together, as they never had done before, under his
control. Some writers have asserted, that he engaged the various Atlantic tribes as far south as
Virginia to assist him ; but of this there is no proof,
and it is rendered improbable by the great want of
inter-communication among these tribes.

Nor is it true, as other writers have stated, that
all the natives of New England itself were involved

with Philip. On the other hand, it was the most trying circumstance of the great struggle of the sachem, that he had not only to rely upon bringing and keeping together scores of petty cantons, as jealous of each other from time immemorial as so many Highland clans; but he had to watch and resist, openly and secretly, all who would not join him, besides the multitudes who deserted, betrayed and opposed him. The New Hampshire tribes mostly withdrew from the contest. The praying Indians, of whom there were then thousands, either remained neutral, or like Sassamon turned against their own race. One of Philip's own tribes forsook him in his misfortunes; and the Pequots and Mohegans of Connecticut kept the field against him from the very first day of the war to the last. It may be supposed, that some of these tribes were surprised, as Philip himself was, by the sudden breaking out of the war, a year before the time which had been fixed for it. This was occasioned by the proceedings in which Sassamon was concerned, and by the ungovernable fury of a few of the young warriors.

Philip is said to have wept at these tidings of the first outrage of the war. He relented, perhaps, savage as he was, at the idea of disturbing the long amity which his father had preserved; but he may well have regretted, certainly, that being once forced upon the measure, he should enter the battle-field unprepared for what he well knew must be the last, as it was the first, great contest between the red men and the whites. But the die was cast, and though Philip never smiled after that memorable hour just alluded to, his whole soul was bent upon the business before him. Day nor night, scarcely was there rest for his limbs or sleep for his eyes. His resources must have been feeble enough, had his plans, now embarrassed, succeeded to his utmost wish; but he girded himself, as it was, with a proud heart for the mortal struggle. The strength of his own dominions was about six hundred warriors, ready, and

more than ready, long since, for the war-cry. The
whole force of his old enemies, the Narraghansetts,
was already engaged to him. He had negotiated,
also, with the Nipmucks and the tribes on the Connecticut and farther west, and one after another, these
were soon induced to join him. Nor was it six
weeks from the first hostilities, before all the Indians
along the coast of Maine, for a distance of two hundred miles, were eagerly engaged, in what Philip
told them was the common cause of the race.

That no arts might be left untried, even while the
court were condemning his three subjects, he was
holding a grand war-dance at Sowams, and mustering his tawny warriors around him from all quarters.
Several tribes afterwards confessed to the English,
that Philip had thus inveigled them into the war
And again, no sooner were his forces driven back upon
the Connecticut river tribes, about the first of September, 1675, than he enlisted new allies among *them.*
The Hadley Indians, who had joined the English,
—very likely at his instigation,—were suspected,
and fled to him. Their Springfield neighbors, soon
after, joined three hundred of Philip's men, in an
attack upon that town; and thus the whole Nipmuck
country was involved. In the course of the ensuing
winter, the sachem is said to have visited the Mohawks in New York. Not succeeding in gaining
their alliance by fair argument, he was desperate
enough to kill some of their straggling young men in
the woods, in such a manner that the blame would
obviously be charged upon the English. But this
stratagem was defeated, by the escape of one who
had only been stunned by the sachem. The latter
was obliged to take abrupt leave of his hosts; and
from that time, they were among his worst enemies.

His situation during the last few months of the war,
was so deplorable, and yet his exertions so well sustained, that we can only look upon him with pity and
admiration. His successes for some time past had
been tremendous; but the tide began to ebb   The

whole power of the Colonies was in the field, aided by guides and scouting-parties of his own race. The Saconets, the subjects of a near relation of his own, enlisted under Church. Other tribes complained and threatened. Their territory, as well as his, had been over-run, their settlements destroyed, and their planting and fishing-grounds all occupied by the English. Those of them who were not yet hunted down, were day and night followed into swamps and forests, and reduced to live,—if they did not actually starve or freeze,—upon the least and worst food to be conceived of. Hundreds died of diseases incurred in this manner. "I have eaten horse," said one of these miserable wretches, "but now horse is eating me." Another informed Church, on one occasion, that about three hundred Indians had gone a long way to Swanzey, in the heat of the war, for the purpose of eating clams, and that Philip was soon to follow them. At another time, the valiant captain himself captured a large party. Finding it convenient to attack a second directly after, he bade the first wait for him, and join him at a certain rendezvous. The day after the skirmish, "they came to him as they were ordered," and he drove them all together, that very night, into Bridgewater *pound,* and set his Saconet soldiers to guard them. "Being well treated with victuals and drink," he adds, with great simplicity, "they had a merry night, and the prisoners laughed as loud as the soldiers; *not being so treated for a long time before.*"

The mere physical sufferings of Philip, meanwhile, are almost incredible. It is by his hair-breadth escapes, indeed, that he is chiefly visible during the war. Occasionally, the English come close upon him ; he starts up, like the roused lion, plunges into the river or leaps the precipice ; and nothing more is seen of him for months. Only a few weeks after the war commenced, he was surrounded in the great Pocasset swamp, and obliged to escape from his vigilant enemies by rafting himself, with his best men, over the great Taunton river, while their women and children were left to be captured. On his return to the same neighborhood, the next season, a captive guided the English to his encampment. Philip fled in such haste as to leave his kettle upon the fire; twenty of his comrades were overtaken and killed; and he himself escaped to the swamp, precisely as he had formerly escaped from it. Here his uncle was shot soon afterwards at his side. Upon the next day, Church, discovering an Indian seated on a fallen tree, made to answer the purpose of a bridge over the river, raised his musket and deliberately aimed at him. "It is one of our own party," whispered a savage, who crept behind him. Church lowered his gun, and the stranger turned his head. It was Philip himself, musing, perhaps, upon the fate which awaited him. Church fired, but his royal enemy had already fled down the bank. He escaped from a close and bloody skirmish a few hours afterwards.

He was now a desolate and desperate man, the last prince of an ancient race, without subjects, without territory, accused by his allies, betrayed by his comrades, hunted like a spent deer by bloodhounds, in daily hazard of famishing, and with no shelter day or night for his head. All his chief counsellors and best friends had been killed. His brother was slain in the Pocasset swamp; his uncle was shot down at his own side; and his wife and only son were captured when he himself so narrowly escaped from the fire of Church. And could he have fled for the last time from the soil of his own country, he would still have found no rest or refuge. He had betaken himself once to a place between York and Albany; but even here, as Church says, the *Moohags* made a descent upon him and killed many of his men. His next kennelling-place* was at the fall of

---

* The language of Church. The same name might be as properly applied, we suppose, to a curious cave in the vicinity

Connecticut river, above Deerfield, where, some
time after, "Captain Turner found him, came upon
him by night, killed a great many men, and frightened many more into the river, that were hunted down
the falls and drowned." He lost three hundred
men at this time. They were in their encampments,
asleep and unguarded. The English rushed upon
them, and they fled in every direction, half-awaken-
ed, and crying out, "Mohawks! Mohawks!"

We cannot better illustrate Philip's character, than
by observing, that within a few days of this affair,
he was collecting the remnants of the Narraghansetts and Nipmucks among the Wachuset hills, on
the east side of the river; that they then made a
descent upon Sudbury; "met with and *swallowed up
the valiant Captain Wadsworth and his company;* and
many other doleful desolations in those parts." We
also find, that Philip was setting parties to waylay
Church, under his own worst circumstances; and
that he came very near succeeding. He is thought
to have been at the great swamp-fight in December,
1675; and to have led one thousand Indians against
Lancaster on the ensuing 8th of February. In
August of the former season, he made his appearance among the Nipmucks, in a swamp ten or twelve
miles from Brookfield. "They told him at his first
coming," said one of them who was taken captive,

---

of Winnecunnett pond, in Norton (Mass.) In the midst of a
cluster of large rocks, it is formed by the projection of one
over another which meets it with an acute angle. It is five
feet high, and the area at the base is seventeen feet by nine.
Tradition represents it as one of the Sachem's secret retreats,
and it bears the name of ' Philip's-Cave' to this day.

* This strong expression of the Captain's may refer to the
really savage treatment which the unfortunate prisoners met
with in this case. We have it on the authority of Mather, at
least, that those " devils incarnate " inflicted a variety of tortures not necessary to be enlarged upon here; " and so with
exquisite, leisurely, horrible torments, roasted them out of the
world." *History of New England*, Book VII. p. 55.
London Ed. 1702.

"what tney had done to the English at Brookfield
[burning the town.] " *Then he presented and gave
to three sagamores,* namely, John *alias* Apequinast,
Quanansit, and Mawtamps, to each of them *about a
peck of unstrung wampum.*"* Even so late as the
month before the sachem's death, a negro, who had
fought under him, informed the English of his
design of attacking certain towns, being still able to
muster something like a thousand men. In his last
and worst days, he would not think of peace ; and
he killed with his own hand, upon the spot, the only
Indian who ever dared to propose it. It was the
brother of this man by whom he was himself soon
after slain.

These are clear proofs, then, that Philip possessed
a courage as noble as his intellect. Nor is there any
doubt that history would have furnished a long list
of his personal exploits, but that his situation compelled him to disguise as well as conceal himself.
If any thing but his face had been known, there was
nothing to prevent Church from shooting him, as we
have seen. And universally influential as he was,
—the master-spirit every where guiding, encouraging, soothing and rewarding,—it is a fact worthy of
mention, that from the time of his first flight from
Pocasset until a few weeks before his death, no
Englishman could say, that he had either seen his
countenance or heard his voice. Hence Church.
describes him as being always foremost in the flight.
The price put upon his head, the fearful power
which pursued him, the circumstance that some of
his own acquaintance were against him, and especially the vital importance of his life to his cause,
all made it indispensable for him to adopt every
stratagem of the wary and cunning warfare of his
race.

---

* Note to Hutchinson's History of Massachusetts. Mather
says, that these very Indians had covenanted by a formal treaty
a month before, that they would not assist Philip

We have said something of Philip's ideas of his own sovereign dignity. Hence the fate of Sassamon, and of the savage who proposed peace. There is a well settled tradition, that in 1665 he went over to the island of Nantucket, with the view of killing an Indian called John Gibbs.* He landed on the west end, intending to travel along the shore, undiscovered, under the bank, to that part of the island where Gibbs resided. By some lucky accident, the latter received a hint of his approach, made his escape to the English settlement, and induced one Mr. Macy to conceal him. His crime consisted in speaking the name of some deceased relative of Philip (his brother, perhaps,) contrary to Indian etiquette in such cases provided. The English held a parley with the sachem, and all the money they were able to collect was barely sufficient to satisfy him for the life of the culprit. It was not a mere personal insult, but a violation of the reverence due from a subject to his king.

It appears, that when he visited Boston, before the war, he succeeded in persuading the government,—as, no doubt, was the truth of the case,—that notwithstanding the old league of his father, renewed by himself, or rather by force of it, he was still independent of Plymouth. "These successive engage ments were agreements of amity, and not of subjec tion any further, as he apprehended." He then desired to see a copy of the treaty, and requested that one might be procured for him. He knew, he added, that the praying Indians had submitted to the English; but the Pokanokets had done no such thing, and they were not subject. The letter of the Massachusetts to the Plymouth Government, written just after this interview with the sachem, is well worthy of notice. "We do not understand," say the former, "how far he hath subjected himself to you;

---

* The fact, as to the visit itself, is authenticated by the extant records of Nantucket.

T.—O

but the treatment you have given him, does not ren
der him such a subject, as that, if there be not present
answering to summons, there should presently be a
proceeding to hostilities."

Philip had himself the same notion of a Plymouth
summons; and yet either policy or good feeling induced him to *visit* the Plymouth Governor, in
March, 1675, for the purpose of quieting the suspicious of the Colony : nothing was discovered against
him, and he returned home. He maintained privately
the same frank but proud independence. He was
opposed to Christianity as much as his father was,
and would make no concessions upon that point.
Possibly the remembrance of Sassamon might have
rankled in his bosom, when, upon the venerable Eliot
once undertaking to convert him, he took one of his
buttons between his fingers, and told him he cared
no more for the Gospel than for that button. That
he was generally more civil, however, may be inferred from Gookin's statement ; " I have heard him
speak very good words, arguing that his conscience
is convicted, &c." The sachem evidently made him
self agreeable in this case.

In regard to his personal appearance, always a
matter of curiosity in the case of great men, sketches
purporting to be portraits of him are extant, but none
of them are believed to have more verisimilitude
than the grotesque charicature prefixed to the old
narrative of Captain Church (the model of the
series) ; and we must therefore content ourselves to
remain ignorant in this matter. As to his costume,
Josselyn, who saw him at Boston, says that he had a
coat on, and buskins set thick with beads, " in pleasant wild works, and a broad belt of the same ;" his
accoutrements being valued at £20. A family in
Swanzey, (Mass.), is understood to be still in posses-
session of some of the royalties which were given
up by ANAWON, at the time of *his* capture by Church.*

---

* Anawon is said to have been Philip's chief counsellor and
captain during the war ; and also to have fought under Massa-

There were two horns of glazed powder, a red-cloth blanket, and three richly and beautifully wrought wampum belts. One was nine inches wide, and so long as to extend from the shoulder to the ancles. To the second, which was worn on the head, were attached two ornamented small flags. The third and smallest had a star figured in beads upon one end, which came over the bosom.

Philip was far from being a mere barbarian in his manners and feelings. There is not an instance tc be met with, of his having maltreated a captive ir any way, even while the English were selling h˙ own people as slaves abroad, or torturing and hang ing them at home. The famous Mrs. Rowlandsor speaks of meeting with him during her *doleful* cap tivity. He invited her to call at his lodge ; and whei she did so, bade her sit down, and asked her if she would smoke. On meeting her again, he requestea her to make some garment for his child, and for this he paid her a shilling. He afterwards took the trou ble of visiting her for the purpose of assuring her, that " in a fortnight she should be her own mistress." Her last interview, it must be allowed, shows his shrewdness to rather more advantage than his fair dealing. It was Indian stratagem in war-time, how-

---

soit. But the latter was not a very belligerent character; noi do we find mention of Anawon's services under Philip, previous to the time of his fall at the swamp-skirmish, when the counsellor made his escape. Hubbard states that he boasted of having killed ten whites in one day; but nearly all that is known of him we derive from the picturesque account of his capture by Church, who headed an expedition for the express purpose. Anawon met his misfortune, and even entertained his conqueror, most manfully on that occasion; and Church recip rocated his courtesies; but all in vain—the old warrior, with many others of his tribe, was soon after beheaded at Plymouth To the traveller from Taunton to Providence, through the south-east corner of Rehoboth, *Anawon's rock* is pointed out to this day—an enormous pile, from twenty-five to thirty feet high, on a sort of island in a swamp of some thousand acres.

ever; and the half-clad sachem was at this very
time living upon ground-nuts, acorns and lily-roots.
"Philip, smelling the business, [her ransom,] called me to him, and asked me what I would give him
to tell me some good news, and to speak a good
word for me, that I might go home to-morrow. I
told him I could not tell,—but any thing I had,—and
asked him what he would have. He said two coats,
and twenty shillings in money, half a bushel of seed-
corn, and some tobacco. *I thanked him for his love,
but I knew that good news as well as that crafty fox.*"
It is probable he was amusing himself with this good
woman, much as he did with the worthy Mr. Gookin; but at all events, there are no traces of malevo-
lent feeling in these simple anecdotes.

What is more striking, we find that when one
James Brown, of Swanzey, brought him a letter from
Plymouth, just before hostilities commenced, and the
young warriors were upon the point of killing him,
Philip interfered and prevented it, saying, that "his
father had charged him to show kindness to Mr.
Brown." Accordingly, it is recorded in Hubbard,
that a little before *his* death, the old sachem had
visited Mr. Brown, who lived not far from Montaup,
and earnestly desired that the love and amity *he* had
received, might be continued to the children. It
was probably this circumstance, which induced
Brown himself, to engage in such a hazardous enter-
prize, after an interval, probably, of some twenty
years.

Nor should we pass over the kindness of Philip
to the Leonard family, who resided near Fowling
Pond, in what is now Raynham. Philip, who wintered at Montaup,—for the convenience of fishing
perhaps,—was accustomed to spend the summer at
a hunting-house, by this pond. There he became
intimate with the Leonards, traded with them, and
had his arms repaired by them frequently. On the
breaking out of the war, he gave strict orders that

*t*hese men should never be hurt, as they never were ;*
and, indeed, the whole town of Taunton,—as it then
was,—remained almost entirely unmolested throughout the war, and amid all the ravages and massacres
which daily took place upon its very borders. How
much of provocation and humiliation he was himself
enduring meanwhile, we have already seen. All his
relations were killed or captured, and a price set
upon his own life.

It is a matter of melancholy interest to know, that
the sachem, wretched and hopeless as he had become
in his last days, was still surrounded by a band of
his faithful and affectionate followers. At the very
moment of his fatal surprise by the English, he is
said to have been telling them of his gloomy dreams,†

---

* A forge is still in operation upon the site of the one here
mentioned. The original LEONARD HOUSE, where tradition
says that Philip's head was deposited for some time, is represented in the Vignette prefixed to this volume. It is still
occupied by one of the family, of the sixth generation from the
builder, and, so far as we are informed, is the oldest mansion
now standing in this country. The vane, at one of the gable-
ends is inscribed with the date 1700; but there is little doubt of
the house having been erected at least thirty years previous.
The workmanship, especially within, is remarkably massive and
sound. It is apparently modelled after an English fashion of the
eighteenth century, with some modifications proper for defence
against the Indians. It was garrisoned during the war.—The
Fowling Pond, still so called, has become a thick swamp.
An aged gentleman was living not many years since, who in
boyhood had frequently gone off in a canoe, to catch fish in its
waters. Indian weapons and utensils are still found on its
borders.

† The violent prejudice existing against Philip, unmitigated
even by his sufferings and death, appears singularly in a pa-
renthetical surmise of Hubbard, " whether the devil appeared
to him that night in a dream, foreboding his tragical end, *it
matters not.*" So Mather says, he was hung up like *Ahag*,
after being shot through his " venomous and murderous heart "
Church, generally an honorable and humane man, speaks of
his fallen foe, in terms which we regard his reputation too
much to repeat.

and advising them to desert him and provide for their own safety. A few minutes after this, he was shot in attempting to escape from the swamp. An Engglishman,—one Cook,—aimed at him, but his gun missed fire ; the Indian who was stationed to watch at the same place, discharged *his* musket, and shot him through the heart. The news of this success was of course received with great satisfaction; Church says, that "the whole army gave three loud huzzas." It is to be regretted that the honest captain suffered his prejudices to carry him so far, that he denied the rites of burial to his great enemy. He had him quartered, on the contrary, and his head carried to Plymouth, where, as Mather is careful to tell us, it arrived on the very day when the church there were keeping a solemn thanksgiving. The conqueror's temper was soured by the illiberality of the Government toward himself. For this march he received but four and sixpence a man, together with thirty shillings a head for the killed. He observes that Philip's head went at the same price, and he thought it a "scanty reward and poor encouragement." The sachem's head was carried about the Colony in triumph ; * and the Indian who killed him was rewarded with one of his hands. To finish the wretched detail, several of his principal royalties were soon after given up by one of his chief captains ; and the lock of the gun which was fatal to him, with a *samp*-dish found in his wigwam, are still to be seen among the antiquities of the Historical Society of Massachusetts. Montaup, which became the subject of a dispute between the Massachusetts and Plymouth Colonies, was finally awarded to the latter by a special decision of King Charles.

Last and worst of all, his only son, a boy of nine

---

* It was kept many years at Plymouth, Dr. Mather says in 1700. "It is not long since the hand which now writes upon a certain occasion took off the jaw from the exposed skull of *that blasphemous leviathan.*"

years of age, whom we have already noticed as among the English captives, was sold as a slave and shipped to Burmuda. It should be stated, however, that this unfortunate measure was not taken without some scruples. The Plymouth Court were so much perplexed upon the occasion, as to conclude upon applying to the clergymen of the Colony for advice. Mr. Cotton was of opinion that "the children of notorious traitors, rebels, and murderers, especially sucn as have been principal leaders and actors in such norrid villanies, might be involved in the guilt of their parents, and might, *salva republica,* be adjudged *to death.*" Dr. Increase Mather compared the child to Hadad, whose father was killed by Joab; and he intimates, that if Hadad himself had not escaped, David would have taken measures to prevent his molesting the next generation. It is gratifying to know, that the course he recommended was postponed, even to the ignominious and mortifying one we have mentioned.

Such was the impression which had been universally forced upon the Colonists by the terrible spirit of Philip. And never was a civilized or an uncivilized enemy more generally or more justly feared. How much greater his success might have been, had circumstances favored, instead of opposing him, it is fortunately impossible for us to estimate. It is confessed, however, that had even the Narraghansetts joined him during the first summer of the war,— as nothing but the abrupt commencement of it prevented them from doing,—the whole country, from the Piscataqua to the Sound, must have been over-swept and desolated. But as it was, Philip did and endured enough to immortalize him as a warrior, a statesman, and we may add, as a high-minded and noble patriot. Whatever might be the prejudice against him in the days of terror produced by his prowess, there are both the magnanimity and the calmness in these times, to do him the justice he deserves.   He fought and fell,—miserably, indeed, but gloriously,—the avenger of his own household, the worshipper of his own gods, the guardian of his own honor, a martyr for the soil which was his birth-place, and for the proud liberty which was his birth-right.

CHAPTER IX.

Tle Narraghansett tribe; territory and power—-Chief Sachems at the date of the English settlements in New England
—CANONICUS associates with himself MIANTONOMO, his
nephew—Their treatment of Roger Williams in 1634—
Hostility to the Plymouth Colony—Invited by the Pequots
to fight the English—Treaty negotiated at Boston, in 1636,
by Miantonomo—War with the Pequots and result of it—
Subsequent hostility between Miantonomo and UNCAS—
SEQUASSEN—Battle of the Sachem's-Plain—Capture of
Miantonomo—Sentence of the English commissioners upon
him—Execution of it.

NEXT to the Pokanoket confederacy, none has a
stronger claim on the early notice of the historian,
than the Narraghansett; a nation, composed of
various small tribes, inhabiting a large part of the
territory which afterwards formed the colony of
Rhode-Island. Their dominion extended also over
the islands in the bay of their own name ; and the
Sagamores of a part of Long-Island, Block-Island,
Cawesit, and Niantick were either their tributaries
or subject to them in some other way. They had
once been able to raise more than four thousand
warriors ; and so late as Philip's time, we have seen
they could muster two thousand, one half of whom
were provided with English arms, and were skilful
in the use of them. From time immemorial, they had
waged war with both the Pokanokets on the North
and the Pequots on the West.

It might be expected, that the rulers of such a
confederacy, thus situated, should be men of talent
and energy ; and this expectation will not be disappointed. Throughout the history of the New England Indians, as we find no people more resolute in
declaring what they believed to be their rights, or
more formidable in defending them, so we find no
sachems more ready and able than theirs, on all occasions, to sustain the high spirit of their subjects.

10—12

There is an unnecessary confusion in the information conveyed by some of our best annalists, respecting the particular personage who governed the Narraghansetts at the date of the first intercourse between
them and the English.   Governor Hutchinson, for
example, speaks in one case of CANONICUS as being
their chief sachem.   In another, alluding to the
death of MIANTONOMO, while the former was yet
living, he observes, that although they had *lost their
chief sachem*, yet they had divers other stout ones, as
Canonicus, Pessacus and others.

The ambiguity has arisen from the circumstance,
that although Canonicus exercised the chief authority
of the country when the English first arrived, he
soon after became associated in the Government
with Miantonomo, his nephew.   What were the particular conditions of the royal co-partnership, or
what was the occasion of it, cannot now be determined.   Some writers suppose, that the sole authority
belonged to the younger of the two, and that the elder
acted in the capacity of regent ; but considering that
the association continued during the whole term of
the joint lives of the two, it appears more probable,
that Canonicus, finding himself far advanced in
years,* as well as encumbered with the charge of an
extensive dominion, at the period of the first English settlements, thought proper to make such an
alteration in his regal state as seemed to be required
by the exigencies of the times.   He therefore selected as an associate, the most popular and active prince
of his own family.

Mr. Hutchinson himself appears finally to adopt

---

* Roger Williams tells us in his KEY TO THE INDIAN LAN-
GUAGES, first printed in 1643, that he was about fourscore years
of age.   Elsewhere, it is stated, that " Cononicus, being the
sole governor or chief sachem, employed his nephew Mianti-
nomy, to manage his warlike affairs, as general of his army,
*and in his declining years took him as a partner in his
government for assistance.   His. Narr. Country. Mass
His. Coll*

the conclusion we have just stated. In a part of his history* subsequent to the passage above cited, he refers to information derived from authentic manuscripts, which furnished the opinion of the Narraghansetts themselves upon the subject. The oldest of that people reported, when the English first arrived, that they had in former times a sachem called TASHTASSACK, incomparably superior to any other in the whole country in dominion and state. This chieftain, said they, had only two children, a son and a daughter ; and not being able to match them according to their dignity, he joined them together in wedlock. They had four sons; and of these, Canonicus, *" who was sachem when the English came,"* was the eldest.

Mr. Hutchinson observes, that this is the only piece of Indian history, or tradition of any sort, from the ancestors of our first Indians, he had ever met with. The brothers of Canonicus here referred to, are occasionally spoken of by the old writers, but not as having signalized themselves by any thing worthy of notice.

The fact that Canonicus and his nephew administered the government in harmony, as well as in union, is shown most clearly by the letters of Roger Williams.† It is well known that, in 1634, when that reverend gentleman was compelled to leave the Massachusetts colony, (on account of his religious opinions,) he fled to Seekonk. But that place lying within the limits of the Plymouth jurisdiction, and the people of that colony being unwilling to embroil themselves with Massachusetts, Governor Winslow informed him of the difficulty which was apprehended, and advised him to occupy a spot on the other

---

* *History of Mass. Vol. I.* pp. 72. and 458.

† See Vol. I. Mass. His. Coll. 3d Series. The same writer says in his Key to the Indian Languages—" Their agreement in the government is remarkable. The old Sachem will not be offended at what the young Sachem doth ; and the young Sachem will not do what he conceives will displease his uncle."

side of the river, without the boundaries of either
iurisdiction. Upon this, Mr. Williams, utterly forlorn,
crossed the river, and threw himself on the mercy
of Canonicus.

The savage chieftain—to his eternal praise, be it
recorded—received him with a hospitality worthy of
an emperor. At first, indeed, he was suspicious of
his visiter's motives ; and he was none the more prepossessed in his favor, from his subjects having recent-
lv suffered excessively from a formidable epidemic,
which he supposed to have been introduced by the
English. " At my first coming among them," Mr.
Williams writes, " Caunounicus* (morosus aeque ac
barbarus senex) was very sour, and accused the
English and myself of sending the plague among
them, and threatening to kill *him* especially." Soon
afterwards, however, he not only permitted the
refugee, and the poor wanderers who had followed
him from Salem, to have a resting place in his
domain, but he gave them all " the neck of land
lying between the mouths of Pawtucket and Mosha-
suck rivers, that they might sit down in peace upon
it, and enjoy it forever." Mr. Williams divided this
land equally among his followers, and founded the
town of Providence. The settlement of Rhode
Island commenced at Patuxet a short time afterwards,
Canonicus conveying to Williams nearly the whole
of what is now Providence county at one time.

The kindness of the Narraghansett rulers is the
more creditable to their feelings, inasmuch as the
former relations between them and the English colonies had been far enough from friendly. Early in
1622, their threats of hostility were so open, that the

---

* The following are but a few of the other modifications of this
name in use.

CONONICUS.   Trumbull's mss. Vol. 19th.
CAUNONICUS   Baylies' History of Plymouth.
CONAUCUS.   Winslow's GOOD NEWS FROM NEW ENGLAND
CANNONICUS. Gookin.
CANANACUS.   Documents in Hazard's Collection.
COONOONACUS, CANOONACUS and CONOWNACUS   Same.

English were receiving constant intelligence of their designs from the Indians in their own alliance; and not long afterwards, Canonicus sent a herald to Plymouth, who left a bundle of arrows enclosed in a rattle-snake's skin—the customary challenge to war. The Governor despatched a messenger in return, bearing the same skin stuffed with gunpowder and bullets; assuring the chieftain also, that if he had shipping, instead of troubling *him* to come so far as Plymouth to gratify his wish for fighting, he would have sought him in his own country;—and furthermore, that whenever he did come, he should find the English ready for him. This resolute message had the desired effect, and the sachem's superstition confirmed it. Fearful of some mysterious injury, he refused to touch the skin, and would not suffer it even to remain in his house. It passed through several hands, and at length was returned to the col ony, unopened.

In 1632, the sachem made an attack on Massasoit, who fled for refuge to an English house at Sowams; and sent despatches for the assistance of his English allies. As Captain Standish took a special interest in this case, there must soon have been a warm contest between the parties, had not the Narraghansetts hastily retreated, on account of a rumor that the Pequots were invading their own territory. Four years afterwards, when the last named nation formed the design of completely extirpating the English from New England, they applied to their old enemies, Canonicus and Miantonomo, to conclude a peace, and to engage them with as many other tribes as possible in a common cause against the colonists.

The sachems are said to have wavered on that occasion, between the gratification of present revenge upon the Pequots, and the prospect of an ultimate triumph over the English power by uniting with them. Their friendship for Roger Williams, and the influence he was consequently enabled to exercise, probably turned the scale. Miantonomo inform-

ed him of the Pequot application ; Mr. Williams for
warded the news immediately to Governor Winthrop
at Boston ; and Canonicus, by the same messenger,
sent word of recent depredations which he had just
understood to have been committed by the Pequots
at Saybrook. The Governor, probably following the
suggestion of Mr. Williams, sent for Miantonomo to
do him the honor of a visit.

He came to Boston accordingly in September
1636, attended by two of the sons of Canonicus, another sachem, and about twenty sanops (or male
adults.) As he had given notice of his approach the
day previous, the governor sent a corps of musketeers
to meet him at Roxbury ; and they escorted him
into town about noon. By this time, Mr. Winthrop
had called together most of the magistrates and
ministers of Boston, but it being now dinner time,
ceremony and business were both postponed. The
sachems dined by themselves in the same room
with the governor, while the sanops were amply
provided for at an inn. In the afternoon, Miantonomc
made his proposals of peace ; and said that, in case
of their acceptance, he should in two months send a
present to confirm them. The governor, according
to their own custom, asked time to consider this proposal. At the second conference, which took place
the next morning, the following terms were agreed
upon, and subscribed by the governor on the one
hand, and the marks of the sachems on the other.

1. A firm peace between the Massachusetts colony, and the other English plantations, (with their
consent,) and *their* confederates (with *their* consent.)

2. Neither party to make peace with the Pequots,
without consultation with the other.

3. Not to harbor the Pequots.

4. To put to death or deliver over murderers, and
to return fugitive servants.

5. The English to notify them, when they march
ed against the Pequots, and *they* to send guides.

6. Free trade between the two nations.

7. None of them to visit the English settlements during the war with the Pequots, without some Eng-.ishman or known Indian in company.

The treaty was to continue to the posterity of both nations. On its conclusion, the parties dined together as before. They then took formal leave of each other; and the sachems were escorted out of town, and dismissed with a volley of musketry. The present promised by Miantonomo appears to have been sent in early in 1637, when a deputation of twenty-six Narraghansetts came to Boston, with forty fathom of wampum and a Pequot's hand. The governor gave each of the four sachems in the company, " a coat of fourteen shillings price, and deferred to return his present till after, according to their manner."* It is well. known, how fully the Narraghansetts discharged their engagements in the expedition which took place about this time against the Pequots. They also furnished, through Mr. Williams, not a little useful information respecting the common enemy, by which the expedition was guided at the outset; and offered the use of the harbors of the Narraghansett coast, for the English vessels.

The joint invasion of the allies took place in May. The English forces, taking the Narraghansett country in their way, acquainted Canonicus and Miantonomo with their arrival and plan of campaign. The latter met them, the next day, with about two hundred of his chief counsellors and warriors. Mason made a formal request for permission to pass through his territories, on his way to the Pequot forts. Miantonomo, after a solemn consultation, replied, that he highly approved of the expedition, and would send men, especially as the English force appeared to him quite too insignificant to meet the Pequots, who were great warriors. About five hundred warriors accordingly marched against the enemy, under the command of Mason; and some of them did active service.

---

* Winthrop's Journal, p. 217

The chief sachems took no part, personally, in the campaign.*

In September 1638, the Pequots being complete-'y conquered, Uncas, the chief sachem of the Mohegans, (who had assisted in the war,) and Miantonomo were invited to meet the Connecticut magistrates at Hartford, to agree upon a division of captives. These were two hundred in number, besides women and children. Eighty of them were allotted to the Narraghansett sachem ; twenty to a neighboring chief, Ninigret ; and the other one hundred to Uncas. The Pequots were to pay an annual tribute of wampum at Hartford. It was also covenanted, that there should be a perpetual peace between Miantonomo and Uncas ; that all past injuries should be buried ; that if any should be committed in future, complaints should be submitted amicably to the arbitration of the English, both parties being bound to abide by their decision on pain of incurring their hostility. No open enemies of the English were to be harbored, and all individual criminals were to be given over to justice.

---

* According to some writers they did not even meet Major Mason, in conference, as above related. Mr. Wolcott, (Gov. of Conn. from 1751 to 1754,) in his *poetical* " Account of Mr. Winthrop's agency in obtaining a charter for Connecticut " gives the following notice of that interview:

> The news of this our march, fame doth transport
> With speed to great Miaantinomoh's court.
> Nor had that pensive king forgot the losses,
> He had sustained through Sassacus's forces.
> Cheer'd with the news, his captains, all as one,
> In humble manner do address the throne,
> And press the king to give them his commission
> To join the English in this expedition.
> To their request the cheerful king assents,
> And now they fill and form their regiments
> To war: a cohort which came marching down
> To us, who lay encamp'd before the town.
> Their chiefs go to our general, and declare
> What 's their intention and whose men they are, &c

The terms of this treaty did not long remain inviolate. Whatever were the motives of Miantonomo, and whatever his justification, he soon became bitterly hostile to the Mohegans at least. It might have been reason enough with him for opposing both them and the English, that *either* was his enemy; because he knew them to be bound together by alliance of offence and defence. But it seems probable, that he intended only to fight the Mohegans. His old grudge against the Pequots revived against *them*, as a branch of the Pequot stock. Uncas, too, was his greatest personal rival: and Miantonomo was ambitious to stand at the head of all the New England Indians. If, however, as has been asserted by some, his main design was to resist the growing power of the English, from merely patriotic motives, it was clear, that an essential step towards the attainment of this object, and especially towards a hostile union of all the tribes, must be the death of Uncas, and the suppression of *his* tribe. Other causes of hostility will be considered hereafter.

But be the reasoning of the sachem what it might, his measures were of a character not to be mistaken Great efforts were made for a general co-operation of the tribes, especially in Connecticut. They were observed to be collecting arms and ammunition, and to be making a general preparation for war. The colonists thought themselves obliged to keep guard and watch every night, from sunset to sunrise, and to protect their inhabitants from town to town, and even from one place to another in the same neighborhood.

Meanwhile Miantonomo is said to have hired a Pequot, subject to Uncas, to kill him. The assassin made an attempt, in the spring of 1643. He shot Uncas through the arm, and then fled to the Narraghansetts, reporting through the Indian towns that he had killed him. When it was understood, however, that the wound was not fatal, the Pequot circulated a rumor that Uncas had purposely cut his

I.—P

own arm with a flint, and then charged the Pequot with shooting him. But, Miantonomo soon after going to Boston in company with the refugee, the governor and magistrates, on examination, found clear evidence that the latter was guilty of the crime with which he was charged. They proposed sending him to Uncas to be punished; but Miantonomo pleaded that he might be suffered to return with himself; and gave them to understand, it is said, that *he* would send him to Uncas. He took occasion to exculpate himself of all blame in the affair, and convinced them so completely, that his requests were granted. Two days afterwards, he killed the Pequot with his own hand.

About the same time, an event took place in another direction, under circumstances which strongly indicated the same authorship. SEQUASSEN, a sachem on the Connecticut river, killed a principal Indian of the Mohegan tribe; and waylaid Uncas himself, as he was going down the river, and shot several arrows at him. Uncas complained to the governor and court of the colony, who took great pains to settle the affair, but without success. He was finally induced to accept of one of Sequassen's Indians, to be given up as an equivalent for the murdered man; but Sequassen would not consent to submission or concession of any kind. He insisted upon fighting. Uncas accepted his challenge, and invaded his territory; and Sequassen was defeated, with the loss of many of his wigwams burned, and his men killed.*

As the conquered sachem was nearly allied to Miantonomo, and upon intimate terms with him, it was generally *believed* that he acted from his instigation, and with the promise of his assistance in case of necessity. He even expressed, openly, his reliance on the aid of Miantonomo.

The Narraghansett chief was not a man to desert

---

* Trumbull's Connecticut.

his ally or to retreat from his foe. Having hastily matured a plan of campaign, it was the next object to strike the intended blow with the most possible effect, and that implied the least possible notice. He raised an army of between five hundred and one thousand men, and marched towards the Mohegan territory. The spies of Uncas discovered their approach, and gave him intelligence. The enemy was already near, and Uncas was unprepared; but he hastily rallied four or five hundred of his men, and telling them that the enemy must by no means be suffered to surprise them in their villages, marched out to meet him forthwith. At the distance of three or four miles, the two armies encountered each other upon a large plain. Meanwhile, Uncas, who found himself obliged to rely more upon stratagem than strength, had acquainted his warriors on the march with a plan which he now proceeded to put in execution.

He desired a parley, and the two armies halted in the face of each other. Then advancing in the front of his men, he addressed Miantonomo : " You have a number of stout men with you, and so have I with me. It is a great pity that such brave warriors should be killed in a private quarrel between us only. Come on, then, like a man, as you profess to be, and let us fight it out. If you kill me, my men shall be yours.—If I kill you, your men shall be mine." Miantonomo saw his advantage too clearly to accept such a proposal. "My warriors," said he, "have come a long way to fight, and they *shall* fight." The reply was anticipated, and it was scarcely uttered, when Uncas fell to the ground. His men discharged over him a shower of arrows upon the Narraghansetts; and then following up the surprise without a moment's interval, rushed upon them furiously with a hideous yell, and soon put them to flight.

The pursuit was sustained with a ferocious eagerness. The enemy were chased down rocks and precipices, like the doe flying from the huntsman

About thirty were slain, and a much greater number wounded. Miantonomo was exceedingly pressed. Some of the bravest men of Uncas at length came up with him; but not daring actually to skirmish with him, or preferring to leave that honor to their leader, they contrived to impede his flight by twitching him back, and then passed him. Uncas now came up, and rushing forward like a lion greedy of his prey, he seized him by the shoulder. The Narraghansett saw that his fate was decided—Uncas was a man of immense strength, and his warriors were thick around him. He stopped, sat down sullenly, and spake not a word. Uncas gave the Indian whoop, and called up a party of his men, who gathered about the royal captive and gazed at him. He still continued moody and speechless. Some of his sachems were slain before his eyes, but he moved not a muscle. "Why do you not speak," inquired Uncas, at length; "had you taken me, I should have besought you for my life." But the Narraghansett was too proud to ask such a boon of his enemy, and especially of his rival. Uncas however spared his life for the present, and returned in great triumph to Mohegan, leading along with him the splendid living evidence of his victory.

The notorious Samuel Gorton having purchased lands of Miantonomo, under the jurisdiction of Plymouth and Massachusetts, and expecting to be vindicated by him in his claims against those colonies, and against other Indian tribes, he immediately sent word to Uncas to give up his prisoner, and threatened him with the vengeance of the colonies if he refused a compliance. But Uncas shrewdly bethought himself of a safer course. He carried his prisoner to Hartford, and asked advice of the governor and magistrates. There being no open war between the Narraghansetts and English, these authorities were unwilling to interfere in the case, and they recommended a reference of the whole affair to the commissioners of the United Colonies, at their next

meeting in September. Meanwhile, Miantonomo
had recovered his speech. He probably expected
better treatment with the English than with Uncas,
and he now earnestly pleaded to be committed to
their custody. Uncas consented to leave him at
Hartford, but insisted on having him kept as *his*
prisoner.

At the meeting of the commissioners the whole
affair was laid before them. In their opinion it was
fully proved that Miantonomo had made attempts
against the life of Uncas, by all the means and
measures heretofore alluded to, and by poison and
sorcery besides; that he had murdered the Pequot
assassin with his own hand, instead of giving him up
to justice; that he was the author of a general plot
among the Indian tribes against the colonies; and
that he had moreover gone so far as to engage the
aid of the Mohawks, who were now within a day's
journey of the English settlements, waiting only for
Miantonomo's release to serve him according to his
pleasure.

"These things being duly weighed and consider
ed," say the commissioners in their report,* "we
apparently see that Vncas cannot be safe while
Myantenomo† lives, but that either by secret treachery
or open force his life will still be in danger. Wherefore we thinke he may justly putt such a false and
blood-thirsty enemie to death, but in his owne Juris-

---

* Hazard's Collections, Vol. II. p. 7.

† Haz. Coll. Vol. II. p. 7.—The reader will observe the
variation of the Sachem's name here used. There are several
others in Hazard. Hutchinson writes MYANTINOMO and
MIANTONOMO in the same volume; Baylies, both terms in the
course of the same page; Trumbull adds an *h*. Winthrop
admits this spelling with the qualification that the chief was
otherwise called MECUMEH (as he was); but he afterwards
regularly uses MIANTUNNOMOH. Mason, (*account of the
Pequot war*,) writes MYANTONIMO and MIANTOMO; Wolcott, MIAANTINOMOH; Roger Williams, MIANTUNNOMU,
and several other variations. We are thus particular only in
the hope of amusing the curious.

diccon, not in the English plantacons; and advising
that in the manner of his death all mercy and moderacon be shewed, contrary to the practice of the Indians who exercise tortures and cruelty, and Vncas
haveing hitherto shewed himself a friend to the English, and in this craveing their advice, if the Nano-
higgansetts Indians or others shall unjustly assault
Vncas for this execucon, vpon notice and request the
English promise to assist and protect him, as farr as
they may, against such vyolence."

The commissioners further directed, that Uncas
should immediately be sent for to Hartford, with some
of his trustiest men ; an l informed of the sentence
passed upon his captive. He was then to take him
into the nearest part of his own territory, and there
put him to death in the presence of certain discreet
English persons, who were to accompany them,
" and see the execucon for our more full satisfaccon,
and that the English meddle not with the head or
body at all." The Hartford Government was subsequently to furnish Uncas with forces enough to
defend him against all his enemies.

These directions were promptly obeyed. Uncas
made his appearance at Hartford, received his prisoner, and marched off with him to the very spot
where the capture had happened. At the instant
they arrived on the ground, a Mohegan who marched
behind Miantonomo split his head with a hatchet,
killing him at a single stroke ; so that he was probably unacquainted with the mode of his execution.
Tradition says that Uncas cut out a piece of his
shoulder, and ate it in savage triumph. " He said it
was the sweetest meat he ever eat—it made his heart
strong." The royal victim was buried, by the conqueror's order, at the place of his death ; and a great
heap or pillar was erected over his grave. The field
of battle, situated in the eastern part of the town of
Norwich, is called the *Sachem's Plain* to this day

CHAPTER X.

Consideration of the justice of the Commissioners sentence upon Miantonomo—Their reasons, as alleged—The charge against him of ambitious designs—Of employing the Mohawks —Of breaking the league of 1638—" Concerning the Pequot squaws"—Of hostility to the English—Of peculation—Proofs of his fidelity and friendship—Causes of complaint by him and Canonicus against the English—Character of both Sachems—Their treatment of Roger Williams—Letters of that gentleman—Anecdotes—Death of Canonicus.

It is not easy to determine, at this period, the justice of the sentence by which Miantonomo was led to the slaughter. As between himself and his enemy, considering Indian custom and character, it might be considered just ; and the sufferer would certainly have been the last to complain of it. But though Uncas may not be blamed for using the privilege of the victor, a different opinion has been entertained of the interference of the English. Their justification, as laid before the Narraghansett nation, after Miantonomo's death, was as follows :

" They may well vnderstand that this is without violacon of any couenant betweene them and vs ; for Vncus being in confederacon with vs, and one that hath diligently observed his couenants before mentioned for aught we know, and requiring advice from vs, vpon serious consideracon of the premises, viz. *his* [Miantinomo] treacherous and murtherous disposition against Vncus &c. and how great a disturber he hath beene of the common peace of the whole countrey, we could not in respect of the justice of the case, safety of the countrey and faythfulness of our frend, do otherwise than approve of the lawfulness of his death. This agreeing so well with the Indians owne manners, and concurring with the practice of other nations with whom we are aquainted, we persuade ourselves howeuer his death may be grieuous at present, yet the peaceable fruits of it will yield not only matter of safety to the Indians, but profite to all that inhabite this continent."

Supposing every thing to be true which is here and elsewhere alleged, it may still be doubted whether the colonies could be justified in the part taken by their commissioners;—but such is not the case.

His killing the Pequot was one point against him, but what could be more natural than for them to misunderstand his promise in that case, or for him to suppose that administering justice with his own hand would be the most satisfactory course he could take. Stress is laid upon Miantonomo's "ambitious designes to make himself vniversal Sagamore or Governor of all these parts;" but this, whether laudable or reprehensible in itself, was clearly no usurpation as against them. As to his hostility towards the English, suffice it to say here, that the evidence of it seems to have been furnished chiefly by his enemies, whose direct interest it was to oppress him by engaging the English interest in their own favor. As to the employment of the Mohawks, in particular, the most that was made to appear, even through this medium, was, that they were awaiting Miantonomo's release—" and then they will carry on their designes, whether against the English or Vncus or both, *is doubtful.*"*

Let us observe the testimony of Mr. Williams in regard to this affair, borrowing from a letter written immediately after it took place. " A fortnight since, I heard of the Mauquawogs coming to Paucomtuckqut, their rendezvous ; that they were provoked by Onkas wronging and robbing some Paucomtuck Indians the last year, and that he [Uncas] had dared the Mauquawogs, threatening if they came to set his ground with gobbets of their flesh &c."

He admits, that a few of the Narraghansetts had

---

* *Hazard's Col. Vol. II. p. 9. Commissioners' Report*

joined the Mohawks: but these, whether they were
well or ill disposed towards the English, were at
all events considered traitors to Miantonomo. Elsewhere he states, "yt ye Narigansetts and Mauquawogs are the two great bodies of Indians in ye
country, and they are confederates, and long have
bene *as they both yet are friendly and peaceable to ye
English.*"*

Miantonomo is said to have violated the league of
1638, by invading the country of Uncas, without
having previously submitted his grievances to the
decision of the English. But did he not think himself absolved from the obligation created by that
league, in consequence of violations of it on the part
of the English. He probably regarded them at this
very time, precisely as they regarded him. Roger
Williams writes on one occasion, when letters of
complaint had been sent to him from Massachusetts,
that "*they* [Miantonomo and Canonicus] thought
they should prove themselvs honest and faithful,
when Mr. Governor understood their answers ; and
that (although they would not contend with their
friends) yet they could relate many particulars,
wherein the English had broken (since these wars)
their promises."

Respecting the alleged violation of the Hartford
league in particular, we might perhaps properly
waive all attempts at justification, inasmuch as the
charge hardly purports to be true. Governor Winthrop gives an account of the affair as received officially from Connecticut, by which it appears that
Miantonomo, before taking part with Sequassen, applied to the authorities of that province for redress
of grievances committed upon him by Uncas. He
was answered, that *the English had nothing to do with
the business* He then applied also to Governor
Winthrop himself, and was very desirous to know if
he would not be offended, by his making war upon

* Ms, Letters. on the Mass. Col. Rec. (File 10. No. 45.)
10—13

Uncas. "Our Governor answered, *if Onkus has done him or his friends wrong, and would not give satisfaction, we should leave him to take his own course.*"*

The account which follows next of the explanation given upon one point by the accused parties, is sufficiently characteristic of their intelligence, at least, to be quoted at length. "First then, concerning the Pequot squaws. Canaunicus answered that he never saw any, but heard of some that came into these parts, and he bade carry them back to Mr. Governour; but since he never heard of them till I came, and now he would have the country searched for them. Miantunnomu answered, that he never heard of but six; and four he saw which were brought to him, at which he was angry, and asked why they did not carry them to me, that I might convey them home again Then he bid the natives that brought them to carry them to me, who departing brought him word that the squaws were lame, and they could not travel, whereupon he sent me word, that I should send for them. This I must acknowledge, that this message I received from him, and sent him word, that we were but few here, and could not fetch them nor convey them, and therefore desired him to send men with them, and to seek out the rest. Then, saith he, we were buzy ten or twelve days together, as indeed they were in a strange kind of solemnity, wherein the sachems eat nothing but at night, and all the natives round about the country were feasted. In which time, saith he, I wished some to look to them, which notwithstanding, in this time, they scaped, and now he would employ men instantly to search all places for them, and within two or three days to convey them home. Besides he profest he desired them not, and was sorry the governour should think he did. I objected that he sent to beg one. He answered, that Sassamun, being sent by the governour with letters to Pequot, fell lame, and lying at his

---

* *Journal Vol. II.* and *Records of the Colonies*

house, told him of a squaw, which was a sachem's daughter, who while he lived was his, Miantunnomue's, great friend. *He* [Miantonomo] *therefore desired in kindness to his dead friend, to beg her or redeem her* [of Mr. Williams.]

In reply to a charge touching his fidelity to the English alliance, Canonicus declared that the Narraghansetts " had stuck to the English in life or death, without which they were persuaded that Okace [Uncas] and the Mohiganeuks had proved false, as he fears they will yet." He then went on to specify his reasons for this persuasion and this fear. He also stated, that although the Mohegans had yet brought in no captives, his own brother, Yootash, had on one occasion " seized upon Puttaquppuunk, Quame and twenty Pequts and three-score squaws ; *they killed three and bound the rest, watching them all night, and sending for the English delivered them into their hands in the morning.*" It seems that soon afterwards Miantonomo passed the house where the Pequots were kept confined by the English, and having a curiosity to see one of the captive sachems—a man of considerable note—he made application for that purpose —but was thrust at with a pike several times by the English sentinels, and finally driven off. Mr. Williams suggested, that probably he was not recognised ; but he thought that he was, and several of the Narraghansetts were of the same opinion, and asked if *they* should have dealt so with " Mr. *Governour.*" Mr. Williams still denied, that he could have been known ; to which Miantonomo answered that, at least, his whole company* were disheartened, " and they all and Cutshamquene desired to be gone : and yet, saith he, two of my men (Waqouckwhut and Maunamoh) were their guides to Sesquanket from the river's mouth."

---

* He was at the head of two hundred of his warriors, just returned from an expedition against the Pequots, in which they had taken ten prisoners, and had faithfully brought them in at this time. See the LIFE of CUTSHAMEQUIN in a succeeding Chapter.

To a third accusation, that he had received prison-ers and wampum of the enemy, which belonged to the common stock, and were nevertheless monopo-lized by himself, Canonicus replied, that although he and Miantonomo had paid their own warriors many hundred fathom of wampum, he never had received one Pequot or one yard of beads. Mianto-nomo added, that *he* had received nothing but one small present from four women of Long-Island, who were no Pequots, but of that Island, and who, for safety's sake, had thereby put themselves under his protection.

Other facts, if not opinions, appear in some of the early annals, which would lead to similar conclusions respecting the fidelity of the Narraghansett chiefs. Governor Winthrop says, in his journal of February 1637—"Miantunnomoh &c. sent twenty six, with forty fathom of wampum, and a Pequot's hand." In March, he records intelligence received from the same source, concerning the Pequot movements, with proposals of fresh assistance. On the 22d of the month, "Miantunnomoh sent us word, that Mason had surprised and slain eight Pequods" &c. Again, during the same summer, "Miantunnomoh *sent here some Pequod squaws*, which had run from us ;" and five days afterwards, "the Narraghansetts *sent us the hands of three Pequods*" &c. The two last statements agree with the declaration of the sachems to Mr. Williams, apparently upon the same points.

We have seen that Canonicus accused the English of having broken their promises. Omitting the proof of that statement, it is impossible to doubt at least, that it was made in the most earnest sincerity. The writer just cited informs us incidentally in his KEY TO THE INDIAN LANGUAGES, that Canonicus, in a solemn address to himself, before a large assembly, had once used the following expression—"I have never suffered any wrong, to be offered to the Eng-lish since they landed, nor never will. If the Eng-lishmen speak true," he added, "then I shall go to my grave in peace, and hope that the English and my posterity will live in peace and love together." Mr Williams observed, that he hoped he had no occasion to question the friendliness of the English. Upon this the sachem took a stick, broke it into ten pieces, and related ten instances, laying down a stick to every instance, which gave him cause for apprehension or suspicion. With regard to some of them, he was afterwards convinced of his being mistaken, and readily acknowledged himself to be so ; but not as to all.

The truth probably is, that provocations of some sort had been received upon both sides ; but that the English had any peculiar reason to complain, and especially to assume the violent administration of punishment or prevention, certainly cannot be admitted. There is no evidence extant to support such a position. Mr. Williams indeed acknowledges, with his usual frankness, that individual Narraghansetts had perhaps now and then committed offences in " matters of money or pettie revenging of themselves in some Indians *upon extream provocation*:" but he also states, in the same paragraph, that he "could not yet learn y*t* ever it pleased y*e* Lord to permit y*e* Narighansetts to staine their hands with any English blood, neither in open hostilities nor secret murthers, as both Pequts and Long Islanders did, and Monhiggans also in y*e* Pequt wars."*

This statement we suppose to be uncontradicted, and the authority is certainly deserving of credit. Now, for a moment, let us examine the other side of the question, bearing in mind how little likely we are, under the circumstances, to be furnished by history with the truth, and least of all with the whole truth.

Some instances in point have already been given. The excessive jealousy and the frequent complaints of the English were in themselves calculated to produce, if not to justify, what they referred to   " The

---

* Ms. Letters.

governor of the Massachusetts"—says Mr. Winthrop, in his journal of 1638—" wrote also to Mr. Williams to treat with Miantunnomoh *about satisfaction, or otherwise to bid them look for war.*" This was a harsh message, at the best, to send to a sovereign ally, who had faithfully served the English cause. The only reason for it which appears in the context is, that Janemoh, a Niantick chief, was understood to have committed certain depredations on a settlement of Long Island Indians who were tributary to the English. Now some of that tribe, we have seen, put themselves under Miantonomo's protection : and there are no means of determining whether that chieftain did not in this case, like the English, feel *himself* aggrieved by Janemoh. We do find it recorded, however, that, in the summer of 1637, Miantonomo came to Boston. The governor, deputy, and treasurer, treated with him, and they parted upon fair terms. He acknowledged on this occasion, that all *the Pequot and Block Island* country belonged to the English, and promised that he would not meddle with them but by their leave. " In fine, we gave him leave to right himself for *the wrongs which Janemoh* and Wequash Cook *had done him :* and for the wrong they had done us, we would right ourselves in due time."*

Not far from the time when the above mentioned complaint seems to have been made through Mr. Williams, the latter writes to Governor Winthrop as follows. " Sir, there hath been a great hubbub in all these parts, as a general persuasion that the time was come for a general slaughter of natives, by reason of a murther committed upon a native [Narraghansett] within twelve miles of us, four days since, by four desperate English. * * An old native comes to me, and tells me, that the natives round about us were fled, relating that those four had slain an Indian, who had carried three beaver-skins and beads for

---

* Winthrop's Journal, Vol. I. 243.

Canaunicus's son, and came home with five fathom and three coats; that three natives which came after him found him groaning in the path; that he told them, &c." The particulars of this flagrant outrage —even to the christian and surnames of the four murderers—are given with a minuteness which precludes the possibility of mistake. And yet we find no mention of this transaction in the English histories. Miantonomo perhaps made *his* complaint to the proper authority, without success. But more probably he endured the injury in silence, as a new evidence that his allies were become his enemies.

Still, it should not be omitted, that Miantonomo never declined to make all the explanation for which a fair opportunity was given him.* As late as 1642, two messengers were sent to him by the Massachusetts government, with articles of complaint; requiring him to come himself or send two of his chief counsellors to the governor, in order to give satisfaction for certain grievances alleged. He attended this summons promptly and personally. On his arrival at Boston, he came forward in court, and demanded that his accusers should be brought before him face to face; and that if they failed in their proof, they should suffer the same punishment which their accusations were calculated to bring upon himself. The whole deportment on this occasion was grave and dignified. His answers were given with great deliberation, and never except in the presence of the counsellors who attended him, that they might be witnesses of every thing which passed. Two days were spent in treaty. He denied all he was charged with, and affirmed—what we have already suggested —that the reports to his disadvantage were raised and circulated, either by Uncas, or some of his people. Such an effect, (it should be here observed) had

---

* "The messengers coming to him, he carried them apart into the woods, taking only one of his chief men with him, and gave them very rational answers to all their propositions, &c." *Win. Journal, Vol. II.*

these reports already produced, that the Connecticu
people were importunate for open war with the Narraghansetts at this very time; and it required the
whole influence of the Massachusetts authorities,
(who doubted, " whether, they had sufficient proofs of
the designs of the Indians to justify a war,") to prevent immediate hostilities.   Such alarm existed, that
places of refuge for the women and children were
provided in most of the towns and plantations.
Beacons were set up, in readiness to be fired; and
smiths were ordered to postpone other business until
all the arms in the colony were put in complete repair.   A great excitement was produced in the towns
about Boston, by a poor man, in a swamp at Watertown crying out for help against a kennel of wolves
which he heard howling around him in the night.
And although Massachusetts was opposed to war,
" Yet the governor, with the magistrates, before the
court met, thought it necessary to disarm the Indians
within the colony, which they readily submitted
to."*

Miantonomo, as was very natural, not only noticed
these symptoms of jealousy on his visit to Boston,
but felt keenly the ill-will they implied, and inquired the cause of them.   Governor Winthrop gave
him an evasive answer, with which, however, he politely professed to be satisfied.   He then entered into
quite an argument, to show that the suspicions which
had been entertained of him were unjust, and were
owing to the machinations of his enemies.   He offered to meet Uncas either at Hartford or at Boston,
and to prove his treachery to the English, in their
presence.   He should stand ready to come at any
time, he added; and this notwithstanding he had
been advised not to visit the English again, lest they
should seize upon his person.   He relied upon his
innocence, and he *would* visit them, whenever it
was deemed necessary that he should.

* Hutchinson, Vol. I

It is acknowledged in fine, that he gave perfect satisfaction at this time. Considering the entertainment which was given him, and his great pride of character, that was quite as much as could be expected. "When we should go to dinner"—it is recorded in the Governor's Journal –"there was a table provided for the Indians, to dine by themselves, *and Miantunnomoh was left to sit with them*. This he was discontented at, and would eat nothing till the governor sent him meat from his table. So at night, and all the time he staid, *he sat at the lower end of the magistrates' table*." But he overlooked the indignity, and parted upon good terms. "We gave him and his counsellors coats and tobacco ; and when he came to take his leave of the governor, and such of the magistrates as were present, *he returned and gave his hand to the governor again*, saying, that was for the rest of the magistrates who were absent." It may be observed, that the examination in this case, which resulted thus satisfactorily to Massachusetts, was a deliberate and thorough one. The court was already assembled, when he arrived at Boston ; and even before his admission, all the points and order of inquiry were agreed upon : "For we knew him,' says the governor, " to be a very subtle man."* The same authority admits, that he showed, in his answers, " a good understanding of the principles of equity and justice, and ingenuity withal."

The attack of Miantonomo upon Uncas, independently of the interest which the English had in it, has been regarded as a moral if not legal outrage— an unprovoked, unprincipled aggression—the off spring of hatred, envy, or at best of mere ambition. But even here we do not happen to be without

---

* A phraseology, which, as implying prejudice, is rather more creditable to the subject than the writer. Hubbard describes him as a very goodly personage, of tall stature, *subtile and cunning in his contrivements, as well as haughty in his designs.*

I.—Q

proof, as well as probability, in favor of the accused.
In more than one case, if not generally, the fault was
on the side of Uncas; and that being true, it must
naturally occur to every reader, to inquire, in the
language applied to a similar case by Mr. Williams,
—" Graunt these subjects, *What capacitie hath their
late massacre of y*e* Narrgansetts (with whom they had
made peace) without y*e* English consent, tho' still under
y*e* English name, put them into ?*"* A very forcible
query, it must be admitted; and to show its relevancy
to the present subject, let us look again for a few
facts.

Soon after the Pequot war, when the chieftains
who had assisted the English in carrying it on, convened at Hartford for a division of the spoil, Mr.
Williams accompanied Miantonomo on his journey.
" By the way," says he, ("lodging from his house
three nights in the woods,) we met divers Nanhiggontick [Narraghansett] men complaining of robbery
and violence, which they had sustained from the
Pequts and Monahiggins in their travel from Cunnihticut [Connecticut]; as also some of the Wun-
nashowatuckoogs [subject to Canaunicus] came to us
and advertised, that two days before about six hundred and sixty Pequts, Monahiggins and their confederates had robbed them and spoiled about twenty-
three fields of corn; and rifled four Nanhiggontick
men amongst them; as also that they lay in way and
wait to stop Miantunnomue's passage to Cunnihticut, and divers of them threatened to boil him in
the kettle."

These tidings being confirmed by various authorities, Mr. Williams and the other English in the company, were strongly in favor of turning back, and
going to Hartford by water. But Miantonomo declared that not a man should retreat; he would keep
strict watch by night, and in dangerous passes the
sachems should all march with a body-guard, but

---

* Ms. Letters, dated 1654.

they should die, as he himself would, rather than turn back. They moved on, therefore, the English with Miantonomo and his wife in front, and a flank-guard of forty or fifty men on either side to prevent surprisal. They arrived safely at Hartford, and the conference took place. Uncas was accused of con-niving at the trespasses of his men upon the Nar-raghansetts, and he retorted with charges of the same kind upon Miantonomo. The result of this angry discussion was, as follows. "At last we drew them to shake hands, Miantunnomu and Okace; and Miantunnomu invited (twice, earnestly) Okace to sup and dine with him, he and all his company (his men having killed some venison:) but he would not yield, altho' the magistrates persuaded him also to it."

The magnanimity manifested by the chieftain on this occasion, was uniformly a prominent part of his character. When he visited Boston in 1640—as he always did, at the request of the Massachusetts gov-ernment—he was entertained first by the govern-ment at Roxbury; but when the parley was to com-mence, he refused to treat through the medium of a Pequot interpreter. The governor being unwilling to yield this point to him—as good policy, if not manners apparently required that he should—he departed abruptly for Boston, without so much as taking leave of his host. The latter informed the court of this conduct, "and would show him no countenance, nor admit him to dine at our table as formerly, until he had acknowledged his failing, *which he readily did as soon as he could be made to understand it.*"* He observed, however, with some dignity, that when the English should visit *him*, he should cheerfully permit them to use their own fash-ions, as they always had done.

Previous to the expedition against the Pequots, both Miantonomo and Canonicus had expressed a

* Win. Jour. Vol II.

wish that whatever was done with the warriors of the enemy, their women and children should be spared. There was a chivalry in this request—and it does not seem to have been soon forgotten—which accords with all that is known of both these chieftains. Canonicus might have suppressed the Plymouth colony in 1622, at a single blow; but he thought it more honorable to give them formal notice of his hostile intentions, by a messenger; and when he became convinced that *they* had been misrepresented to *him*, he at least ceased to be their enemy if he did not become their friend. In the same spirit, Miantonomo, while in the custody of the governor of Connecticut, cautioned him to increase his guard. He openly declared—what was the fact—that attempts were and would be made by his Narraghansett sub jects for his rescue.

There is a most affecting evidence of the same noble disposition, in the report of the commissioners for 1644. The Narraghansetts, now constantly complaining of the conduct of Uncas and his tribe, brought a charge, among other things, that the latter had embezzled a quantity of wampum which had been put into their hands for the ransom of Miantonomo, while the chief was yet living. How much truth there might be in the allegation, cannot well be ascertained. The commissioners however report, that they gave a fair hearing to the ' Narrahiggansett' deputies on the one hand, and to Uncas on the other The result is thus stated ·

" That though severall discourses had passed from Vncus and his men that for such quantities of wampom and sucn parcells of other goods to a great value there might have been some probabilitie of spareing his life, yet no such parcells were brought. But Vncus denyeth ; and the Narrohiggansett Deputies did not allready, much less proue that any ransome was agreed, nor so much as any treaty begunn to redeeme their imprisoned Sachem. And for that wampoms and goods sent as they were but smal parcels and scarce considerable for such a purpose, a part of them disposed by Myantinomo himself to Vncus his counsellors and captaines for some favour either past or hoped for *and part were giuen and sent to Vncus and to his Squa for preseruing his life so long and vssing him curteously during his Imprisonment.*" What could be nobler than this?

The warm and constant friendship of the two sachems for Williams himself, is a sufficient indication of noble natures. Canonicus was suspicious of him at first; "but with Miantunnomu," writes Mr. Williams soon after his removal, "I have far better dealing. He kept his barbarous court lately at my house. He takes some pleasure to visit me, and sent me word of his coming over again some eight days hence." When the treaty of 1636 was negotiated at Boston, Miantonomo not being able to understand perfectly all the articles, or perhaps not placing entire confidence in the Massachusetts government, desired that a copy should be sent to his friend Williams—if *he* was satisfied, it was intimated, no objection or difficulty would arise upon his own part. The conveyances of land heretofore spoken of, were made to him in the same feeling. "It was not price or money," says the grantee, "that could have purchased Rhode Island: but 't was obtained by love, that love and favor which that honored gentleman, Sir Henry Vane, and myself, had with the great sachem, Miantunnomu, about the league which I procured in the Pequod war. The Indians were very shy of *selling* lands to any, and chose rather to make a grant [gift] of them, to such as they affected."

It might be supposed, that Mr. Williams had peculiar facilities for instructing the sachems in the doctrines of Christianity: but he did not attempt a great deal in this way, and his reasons for it are given in his KEY TO THE LANGUAGES.* He observes, that he

---

* In 1654, (Mass.) he writes " at my last departure for

once heard Miantonomo conversing with several of his chief warriors about keeping the English Sabbath At another time, a Connecticut Indian undertook, in Miantonomo's presence, to dispute Mr. Williams's doctrine, that the souls of the good should go to heaven, and those of the wicked to hell. Our Fathers have told us, said he, that all go to the South-West, and this I believe. "And why so," asked the sachem, "did you ever *see* a soul go to the South-West?" To this the other rejoined, that the evidence was the same in this respect for the Indian doctrine as for that of Mr. Williams. "Ah!" answered Miantonomo, "but he has books and writings, and one which God himself has made; he may well know more than we or our fathers." The anecdote certainly shows a great confidence of the sachem in his English acquaintance.

We shall close our remarks upon this part of our subject with citing at large one of the letters to which we already have been so much indebted for facts. It is sufficiently characteristic of both the writer and the chieftains his friends, to repay us for the labor of perusal. It is supposed to have been written in October 1637.

"*The last of the week. I think the 28th of the 8th.* Sir.

This bearer, Miantunnomu, resolving to go on his visit, [to Boston] I am bold to request a word of advice from you concerning a proposition made by Canaunicus and himself to me some half year since. Canaunicus gave an island in the bay to Mr. Oldam, by name Chibachuwese, *on condition,* as it should seem, *that he would dwell there near unto them.* The

England, I was importuned by ye Narigansett sachims, and especially by Nanekunat, to pressent their petition to ye high sachims of England, yt they might not be forced from their religion, and for not changing their religion be invaded by war: for they said they were daily visited by threatenings by Indians yt came from about ye Massachusetts yt if they would not pray they should be destoyed by war." Ms. Letters.

Lord (in whose hands all hearts are) turning their affections towards myself, *they desired me to move hither and dwell nearer to them.* I have answered once and again, that for the present I mind not to remove. But if I have it from them I would give them satisfaction for it, and build a little house, and put in some swine, as understanding the place to have store of fish and good feeding for swine. Of late I have heard that Mr. Gibbons, upon occasion, motioned your desire and his own of putting some swine on some of these islands, which hath made me since more desire to obtain it. I spake of it to this sachem, and he tells me that *because of the store of fish, Canaunicus desires that I would accept half* (it being spectacle wise, and between a mile or two in circuit, as I guess) and he would reserve the other ; *but I think, if I go over, I shall obtain the whole.* Your loving counsel, how far it may be inoffensive, because it was once (upon a condition not kept) Mr. Oldam's. So with respective salutes to your kind self and Mrs. Winthrop, I rest

your worship's unfeigned, in all I may.

Ro. WILLIAMS."

For his much honored }
Mr. Governour, these." }

A singular paragraph in a previous communication addressed to the same gentleman, indicates that the writer took some pains to requite the various favors conferred upon him. " Sir, if any thing be sent to the princes, [alluding to proposed presents,] I find that Canaunicus would gladly accept of a box of eight or ten pounds of sugar, and indeed he told me he would thank Mr. Governor for a box full."

In fine, we cannot dismiss the biography of Miantonomo without confessing a sensation of sorrow, and even shame, arising from the contemplation of the lofty and noble traits which certainly adorned his character, contrasted with the ignominious death which he met with at the hands of his allies. The learned editor of a recent edition of Winthrop's Jour-

nal, calls it a case of "perfidy or cruelty, or both.
He also expresses an opinion, that the argument
which really though secretly decided the minds of
the commissioners against the sachem, was his encouragement of the sale of Shaomet and Patuxet to
Gorton and his associates. Without going as far as
this, we may be permitted to say, that the case requires all the apology which can be derived from the
great excitement of the times, occasioned especially
by the power and movements of the Indians.

Such seems to have been the opinion of Governor
Hopkins,* who, it will be observed, also intimates a
new explanation of the conduct of the colonies, towards the Narraghansett chief. His eloquent and
generous tribute to the memory of the latter, we do
not think ourselves at liberty to omit or abridge.

" This," says that eminent scholar, and patriot, " was
the end of Myantinomo, the most potent Indian prince
the people of New-England had ever any concern
with ; and this was the reward he received for assisting them seven years before, in their war with the Pequots. Surely a Rhode-Island man may be permitted
to mourn his unhappy fate, and drop a tear on the ashes
of Myantinomo; who, with his uncle Conanicus, were
the best friends and greatest benefactors the colony
[of R. I.] ever had. They kindly received, fed, and
protected the first settlers of it, when they were in
distress, and were strangers and exiles, and all mankind else were their enemies ; *and by this kindness
to them,* drew upon themselves the resentment of the
neighboring colonies, and hastened the untimely end
of the young king."

Nothing of great interest can be added to the history of Canonicus, subsequent to the death of his
colleague. Messengers were sent to him, the same

---

* See his *Account of Providence Colony,* first published in
the Providence *Gazette* of 1765, and preserved in the *Mass.
His. Coll.* He was governor of Rhode-Island for nine years,
but is better known as one of the signers of the *Declaration
of Independence.*

year, to explain the circumstances of that event, and to take measures for preserving peace. In 1644, he is said to have subjected himself and his teritory to the Government of Charles I. of England, by a deed dated April 19th.* He must have been near ninety years of age at this time, and if actually in the exercise of government, no doubt was more disposed than ever to live peaceably with his English neighbors.

Mr. Winthrop states, that he died June 4th, 1647. Mr. Hubbard says 1648, and he has been copied by late writers (including Holmes :) but the former date is believed to be the better authenticated of the two. One or two historians indeed seem to confound the old sachem with a younger man, who was killed in Philip's war, by the Mohawks, in June 1676. This person bore the same name, and may have been one of his descendants. Between twenty and thirty years before this, Mr. Williams, (the best authority on all that relates to the Narraghansetts,) writes, that "their late famous long-live Caunnonicus so liv'd and died, and in ye same most honorable manner and solemnitie (in their way) as you laid to Sleepe your Prudent Peace-Maker, Mr. Winthrop, did they honour this, their Prudent and Peaceable Prince."†

---

* Report of Commissioners appointed in 1683 by Charles II to enquire into the claims and titles to the NARRAGHANSETT COUNTRY. *5th. Vol. of Mass. His. Coll. 1st. Series.*

† *Ms. Letters.*

10—14

CHAPTER XI.

Canonicus succeeded by PESSACUS—MEXHAM—NINIGRET
Sachem of the Nianticks—Proposals made by them to the
English, and by the English in return—They commence hostilities against Uncas—The English resolve to make war
upon them—They make concessions—Their visits to Boston
—Subsequent movements against Uncas. An armed party
sent against Ninigret and Pessacus—They are accused of a
league with the Dutch against the English.

STRICTLY speaking, there was no *successor* to Canonicus in the government of the Narraghansetts,
the lineage, talents and age of that sachem having
given him a peculiar influence over his countrymen,
which none other among them could command
At his death, therefore, the authority which he had
monopolized at one time, and afterwards shared with
Miantonomo and others, reverted into that form of
dominion (half way between oligarchy and democ
racy, and occasionally vibrating to each extreme,)
which is common among the Indian tribes.

One of the Narraghansett chiefs, after that period,
was his son, MEXHAM, otherwise called Mexamo,
Mixamo, Meihammoh, and by Roger Williams
also Mriksah and Mejhsah. Considering the multitude of his names, he is rather less distinguished
than might be supposed. Mr. Williams however
gives him the credit of inheriting 'his father's spirit'
of friendliness for the English. In another passage,
speaking of the Nipmucks, he says 'they were unquestionably subject to ye Narrhigansett sachims,
and in a special manner to Mejhsah, ye son of Caun-
onnicus, and late husband to this old SQUA-SACHIM
now only surviving.'* This letter bearing date of
May 7th, 1668, Mexaham must have died previous
to that time. The name of his widow and succes-

_____

* MS. Letters.

sor, (sometimes called QUAIAPEN, and more frequently MAGNUS,) who was a woman of great energy, figures not a little in the history of King-Philip's war. We may hereafter have occasion to mention both husband and wife.

A more distinguished character was PESSACUS, generally believed to have been the brother of Miantonomo,* and therefore *nephew* of Canonicus—a better authenticated theory than that of Johnson's, who (in his WONDER-WORKING PROVIDENCE,) calls him a *son.* He was born about the time of the English settling at Plymouth, and was therefore not far from twenty years old when his brother was killed. His name being associated with that of Canonicus in the deed of 1644, alluded to in the preceding chapter, it may be presumed, that the mantle of Miantonomo, after *his* death, fell upon the shoulders of Pessacus. It will soon appear, how much he interested himself, both as sachem and brother, in the revenge of that outrage.

It is impossible to pursue the career of either of these chieftains, eminent in history as some of them are, without connecting them not only with each other, but with a foreign party who still remains to be named. We refer to NINIGRET,† chief sachem of the Nianticks, generally considered a Narraghansett tribe, and certainly the most considerable of all those which profited by the alliance of that people. Miantonomo spoke of them to Governor Winthrop, in 1642, " as his own flesh, being allied by continual intermarriages ;" and the governor consequently had

---

* Winthrop.
† Variously entitled by various writers.
● g. NINIGRATE, by Hutchinson.
  NYNIGRETT,   Mason's Pequot war
  NINICRITE,   Hubbard.
  NINICRAFT,   Same and others.
  NINEGRAD,   Prince.
  NENNEGRATT and NENNEGRATE, &c. Hazard.
  NANEKUNAT, NINIGLUD, &c. R. Williams and others.

"some difficulty to bring him to *desert* them" In fact, they were rather confederates than tributaries to Canonicus during *his* life, and the relationship of blood, with no other bonds of sympathy, would have abundantly sufficed to keep up an intimate connexion after his death. Prince states that Ninigret was the uncle of Miantonomo; but other writers represent him as the brother or brother-in-law; and considering the age of the parties especially, the latter supposition is much the more plausible. Either will explain the regard which he will be found to have cherished for the memory of the dead chieftain, and for the person of Pessacus, the living brother.

We first hear of Ninigret in 1632, from which time to 1635 a violent war was carried on between the Narraghansetts and Pequots. In this he is said to have taken no part; and the fair inference is, that he was not from his relation to the former under any necessity, and probably not under obligation, to assist them.

A similar conclusion might be drawn from the division of captives made at the close of the war of 1637, when Ninigret's services were acknowledged by the compliment of twenty Pequots—in the same manner, though not in the same measure, with those of Uncas and Miantonomo. Like the latter, however, Ninigret took no personal or active part in that war: and like him, he permitted his subjects to go volunteers under Mason. Mr. Wolcott thus mentions him on the occasion of Underhill's arrival in his territory,* on *his* way to the Pequots:

And marching through that country soon they met
The Narraghansett Prince, proud Ninigrett,
To whom the Engilsn say, we lead these bands,
Armed in this manner, thus into your lands,

* The principal residence of Ninigret, and the centre of his dominion, was at Wekapaug, now Westerly, R. I. It was formerly a part of Stonington, Conn

Without design to do you injury,
But only to invade the enemy ;
You, who to the expense of so much blood
Have long time born their evil neighborhood,
Will bid us welcome, and will well excuse
That we this way have took our rendezvouz, &c."*

If what is here intimated was true, that the Pequots had been bad neighbors to the Nianticks, as they certainly had been to the Narraghansetts, it is no matter of wonder that numbers of those tribes engaged in the English expedition ; and it indicates the pride, if not magnanimity, of their two young chiefs, on the other hand, that neither would consent to fight against the common enemy of both.

From Major Mason's account of the affair, it would appear that the English took this independence of Ninigret rather in dudgeon. "On the Wednesday morning," says that writer, "we marched from thence to a Place called Nayanticke, it being about eighteen or twenty miles distant, where another of those Narraghansetts lived in a Fort; it being a Frontier to the Pequots. They carryed very proudly towards us ; not permitting any of us to come into their Fort." Upon which Mason set a guard about them, forbidding the Indians to go in or out, and quartered in the neighborhood over night. Whether this 'Sachem' was Ninigret or one of his subjects, the conduct of Mason could hardly have left a very gratifying impression on the mind of that chieftain. Possibly, if borne in mind by the reader, it may throw some light upon subsequent events.

From the time of Miantonomo's death, all the sachems we have mentioned as succeeding to his power, came prominently into intercourse with the English. Ninigret and Pessacus, particularly, were

* " A Brief Account of the Agency of the Hon. John Winthrop Esq. in the Court of King Charles the second, Anno Dom. 1632; when he obtained a charter for the Colony of Connecticut." *Vol. IV. Mass. His. Coll.*

distinguished by a continual series of controversies
alternately with that people, and the Mohegans, and
very often with both. They inherited the strong
prejudice of the slaughtered Narraghansett against
Uncas and his tribe; and most bitterly was that
prejudice exasperated by the slaughter itself.

Anticipating such an excitement, the commission
ers, immediately after the execution of the sentence,
despatched messengers to Pessacus, who were directed to inform him that they had heard of the quarrel between himself and Uncas; and to propose that
he should send delegates to Hartford: these should
meet delegates from Uncas, and thus all differences
be adjusted. A conference accordingly was agreed
upon, and it took place as proposed. The result
was stated, in the commissioners Report: "They
did require that neither themselves [the Narraghan-
setts] nor the Nayanticks should make any warr or
injurious assault vpon Vncus or any of his company
vntil they make proofe of the ransome charged &c"—
alluding to the allegation that Uncas had embezzled
money, deposited in his hands for Miantonomo's redemption.

The following agreement was subscribed by the
four "Narrohigganset Deputies," as they are called in
the Report. It should be observed, that although
"the Nayantick sachems" are ostensibly here represented, the only evidence going to justify such a
phraseology, so far as we know, is in a previous statement (in the Report,) that when the English messengers had been sent to propose this conference, the
Narraghansett sagamores "consulting among themselves *and with Kienemo one of the Nayantick sachims*
had sent a sagamore &c." We copy *literatim* and
punctuatim:

"Weetowisse one of the Narrohiggansett sachims
Pummumsh (alias) Pumumshe and Pawpianet two
of the Narrohigganset Captaines being sent with two
of the Narrohiggansett Indians *as Deputies from the
Narrohigganset and Nayantick* sachims to make

proofe of the ransome they pretended was given for
their late sachim's life as also to make knoune some
other greevances they had against Vncus sachim of
the Mohiggins did in conclusion promise and engage
themselves (*according to the power committed to them*)
that there should be no war begun by any of the
Narrohiggansets *or Nayantick* Indians with the Mohegan sachim or his men till after the next planting
tyme, and that after that, before they begin warr, or
vse any hostility towards them, they will give thirty
dayes warneing thereof to the Government of the
Massachusetts or Conectacutt.

Hartford the XVIIjth of September, 1644
(Signed with the marks of) WEETOWISSE
PAWPIANET
CHIMOUGH
PUMMUMSHE."

This, considering it an agreement authorised by
Pessacus, was certainly as much as could be reasonably expected of him ; for such was his eagerness to
revenge the death of his brother, that he had himself
sent messengers to confer upon the subject with the
Massachusetts Government. Only a month or two
after that event, they carried a present from him, of
an otter coat, with wampum to the value of fifteen
pounds. Proposals of peace and friendship were
tendered ; but a request was added, that the Governor should not assist Uncas, whom he (Pessacus)
intended shortly to make war upon. The Governor
replied, that *he* desired peace, but wished that all the
Indian tribes, including the Mohegans, might be partakers of it ; and that unless Pessacus would consent
to these terms, his present could not be received.
The messengers said, they had no instructions upon
this point ; they would however return, and consult
with Pessacus ; and meanwhile the Governor was
requested to retain the present, which he did.

After this, (in April, 1644) and previous to the
Hartford conference, the Governor sent messengers
on his own part to the Narraghansetts, probably to

sound the disposition of Pessacus. They went first
to the wigwam of the old sachem Canonicus, whom
they found in such ill humor that he did not admit
them, (as they stated) for two hours, during which
time they were not altogether at ease, being obliged
to endure the pelting of a rain-storm. On entering,
they found him lying upon his couch. He noticed
them, not very cordially, for the purpose of referring
them to Pessacus; and for *him* they waited four
hours more. When he came, he took them into a
shabby wigwam, and kept them talking with him
most of the night. On the whole, he appeared determined to wage war on Uncas forthwith; not in
the manner of Miantonomo, but by sending out
small war-parties, to cut off the straggling Mohegans, and to interfere with their hunting and fishing.

There is reason to believe, that he either had taken,
or was about taking some measures in pursuance
of this scheme; and that the message of the commissioners was therefore rather as much in consequence as in anticipation of his acts. On the 23d.
of April, messengers came to Boston from POMHAM,
(a chief, hereafter noticed at length, who had put
himself under the Massachusetts protection,) with intelligence that the Narraghansetts had captured and
killed six Mohegan men and five women; and had
sent *him* two hands and a foot, to engage him in the
war. If this statement was true—and we know no
particular reason for doubting it—the commissioners
might certainly consider themselves fortunate in
checking hostilities, so far as they did in September.

They convened again, at Boston, early in 1645;
and messengers were again sent to the Narraghansetts, with directions afterwards to visit the Mohegans, inviting all the sachems to meet them for a new
adjustment of difficulties. The instructions given
to these men* imply, that the commissioners supposed
Pessacus to be in a state of warfare with Uncas at

---

* See records of the United Colonies.   Hazard.

that time—whether it was now past " planting-tyme,"
or not—but the same records show that the messengers brought back " a letter from Mr. Roger Williams
wherein hee assures vs the warr *would presently
break forth* and that the Narrohiggansett sachims
had lately concluded a neutrallyty with Providence
and the Townes upon Aquidnett [Rhode] Island."

It would seem, then, that the treaty was not *yet*
broken—when the messengers were sent. Pessacus
at first told *them*, that he would attend the commissioners' summons, and that meanwhile there should
be no operations against Uncas ; but he soon afterwards said, that his mind was changed. They then
went to Ninigret. He expressed great discontent on
account of certain military assistance which the
English had sent to defend Uncas ; and threatened
haughtily, (said the messengers) that unless that force
were withdrawn, he should consider it a violation of
the treaty. "He would procure as many Mowhauques as the English should afront [meet] them
with, that would lay the English cattell on heapes as
heigh as their houses, and no Englishman should
stir out of his doore but he should be killed."

After meeting such a reception here, the messen ·
gers were afraid to set out for the Mohegan country,
and they therefore went back to Pessacus, and requested him to furnish them with a guide. He offered
them an old Pequot squaw—in derision (as they supposed)—and even while they were speaking, several
of his Indians who stood close behind him, appeared
to them to be frowning rather grimly, besides brandishing their hatchets in a most ominous manner.

"Wherevpon," [on the return of the messengers]
says the Report, "the commissioners considering
the great provocations offered and the necessyty we
should be put unto of making warr vpon the *Narrohiggansets &c.*" it was agreed, "First, that our engagement bound us to ayde and defende the Mohegan
Sachem. 2dly, That this ayde could not be intended onely to defend him and his in his fort or habita

con, but (according to the common acceptacon of such covenants or engagements considered with the fraude or occasion thereof) so to ayde him as hee might be preserved in his liberty and estate. 3dly, That this ayde must be speedy least he might bee swallowed vp in the meane tyme and so come too late."

The engagement here alluded to was made at Hartford in these words : " That if they assualt Vncus the English are engaged to assist him." Whether they had assaulted him or not—whether, if they had, it was under circumstances which started such a *casus fœderis* as to justify the English interference— and whether, under any circumstances, the latter could justify sending an expedition designed " not onely to ayde the Mohegans but to offend the Nar- rohiggansets Nyanticks and other their confede- rates"*—need not now be discussed. Nor shall we inquire whether any blame was chargeable, on the other hand, to Uncas, as having himself secretly pro- voked hostilities—which, it may be observed, is a matter that in its nature cannot easily be deter- mined.

Preparations were made for a war; but, at the suggestion of some of the Massachusetts Govern- ment, it was concluded to make still another of- fer of compromise to the Narraghansetts, returning at the same time, by way of manifesto, the present of wampum 'long since sent and left by messengers from Piscus [Pessacus].' A conference took place between some of the messengers and some of the Sa- chems, at which *Mr. Williams officiated as interpreter,* and the result was almost necessarily pacific. Seve- ral of the allegations of the English ('which Bene- dict upon oath had formerly certified't) were denied,

---

* " Instructions for Serjeant Major Edward Gibbons, com- maunder in chief of our military forces and for such as are joyned to him as a counsell of warr." Hazard.

† *Report of Commissioners*, 1645. Benedict Arnold is here referred to, a person employed as messenger for a long

says the commissioners' Report, and others excused and as the English desired further conference, it was agreed "that Pissicus chiefe-sachem of the Narraghansetts and Mixano Canownacus his eldest sonn and others should forthwith come to Bostone to treat with the commissioners for the restoreing and settleing of peace."

This promise was faithfully kept. The sachems just named, with a Niantick deputy, made their appearance at Boston within a few days, followed by a long train of attendants. Some altercation took place between them and the commissioners, in the course of which the latter charged them (as the Report shows,) that, notwithstanding the Hartford treaty, "they had *this summer* (1645) at severall tymes invaded Vncus &c." At length, with great reluctance, and "after long debate and some private conferrence they had with Sergeant Cullicutt they acknowledged they had brooken promise or covenant in the aforemenconed warrs." They then offered to make another truce, but that not satisfying the commissioners, they wished to know what *would.* Upon which the commissioners, "to show their moderacon required of them but twoo thousand fathome of white wampon for their oune satisfaccon," beside their restoring the boats and prisoners taken from Uncas, and making reparation for all damages. A treaty, containing these and other stipulations, and providing that the payment of one instalment should be made in twenty days, was drawn up and finally subscribed by all the deputies. Four hostages were given for security, including a son of Pessacus; the English army was disbanded; the sachems returned home; and the 4th of September, which had been appointed for a fast, was now ordered to be observed as a day of thanksgiving.

---

series of years. He seems to have been in this case the only witness against the Sachems; and what his testimony amounted to, we have already seen

We have thought it the less necessary to specify all the provisions of this 'treaty,' inasmuch as the circumstances under which it was made, amount, as appears to us, to such a duress as not only must have greatly exasperated the Sachems, but clearly invalidated the treaty itself. This point, however, we shall leave to be decided by every reader who will trouble himself to become familiar with those minutiæ which cannot here be stated. It is sufficient to add, that the Report itself, as above cited, shows the consideration (so to speak) upon which the whole transaction was founded, to have failed, or rather never to have existed. The 'acknowledgements,' indeed, like the agreements, under the circumstances we count nothing; but even these, as the commissioners state them, only intimate that the Narraghansetts had invaded Uncas 'this summer —that is, (for aught we are told) subsequent to 'planting-tyme,' when the former treaty expired—and not then without previous and repeated declarations to the English, as we have seen, of their intended movements. No remarks need be made upon the invasion of the English, or upon the requisitions on the deputies at Boston.

One provision of the treaty was, that the Narraghansetts should meet Uncas at New Haven in 1646, which they failed to do, though Uncas himself attended the meeting of the commissioners at that place. Nor did they make their payments of wampum according to promise. Three instalments, to the amount of one thousand three hundred fathoms, being now due, they sent into Boston one hundred fathoms—mostly, it is said in ' old kettles '—excusing themselves on the score of poverty and the failure of the Nianticks to contribute their proportion. So small a sum the commissioners would not accept; and the messengers who brought it therefore sold their kettles to a Boston brazier, and deposited the money in his hands, to be paid over when they should bring the residue of the debt. Messengers were sent for Pessacus, but he failed to make his appearance.

The summons being repeated in 1647, on the 31st of July, " Thomas Stanton returned with Pessacks answere as followinge. Pessack being charged for not meeting the commissioners at New Haven the last yeare, his answer was, he had no warninge. It is true, said he, I have broken my covenant these two years, and it is and hath been the constant griefe of my spirit. 2dly, The reason why he doth not come at this time is, because he hath bene sicke and is now sicke; had I bene but pretty well, said he, I would have come to them." He also stated, that he *when the last treaty was made, he had acted in fear of the English army;** and he proposed to send Ninigret to Boston forthwith, with full authority to treat in his own name.

Ninigret accordingly came on the 3d of August. When the commissioners demanded an explanation of his past defaults, he at first affected ignorance of what agreements had been made by the Narraghan setts. He then argued the matter, and inquired upon what pretence the alleged debt was originally founded. He was reminded of all the old subjects of complaint, including his own declarations of hostility towards the English. In respect to the latter, he said that the messengers had given him provocation. As to the money, he considered it impossible ever to pay it, but nevertheless wished to know how the reckoning now stood. It appeared, on examination, that Pessacus had paid seventy fathoms of wampum the first year. As for the kettles sold to

---

* Report of the comm. for 1647. " He doth say when he made his covenant he did it in feare of the army that he did see, and tho' the English kept their covenant with him there and let him go from them, yet the army was to goe to Narragensett ymmediately and kill him there, therefore said the commissioners sett your hands to such and such things or els the army shall goe forth to the Narragensetts." **Excellently well stated!**

the braziers, that property had since been attached
by one Woddy, a Boston man, for goods stolen from
him by a Narraghansett Indian. Ninigret excepted
to this procedure. It was neither the property of
Pessacus, he said, nor of the thief; it was deposited
as part payment of the debt, and ought so to be received. Having gained this point, he next proposed
that credit should be given him for one hundred and
five fathoms, sent by the hand of an Indian named
Cutchamaquin.* It was rejoined, that the sum refer
red to had been intended as a present to the Governor. Ninigret, " *being pressed to cleare the questione
himselfe, he answered, his tounge should not belye his
heart, let the debt be satisfied as it may—he intended it
for the Governoure.*" He had sent ten fathoms to
Cutchamaquin for his own trouble ; but that covetous
Indian, unsatisfied with so liberal a commission, had
appropriated all but forty-five fathoms to his own
use and 'lied' about the residue. The facts came out
upon a cross-examination, instituted by Ninigret
in presence of the commissioners.†

---

* Whom we suppose to be the Sachem of Braintree, (near
Boston), so well known for his violent opposition to Mr. Elliot's preaching, and called also Kitchmakin and some half
dozen other names. He submitted to the Massachusetts
Government in 1643. Neal says, that soon after his appearing at Mr. Elliot's lecture, and protesting against the building
of a town for the Christian Indians in what he considered *his*
dominions, ' he himself turned Christian.' But that reverend
missionary does not himself state quite so much. In that old
tract, THE LIGHT APPEARING &c. he says, that after a
certain pungent discourse which he took occasion to level at the
Sachem, and not long after his remonstrance just mentioned,
" Elder Heath his observation of him was, that there was a
great change in him, his spirit was very much lightned, and
it much appeared both in his countenance and carriage, *and
he hath carried all things fairly ever since.*" We are
glad to leave him thus—he died soon after his reformation.

† Hazard Vol. II. p. 80 (quarto 3d. Phil. 1794) " Hereupon
Cutchamaquin was sent for and before Ninegrate questioned
&c. He at first persisted, and added to his lyes, but was at las

He then asked time to give in his final answer, and the commissioners allowed him a day. Having con- sulted meanwhile with his companions, he appear- ed the next morning again. He was sorry to find, he said, that the burden of the business had been shifted from the shoulders of Pessacus upon his own, but he had determined to do what he could; and he would therefore send some of his men home to collect the arrears due to the English. In the course of three days he should know the result, and in ten he thought the wampum might be forwarded. He would himself remain at Boston till that time, and send word to the Narraghansetts of the arrangement. "But if the collection," he added, "should fall short of the sum due, he desired some forbearance, being sure that the residue would be shortly paid, and that the English would at all events perceive his great desire to give them entire satisfaction." The com- missioners accepted these proposals, and Ninigret despatched his messenger.

They returned on the 16th of the month, but brought only two hundred fathom of wampum. The commissoners complained of this new default, and Ninigret was a little embarrassed. He said, it must be owing to his own absence; but as it was, he wished that the wampum intended, but not yet re- ceived, as a present to the Governor, should go in part payment of the debt. For the remainder, he desired a respite till the next spring, when, if it were not fully paid, the English should have his country and his head.* The commissioners accordingly gave him

convinced by Ninegrate &c." A good illustration of the im- propriety of giving implicit credit in such cases.

* The account, which may be considered a curiosity, now stood thus.

Mr. Pelham received allmost two yeares since, above what was given Vncus	70 fathome
Left by the Narraghansetts in Mr. Shrimpton's hands, in kettles and wampum	70 fathome
In Cutchameqvin's hands by Ninegrett	105 do

leave to return home, and allowed him twenty days
for sending in one thousand fathoms ; if he failed, he
must suffer the consequences. If he did what he
could, and *Pessacus* failed, as heretofore he had done,
they should punish *him*, and expect Ninigret's assistance.

At their meeting in 1648, the commissioners received information of new movements of Pessacus
and Ninigret, in disturbance of the common peace.
Both sachems were said to be withdrawing their old
men, women and children into swamps, hiding their
corn, and preparing for the reception of the Mohawk,
whom they had engaged to assist them. The invading army was to consist of eight hundred men. The
Mohawks had four hundred guns, and three pounds
of powder to a gun. Ninigret had made inquiry
whether the English would probably defend Uncas,
and seemed to calculate, in that case, upon the necessity of fighting *them*. The Pocomtock tribe were
also engaged to assist him. But both these and the
Mohawks were finally discouraged from undertaking the expedition, by the prospect of having to
contend with the English.

But depredations were soon after committed by
some of the Narraghansetts upon the English ; and
as for Uncas, the hostility against him was carried so
far, that he came very near losing his life by an
Indian hired to assassinate him, having been run
through the breast with a sword, as he was going
on board a vessel in the river Thames. At the commissioners' meeting in 1649, he appeared, laid his
complaints before them, and demanded the protection
of his ally. Ninigret also presented himself. As to
hiring the Indian to assassinate Uncas, he observed,
the confession of the criminal himself was the only
evidence in the case, and that was forced from him

Received of Ninegrett 16. Aug. 1647. 243½ do

The sum being 448½

oy the Mohegans. As to the arrears of wampum, of which much was said, he thought there had been a mistake in the measure, and that only two hundred fathoms were due, while the English at this time acknowledged the receipt of only one thousand five hundred twenty-nine and a half in the whole. But the commissioners were dissatisfied with his answer; and they therefore once more set themselves to making vigorous preparations for war.

The measures adopted in 1650, may be learned from the following passage of the commissioner's record for that year. "Taking into consideration the seueral offensiue practices of the Narraghausetts whereby they have broken their couenents and endeauoured to disturbe the peace betweene the English and themselves; and how they yet delay to pay the wampum which hath been so long due [having sent but one hundred fathom since the last meeting at Boston:] it was therefore thought meet to keepe the colonies from falling into contempt among the Indians, and to preuent their improuing said wampum to hire other Indians to joyne with themselves against vs or Vncas, that twenty men well armed bee sent out of the Jurisdiccon of Massachusetts to Pessicus to demand the said Wampum which is three hundred and eight fathom, and vpon Refusall or Delay to take the same or to the Vallew thereof in the best goods they can find; Together with so much as will satisfy for their charges &c."

The messengers were farther instructed to go to Ninigret, and make the following complaints. 1. That the commissioners were told he had married his daughter to the brother of the old Pequot chief, Sassacus, and had made some pretensions to the Pequot territory. 2. That *Weekwash Cooke* had complained to them of certain grievances received at his hands. 3. "That about twelve years sence a Mare belonging to Elty Pomary of Winsor in Connecticatt was killed wilfully by Pequiam a Nyantick Indian brother to Ninegrett which Mare cost twenty

10—15

nine pounds, for which satisfaccon hath often been required."&c.   They were then to demand payment
of all charges due the English, and as also categorical
answers to a certain list of questions.

The party sent out by Massachusetts in pursuance
of these orders was commanded by Major Atherton.
On meeting with Pessacus, and stating the purposes of his visit, some altercation ensued.   As the
Narraghansett warriors meanwhile appeared to be
collecting around him, Atherton marched directly to
the door of his wigwam, posted a guard there, entered himself with his pistol in hand, seized Pessacus
by his hair, and drawing him out from among his
attendants, declared he would despatch him instantly
on perceiving the least attempt for his rescue.   This
bold stroke made such an impression, that all arreara-
ges were paid on the spot.   Atherton then visited Ninigret, and having stated the accusations, suspicions
and threats of the commissioners—though without
obtaining any farther satisfaction—returned home.*

In 1653, the commissioners sent messengers to
demand of Ninigret, Pessacus and Mexham, answers
to the following questions.   They are given in full,
as a curious illustration both of the policy of the former and the character of the latter.   The object and
occasion are sufficiently manifest on the face of them.

1. Whether *the Duch Governor* hath engaged him
[Ninigret] and others to healp them to fight against
the English, and how many ?

2. Whether the Duch Governor did not attempt
such a Conspiracy ?

3. Whether hee [Ninigret] hath not received of the
Duch Governor guns powder bullets and swords or
any ammunition to that end ; and how much or
many of the said provision for warr ?

4. What other sachems or Indians to his Knowl-
idg that are so engaged ?

* Trumbull's expression is—" Having in this spirited manner *Accomplished his business*, he returned in safety."   *His*
tory of Conn. Vol. I.

5. Whether himselfe or the Rest are Resolved according to theire engagement to fight against the English?

6. If hee bee Resolved of his way what he thinks the English will do?

7. Whether it bee not safest for him and his men to be true to the English?

8. Whether the Duch hath engaged to healp him and the Rest of the Indians against the English?

9. If hee haue engaged against us to aske vpon what grounds and what wrong wee haue donn him?

10. Whether hee thinks it meet to com or send his messengers to give satisfaction concerning these queries?

11. Whether hee hath hiered the Mohakes to healp him against us?

The answer of Mexham, as reported by the messengers, to the first question, was thus. "I speak vnfeignedly from my hart without Dessimulation that I know of noe such plott that is intended or ploted by the Duch Governour against the English my frinds. Though I bee poor it is not goods guns powder nor shott that shall draw mee to such a plott." Pessacus said, "I am very thankfull to these two men that came from the Massachusetts and to you Thomas and to you Poll and to you Mr. Smith that are come soe fare as from the Bay to bring vs this message, *and to enforme vs of these things wee knew not of before.*"

To the second, Mexham answered 'No.' Pessacus said, "that for the Governor of the Duch, *wee are loth to Inuent any falsehood of him*, though we bee far off from him, *to please the English* or any other that bring these Reports. The Duch Governor did never propound such a thing." He also represented the evident folly of *his* leagueing with a remote people against his nearest neighbors. He gave a negative to the fifth question. The sixth he supposed to be already answered. To the seventh, he said, "wee desire to keepe it [peace] feirmly to our dieing day as neare as we can." The eighth and ninth, both Mexham and Pessacus thought they had answered already. As to the tenth, they replied, that Pessacus was *too old** to "trauell two daies together, but they would send some men into the Massachusetts to speake with [tell] the Sachems that they had sent to Mr. Smith and Voll his man to speake to Mr. Browne that they loved the English sachems and all English in the Bay." The charge implied in the last query they absolutely denied.

The answers of Ninigret, which were given separately, are the more worthy of notice that he was known to have visited New York during the previous winter, and had been accused by various Indians, including some of the Mohegans, of having formed an alliance with the Dutch against the English. He utterly disclaimed such conduct. "But," he added, "whiles I was there att the Indian Wigwames there cam som Indians that told mee there was a shipp com in from Holland, which did report the English and Duch were fighting together in theire owne countrey, and theire were severall other shippes cominge with amunition to fight against the English heer, and that there would bee a great blow given to them, but *this* (said he,) *I had from the Indians*, and I cannot tell how true it is." Next, four queries were answered in the negative. As to the sixth, "What shall I answare these things over and over again? What doe the English thinke that I thinke they bee asleep and suffer mee to do them wronge? Doe we not know they are not a sleepy people? The English make queries for gunpowder, and shot and swords Do they thinke wee are mad to sell our lieus and the liues of all our wiues and children and all our kindred, and to haue our countrey destroyed for a few guns powder shott and swords? What will they doe vs good when wee are dead?" The eighth, ninth, and eleventh, were denied. To the seventh he

---

* Probably meant for *too ill.*

replied, that he knew no reason for breaking his league with his old friends the English; and why should he ally himself to a few Dutchmen, so far off, when he lived next door to *them?* The answer to the tenth would puzzle the most mystifying politician of modern times. "It being indifferently spoken whether hee may goe or send yet hee knowing nothing by himselfe wherein hee hath wronged the English but that hee may goe yet being Indifferently spoken hee would send to speak with the English."*

Letters having been also sent to the sachems from the commissioners, Pessacus and Mexham sent word in return, that they wished for a good understanding, and hoped it might be preserved. They requested, furthermore, that the English would make known *the names of their accusers,* and the other sources of their information respecting their alleged league with the Dutch. Ninigret replied as follows:

"You are kindly welcom to vs and I kindly thanke the Sachems [magistrates] of the Massachusetts that they would Nominate my Name amongst the other to require my answare to the propositions: had any of the other Sachems been att the Duch I should have feared theire folly might have donn some hurt one way or other, but they have not been there. *I am the Man that haue bene there myselfe,* therefore I must answare for what I haue doun. I doe utterley deney and protest against any such acteings doun by mee or to my knowlidge att or with the Duch. What is the story of *these great Rumers that I hear att Pocatocke, that I should bee cut off and that the English had a quarrell against mee.* I know of noe such cause att all for my parte. *Is it because I went thither to take Phisicke for my healthe?* Or what is the cause I found noe such entertainment from the Duch Governour, when I was there to giue mee any Incor-

---

* We copy *punctuatim,* from the Records of the United Colonies, as preserved in Hazard's Collections. Perhaps the Interpreter was to blame for this problematical sentence

ragement to sturr mee upp to such a league against the English my friends. It was winter-time, and I stood a great parte of a day knocking at the Governor's dore, and he would neither open it nor suffer others open it to lett mee in. I was not wont to find such carriage from the English my frinds." The messenger promised to be sent by Pessacus was sent accordingly. The English examined him very closely but ascertained nothing new

CHAPTER XII.

Sequel of the lives of Ninigret and Pessacus, from 1653—Various accusations, deputations, and hostile movements between them and the English—Controversy between Ninigret and Harmon Garrett—Application for justice in 1675—Conduct of Ninigret in Philip's War—Consequences of it—His death—Death of Pessacus—Some of the charges against the former considered—His hostility to Uncas, and the Long Islanders, and ' League with the Dutch'—Remarks on his character.

IN September, 1653, new complaints were made against the Narraghansett and Niantick Sachems. It was reported to the commissioners, that they had attacked the Long Island Indians, and slain two Sachems and thirty others. This was deemed a case requiring their interference; and messengers were forthwith despatched as usual, to demand explanation and satisfaction, on penalty that the commissioners would otherwise " proceed as they should find cause." These men executed their errand, and returned on the 19th of the month. According to their own account, they were not very graciously received, as indeed it was hardly to be expected they should be.

They declared upon oath that, on entering the Niantick country, they saw about forty or fifty Indians, all in arms, who came up to them as they rode by ; and the leader having a gun in his hand, " did, in the presence of Thomas Staunton Serjeant Waite and Vallentyne Whitman, put his hand back as if hee would have cocked it ; Richard Waite said this man will shoote ; whervpon the English men faced about, Rode vp to the said Indians, asked what they intended to doe and bedd them goe before, which some of them did but others would not ; and particularly the said Captaine Refused. The English rode on in the way towards Ninigrett, but coming vp into the Woods, the former company of Indians first

fell on shouting in a triumphing way. After the
English Messengers came to a greater company of
Indians all armed, whoe comaund them to stand to
alight and to tye there horses to a tree showed them,
which the Messengers refused to doe. The Indians
then strove to becompase the English, which they
would not suffer, but being Informed that Ninnigrett
would come thither they stayed awhile, but Ninnigrett
not coming the English tould the Indians that if they
might neither passe nor Ninnigrett come then they
would return home. The Indians answered hee
would com presently, but hee not coming the English
rode forward and mett Ninnigrett; the Indians running on both sides hollowing, the English Messengers made a stand, when they mett Ninnigrett haveing many armed men with him and him selfe a pistoll
in his hand. Ninnigrett sat doune and desir?d them
to alight which they did. The Indians then surrounded them and som of them charged their guns
with powder and bullets and som primed their guns.
The English in the meen time delivering their message to Ninnigrett his men were so Tumultus in
speaking especially one whoe they said was a Mo
hauke that they were much desturbed."*

The messengers were afterwards informed by one
of Ninigret's chief men, " that the aforementioned
Mohauke came to see what news, for *they heard that
the English were coming to warr against the Narraghansetts,* which if true the Mohaukes take what is
doun against the Narraghansetts as doun against
themselues." After leaving Ninigret, two Indians,
with bows and arrows in their hands, came running
out of the woods, and roughly demanded of Staunton
whither he was going, when he was coming back,
and which way he should come.—Upon this report,
the commissioners decided to make war at once,
with the exception of Mr. Bradstreet alone, (the

* This Valentyne is apparently the same whom Ninigret
familiarly called ' Voll,' and another chief, ' Poll '

member from Massachusetts,) who protested against such a proceeding, and thereby prevented it.

In 1654, the commissioners were informed, that Ninigret was not only prosecuting hostilities against the Long-Island Indians as before, but had hired the Mohawks, Pocomtocks and Wampanoags to assist him. They immediately sent messengers demanding his appearance at Hartford, and the payment of the tribute so long due, as they alleged, for the Pequots under his dominion. One article in the messenger's instructions was expressed thus. "That vnlesse hee either com himselfe forthwithe to Hartford or give som satisfying securitie to the commissioners for the true and constant paiment of the said Tribute the commissioners shall thinke of some course forthwithe to despose of the said Pequots some other way." On the 18th of September, the following report was made of the result of the inter view.

1. When Ninigret was told, that the commissioners had perused *the letter he had sent to the governor of Massachusetts* concerning the suspicions he had of Uncas*, he answered, that he knew nothing of such letter, and expressed great wonder at its being charged upon him.

Again, as to the breach of covenant alleged against him, he desired to know who could say that he had any Pequots under him. 2. Mr. Eaton and Mr. Hopkins, being both at New Haven, had told him that he was to pay for the Pequots only ten years. And 3. Those ten years had elapsed three years before.†

---

* We see no previous mention of this letter. It must have been one of many cases where the commissioners were deceived by false testimony.

† Such an agreement *was* made in 1651, between the commissioners, Uncas, and some of Ninigret's men. The ten years were to commence with 1650; but, probably, Ninigret was either uninformed or misinformed respecting this stipulation. Frequently, treaties were not understood even by those who subscribed them.

3. In respect to the Long-Islanders he answered in the following remarkable manner: " Wherfore should he acquaint the commissioners therewith when the long-islanders had slayne a sachem's son and sixty other of his men; and therefore he will not make peace with the long-islanders, but doth desire the English would lett him alone, and doth desire that the commissioners would not Request him to goe to hartford: for hee had doun noe hurt what should he doe there; hee had bene many times in the Bay, and when was Uncas there; Jonathan [the messenger] asked him whether he would send two or three of his men that might act in his Rome and steed if hee would not goe him selfe hee answared what should hee or his men doe att hartford; Adding if youer Governor's sonne were slayne and seuerall other men would [you] aske counsell of another Nation how and when to Right yourselves; and againe said hee would not goe nor send to Hartford."

4. " Concerning the vpland Indians his answare was they are my frinds and came to healp mee against the long-islanders which had killed seuerall of my men; wherfore should I acquaint the commissioners with it; I doe but Right my owne quarell which the long-islanders began with mee."

This spirited reply, alone sufficient to immortalize Ninigret, brought on open war. A body of troops was raised in the three united colonies, and sent into the Niantick country, under Major Willard of Massachusetts, with orders to demand of Ninigret the Pequots subject to his control, the tribute already due from them, and also a cessation of hostilities against the Indians of Long Island. On refusal to comply with these terms, they were to reduce him to submission and tribute by force, and take hostages for security. The place of general rendezvous was appointed at Stanton's house in the Narraghansett country. On arriving there, Major Willard found that Ninigret had fled into a swamp ten or fifteen miles distant from the army. leaving his country, corn, and wigwams, at the invader's mercy. Messengers were sent to him, inviting him to a conference, and pledging the safety of his person. He returned answer that aggressions had *already* been made upon his territory and property, and he did not think it safe for him to visit the Major. He wished to know, too, what had occasioned the present invasion. What had he done to *the English*, that they beset him in this manner?—Whatever the difficulty was, he was ready to settle it by messengers, but not in person.

A day or two afterwards, as he was still in close quarters, six new messengers were sent to him, two of whom, only, after much debate with his guards and scouts, were admitted to his own presence. They began with demanding the Pequots; to which he replied, that most of that people had left him already —(nearly one hundred had deserted to the English army—); and the few that remained were hunting and straggling up and down the country. He however set his mark to the following agreement, dated Oct. 18, 1654.

"Wheras the commissioners of the vnited collonies demaund by theire Messengers that I deliuer vp to the English all the captiue Pequotes in my countrey I heerby ingage myselfe to surrender the said Pequotes within seuen daies to Mr. Winthrope or Captain Mason Witnesse my hand.

Witnesse Thomas Stanton and Vallentine Whitman Interpretors Witnesse alsoe Thomas Bligh."

The messengers next demanded the tribute due for the Pequots. He replied, that he never engaged to pay it. "Why then," said they, "did you pay it, or part of it, at New Haven?" "Because," he readily answered, "I feared they would be taken from me if I did not, and therefore made a gratuity out of my own wampum to please *you*." Being now forbidden in the commissioners' name, to pursue hostilities against the Indians of Long-Island, he stood silent for some time, and then asked if it was right that his men—*such* men—should lose their lives and their blood, and not be revenged. The English observed, that he should have offered his complaints to the commissioners; but to this he made no reply; nor yet to the unceremonious if not uncivil declaration of the messengers, that in case he gave any farther trouble to any of the friends of the English, they should forthwith take the liberty to set his head upon a pole. The conference ended with their requesting him to pay the expenses of the expedition, which he refused to do: "Hee was not the cause of it, but longe-Island Indians killed him a man att Connecticott." Thus the affair ended. The commander was censured by the commissioners, for neglecting a good opportunity of humbling a troublesome enemy, but no farther strictures ensued.* They contented themselves with stationing an armed vessel in the *road* between Neanticut and Long-Island, with orders to prevent hostile movements on the part of Ninigret, and with encouraging his Indian adversaries by promises of English assistance. The next year, Ninigret continuing his attacks, they thought themselves under obligation to furnish it.

From this time forward, there is little of interest in the life either of Pessacus or Ninigret. We hear of them occasionally, but not much farther than is sufficient to indicate their existence. Whether they gave less reason to be complained of than before, or whether the English at length grew weary of sending messages to them, cannot be ascertained; but there is probably some truth in both suppositions.

One of the last deputations to Ninigret, in 1656, was occasioned by complaints which he made to the Eng

---

* A Mss. private letter of Major Willard is extant, (in the possession of Mr. Shattuck, author of a very valuable History of Concord, which we hope may be soon published,) in which, alluding to this expedition, he rather mysteriously speaks of his 'hands being tied.' Whether this alludes to his general instructions, or to something more secret, every reader will judge for himself.

ish of grievances recieved from the Long-Islanders.
He failed to prove them as alleged, and the commissioners took that occasion to remind him of his own
duties and defaults, in their wonted manner. The
lesson was repeated in 1657, some affrays and assaults
having meanwhile occurred, which threatened to
bring on more serious troubles between the Indian
tribes. The most remarkable circumstance connected with the deputation of this season, is the dissent
of the commissioners of Massachusetts, who frequently had occasion to differ with their associates in
regard to intercourse with the Indians. The terms
of this opinion, expressed in the records, are worthy
of notice, as throwing a casual light on the charges
brought against Ninigret.

" There hauing bine," say they, "many messengers
to this purpose formerly sent from the commissioners
to the Indian Sachems, but seldom obserued by them,
which now to Renew againe *when many complaints
have bine made against Vncas by seuerall Sachems and
other Indians of his proud Insolent and prouocking
speeches and Trecherous actions, and with much probabilitie of truth,* besides his hostile attempts at Potunck
&c.—seems vnseasonable ; and can in Reason have
no other attendance in conclusion than *to Render vs
lo and contemptable in the eyes of the Indians, or engage
vs to vindecate our honer in a dangerouse and vnessesarie warr vpon Indian quarrells, the grounds whereof
wee can hardly euer satisfactoryly vnderstand,* &c."
There is manifestly great truth, as well as some
severity, in this declaration. We may hereafter allude again to what is said respecting Vncas.

We now refer to the instructions of messengers
sent two years after the embassy last named, merely
to illustrate the style of diplomacy which still continued to be used. They were directed " to Repaire
to Ninnigrett, Pessicus, Woqnocanoote, and the Rest
of the Narraghansett Sachems, and distinctly and
clearly deliuer to them the following message." One
article of complaint runs thus:

"The comissioners doe require ninety-five fath
om of wampam ordered by them to bee payed the last
yeare for the Insolencyes committed att mistress
Brewster's feet to her great affrightment and stealing
corne &c. and other affronts."

Again: "The comissioners doe charge Ninnigrett with breach of couenant *and high neglect of
theire order sent them by Major Willard six yeares since
not to Inuade the longe Iland Indians;* and doe
account this surprising the longe-Iland Indians att
Gull Iland and murthering of them to be an insolent
carriage to the English and a barbarous and inhu-
maine acte; therefore the comissioners *haue provided for his entertainment at longe-Iland* if hee shall
dare further to attempt vpon them before hee hath
satisfied the comissioners of the justnes of his quarrell, ordering the English there to assist the Indians
and driue him from thence." It will be recollected,
that Ninigret had always disclaimed the right of the
English to interfere in this contest with his neighbors, though he explained to them, so far as to justify
himself on the ground of having been first aggrieved
and attacked by his enemy. More recently he had
chosen—probably for the sake of keeping peace with
the English — to make complaints to them; but
because he had failed to prove them (—and no doubt
they were mostly incapable of being proved, in their
very nature—) the commissioners had taken no other
notice of his suit than to send Thomas Stanton and
others to reprimand him at once for his present insolence and his old sins.

Still, he was not utterly discouraged, for he did
not invariably fail of having justice done him. In
1662, the commissioners being informed of his intention to sell a certain tract of land in his actual
possession, which was nevertheless claimed by one
Harmon Garrett, they sent to him—not a message of
threats by Thomas Stanton—but "a writing vnder
theire hands sertifying the said Harmon Garrett's
claime, which being made knowne to Ninnigrett, the

said Ninnigrett by his Messengers to the comissioners att theire last meeting att Plymouth made claime to the said land, and Refered the Determination therof to the next meeting of the court att Boston, *desireing that notice might bee given to the said harmon Garrett att the said Meeting of the comissioners to appeer.*

This honorable proposition was adopted. Garrett made his appearance, and Ninigret sent his attorney to meet him at Boston. Garrett stated, that his father was a great sachem, and was possessed of the lands in controversy, and that Ninigret was the said Sachem's younger brother. On the other side, *Cornman* in behalf of Ninigret, showed that his master was possessed of said lands according to the Indian custom, being allowed to be the chief sachem, and having married the sister of Harmon Garrett; and that said Harmon was not of the whole [Niantick] blood, because his mother was a stranger. This evidence was furnished orally by divers Narraghansett and Pequot Indians, as also by Uncas and others in writing. The commissioners decided, that it was "not meet to prejudice the title of Ninnigrett, being in posession by any acte of theires, and that the writing giuen vnder theire hand att New-hauen conserning harmon Garrett bee not vnderstood nor made vse of to prejudice Ninnigrett's title and posession, but aduise all the English to forbeare to disturbe Ninnigrett."*

The good effect of this decision is to be seen in the almost total silence of history in regard to Ninigret for the next twelve or thirteen years, when we find him coming forward, confidently and amicably, in a similar case. The particulars may be best gathered from a letter written by Mr. John Easton, (probably a magistrate living near the sachem,) to the Governor of Plymouth Colony. It runs thus:

"Ninigret, one of the two chief sachems of the Narraghansetts in our colony, importuned me thus

---

* Records of the Colonies. Hazard, Vol. II.

to write to you, that, as he saith, it is the Indian
custom or law, that when any sachem's men are
driven and cast ashore, or their goods, upon any
other sachem's jurisdiction, or taken up by any other
sachem's men, that the goods are to be restored to
the sachem whose men they were; and this spring,
twelve Indians, at a time, were drowned in the sea,
coming from an Island, and some of their goods
drove up in your jurisdiction at Dartmouth; and he
desireth you to inform those Indians [at Dartmouth]
that they should restore to him all the goods of those
drowned that they have got."*

This letter was written in March, 1675, just on the
eve of the great war of King Philip. The friendly
disposition of Ninigret was now put to the test. The
Nipmucks, Nashaways, Pocontocks, the Hadley and
Springfield Indians, the Pokanokets of Philip, the
tribes of Maine, and still nearer home the Narraghansetts, were involved in the common controversy of
the times. But Ninigret remained faithful to the
English; and though he took no personal part in
the war, some of his warriors distinguished themselves more than once by their zealous cooperation
with their allies. Ninigret was one of the signers
of the treaty of July, wherein the Narraghansetts
bound themselves to remain neutral; and in October,
his counsellor, Cornman, signed a confirmation of
the same instrument, in *his* name, (at Boston,) with
an additional agreement to surrender up such Pokanoket refugees as might be found in his territories
Several of the Narraghansett sachems did the same,
but Ninigret, alone, seems to have maintained his
fidelity. At all events, he alone had the credit of it,
and the consequent benefit. The Narraghansetts
were completely subdued, and their country overrun
and subjected. The tribe and territory of Ninigret
were spared; and several of their descendants were
living on the premises so late as 1738, when few, if

---

* Sixth volume of the Mass. His Coll 1st Series

any, of the Narraghansett blood could be found within the limits of Rhode Island.*

The precise time of the death of Ninigret is not recorded   It is not probable that he lived long after Philip's war, for two good reasons. He is rarely if at all mentioned, subsequently; and he must have been already quite advanced in age. It was now over forty years since that Pequot war, at the date of which he is mentioned by Prince. Pessacus must have died previous to Phillip's war. We do not find his name in the Colonial Records after 1658, though it would certainly have been among the signatures to the treaty last mentioned, had he been living at the date of its execution. The English regarded him as the leading man of his tribe.

The three principal complaints made against Ninigret, and the occasion of the ill-treatment he received from the English, were his hostility to Uncas, his intercourse with the Dutch, and the wars which he waged with the Long Islanders. Respecting the latter, enough has already been said. Enough appears in the protest of the Massachusetts commissioners, alone, to show that the English had but a poor reason for interfering as they did. They barely alleged that these Indians were their friends; but nothing is more obvious than that *such* reasoning, however satisfactory to themselves, could only render them, in the words of the protest, "low and contemptible in the eyes of the Indians."

"There being noe agreement produced or proved," —said Mr. Bradstreet, of Massachusetts, in 1653— "whereby the collenies are obliged to protect the Long Island Indians against Ninnegrett or others, and so noe Reason to engage them in theire quarrells the grounds whereof they cannot well vnderstand: I therefore see not sufficient light to this vote."

It is obvious that even an 'obligation,' by agree-

---

* Callender's Century Discourse.

ment, to protect those Indians, might not imply a
right to do so as regarded other parties—but granting such a right as consequent upon sufficient provocation, it still remains to prove upon which party
lay the blame of the first attack.   Ninigret always
asserted that he acted in self-defence, and no doubt
such was his real opinion.   The English only rep-
rimanded him upon old scores, when he laid his
grievances before them; and then sent an armed
vessel and a body of troops to fight for his enemies.
The Long Islanders told a different story; but this
was at best but one Indian testimony against another; and how much *theirs* in particular could be relied upon, appears from the fact, that within a year
or two after this same affair, they themselves committed the most flagrant depredations upon the
English.   Trumbull says, that in 1657, "after all
the trouble and expense which the English had been
at for their defence, they became tumultuous, and
did great damage to the inhabitants of Southampton."

To conclude this discussion, we introduce some
passages of a manuscript letter from Roger Williams
to the government of one of the colonies, which has
already been cited.   It bears date of Oct. 5, 1654, and
was written to prevent war.*

"The Cause and Roote of all yᵉ present mischief
is yᵉ Pride of 2 Barbarians, Ascassassôtick, yᵉ Long
Island Sachim, and Nenekunat, of the Narigansett.
The former is proud and foolish.   The latter is
proud and fierce.   I have not seene him these many
years, yet from their sober men I hear he pleads,

First, yᵗ Ascassassôtick, a very Inferior Sachim
(bearing himself upon yᵉ English) hath slain 3 or
4 of his people and since yᵗ sent him challenges and
darings to fight and mend himself.

2dly. He, Nenekunat, consulted by Solemn mes
sengers with the chiefe of the English Governors,
Major Endicott then Govᵣ of yᵉ Massachusetts, who
sent him an Implicite consent to right himselfe.

---

* Col. Rec. of R. I.

3 After he had taken revenge, upon ye Long
Islanders and brought away about 14 Captives, yet
he restored them all again upon ye mediation and
desire of ye English.

4. After this peace made, the Long Islanders pretending to visit Nenekunat at Block Island, slaughtered of his Narigansetts neere 30 persons at midnight, 2 of them of great note, especially Wepiteam-
mock's sonn, to whom Nenekunat was uncle."

Mr. Williams afterwards says;

" 1. I know it is said ye Long Islanders are subjects: But I have heard this greatly questioned, and
indeed I question whether any Indians in this Country, remayning Barbarous and Pagan, may with
truth or honor be cald ye English subjects.

2. But graunt them subjects, what capacitie hath
their late massacre of ye Narigansetts (with whom
they had made peace) without ye English consent,
though still under ye English name, put them into?"

As to a league between Ninigret and 'the Duch
Governor,' his own reply to the charge has been
given. It will furnish some amusement, at least, to
review parts of the evidence upon which it was
founded. Ninigret and Pessacus sent an Indian
named Awashaw to the commissioners, in pursuance
of their agreement to give what satisfaction they
could in regard to this subject; "*whoe being demanded why Ninigret went to the Monhatoes the last winter,*
answared that Ninigret told *him* that hee went
thether to bee cured of his disease, hearing there
was a Frenchman there that could cure him; that
Mr. Iohn Winthorpe knew of his going; that he
carried thirty fathom of wampam, ten whereof he
gave the Doctor and fifteen to the governor; and the
governor gave him in Lieue thereof sleived coates
but not one gun, but the Indians there gave Ninigrett two guns." This was in 1653.

Not long before, it seems that *Uncas*—the last
man whose evidence should have been noticed at
all—had called on Governor Haynes at Hartford.

and informed him of Ninigret's visit to the Dutch, as also that he had made a league with them, bought up a large quantity of ammunition, and negotiated with the New York Indians for a war against Uncas and the English. Furthermore, it was said that Ninigret had sent to a neighboring Sachem, to procure a man skilful in poisoning, and had promised him one hundred fathoms of wampum in return. The wampum was sent by a canoe, which Uncas intercepted, with seven Indians aboard, one of whom *his* men had killed, (according to his own story,) and two others had confessed Ninigret's whole plot. We are inclined to hold, that this testimony should be received only so far as it goes against Uncas himself, showing that he took the liberty, on the strength of his suspicion alone, to assault a canoe belonging to Ninigret, and to murder one of his subjects. When these accusations were stated by the commissioners to Awashaw, the messenger just mentioned, and he was particularly questioned who and what was in the canoe, he replied, "that in the canoe that was sent back which was taken by Vncas his men, hee sent in it sixty fathom of wampam to pay for the two guns which he had of the Indians whiles hee was att the Monhatoes, and the Remainder of the Phissicke he had there." Being asked what corn Ninigret sent to the Dutch *in the Vessel taken by the English* [another aggression it would seem,] he said, "that hee Intended not to send any corne to the Duch Governor, but what corne was aboard the Duch vessel *was for the hier of the vessel that* brought him home." It appears, he had returned by water, while some of his men had walked : and he paid for his passage in corn.

Awashaw on this occasion had an Indian in company with him, named Newcom Matuxes. The means resorted to for obtaining proof of the accusation, are farther illustrated by the information gravely given us in the Records, that this fellow "spake with one Iohn lightfoot of Boston, an Englishman, whoe as Lightfoot saith, told him in Duch that the Duchmen would cutt off the English on Long-island. Newcom also confesseth that Ninnigrett said that hee heard that some shipps were to come from holland to the Monhatoes to cutt off the English; and that when the said Newcom lived att Southhold an Indian tould him that the Duch would come against the English and cutt them of, but they would saue the weemen and children and guns for themselves *But Captaine Simkins and the said Lightfoot doe both affeirme that the said Newcome tould them that the Duch men tould him as before,* tho' he now puts it of and saith that an Indian tould him. Further hee the said Newcom tould captaine Simkins (as hee confidently afeirmeth) that if he would goe to serue the Duch the Duch would giue him an hundred pounds a yeare." It matters but little, we conceive, whether Captain Simkins recollected correctly or not, his reminiscences amounting to nothing in any case. Ninigret had himself expounded the transaction, much more completely than all these witnesses together.

But the examination was still pursued, "Thomas Stanton [Interpreter] being there alsoe to charge it vpon him. The said Newcom not being able to cleare himselfe from *the guilt* of the charge, the comissioners then tould Awashaw that had the said Newcom not bine a Messenger sent by Ninnigrett nee should not have escaped without some punishment, and therfore they willed Awashaw to tell Ninnigrett hee would doe well to send the said Newcom againe to vs, the better *to cleare himselfe from all suspition.*" This manœuvre has a little too much the air of a pretext for getting a farther opportunity to cross-examine and confuse poor Newcom; he had thus far been able to make out a respectably clear statement.

Before leaving town, Awashaw sent a request to the commissioners for another interview; which being granted, he inquired who had informed them of these matters against Ninigret. They mentioned in reply "severall Indians, and more particularly *the Monheage Indian, and the Narraghansett taken by Vncas his men.*" Awashaw then requested restitution of the wampum taken by these men. The commissioners only said, that they had not yet ascertained the truth of that affair ; but when they had thought of it more, he should know their decision.

The following amusing document is a fair specimen of the testimony furnished against Ninigret by other Indians. It is the *deposition*—taken in May, 1653—of one Adam, of whom nothing farther is known. After mentioning what the Dutch Governor had done among the Indians, which is not to our purpose,

"Further hee saith that Ninnegrett the Fiscall [Treasurer] and the Duch Governor were vp two daies in a close Roome with other Sagamores ; and there was noe speaking with any of them except when they came for a cole of fier or the like and much sewam [wampum] was seen at that time in Ninnegret's hand and he carried none away with him ; further hee saith that Ronessocke a Sagamore on longe Island tould the said Addam that the Duch Governor bid him fly for his life ; for that the plott was now descovered : and besides hee sends word dayly that they had as good appear now for when hee is cutt of the English will cut them all of.

This was testifyed aboard Tuson near the white stone   before   JOHN LEVERETT
                                                 WILLIAM DAVIS."

Other evidence, considerably relied upon, was an Indian squaw's relation to a person in Wethersfield, (Conn.)—being an assertion, in general terms, that the Dutch and the Indians were leagued against the English. In fine, the commissioners say, " *wee heare* that some of the Duch att or about the Monhatoes tell the English they shall shortly have an East India breakfast, in which it is conceived they Refer to that horrid Treacheryvs and crewill plott and execution att Amboina. * * * And not to multiply Indian Testimonies which from all parts of the countrey presse vpon the colonies—[we quote the only definite statement we can find]—nine Indian Sagamores whoe liue about the Monhatoes did voullentarily without any Motion or Reward from the English send theire Messengers to Stanford declaring and afeirming that the Duch had solissited them by promising them guns pouder swords weapons war-coates and coates to cutt of the English " &c. It is of no consequence, so far as regards Ninigret, whether these Sagamores conspired to tell a falsehood or to tell the truth. Nor do we intend to enter at length into this ancient controversy between the colonies and the Dutch. It is sufficient to observe, that the charges of the former were officially and distinctly denied by the latter. Governor Stuyvesant. in a letter to the commissioners dated May 26, 1658, and written by the order of the Counsel of New-Netherlands, says—

"As touching what happened in the Amboyna busines in the East Indies is unknown vnto vs, neither hath there been any of vs there, therefore wee sease to answare to the same or to trouble yourselues or vs therein.

It is in parte as youer Worships conclude that about January there came a strange Indian from the North called Ninnigrett, Commaunder of the Narraghansetts. But hee came hither *with a passe from Mr. John Winthrope* vpon which passe as wee remember the occasion of his coming was expressed viz: to be cured and healed," &c. On the whole, the reader of our times, on perusing these records, can hardly go farther with the commissioners than to extenuate their harshness towards Ninigret, like their treatment of Miantonomo, on the score of their exaggerated fears.

Upon the quarrel with Uncas, we shall waste no words. Ninigret and Pessacus no doubt considered the circumstances of Miantonomo's case a sufficient

cause for war upon the English. But this they
waived; and even engaged, at *their* instance, to forbear hostilities against Uncas for some months, expressing at the same time a strong desire to be upon
friendly terms with the English, if they could be
left to pursue their own business in their own way.
It is neither necessary nor possible to determine upon
which side the provocation began between these
sachems and Uncas. It has been seen, that the latter
took many liberties for which the English never
called him to account, as well as some for which they
did; but of still more they must necessarily have remained in ignorance. The truth seems to be most
plainly set forth by Hutchinson, who says, it would
appear to have been good policy not to interpose in
this Indian quarrel; but *the English were afraid of
the success of the Narraghansetts,* and as they had
generally espoused the cause of the Mohegans, it was
feared, that as soon as *they* were subdued, if not in
the course of the war, the Narraghansetts and their
allies would fall upon the plantations of the English,
against whom they were then in a peculiar manner
enraged for the death of Miantonomo. The same
historian acknowledges, that it was with great reluctance the Narraghansetts submitted to the hard terms
of the treaty of 1645, and only in consequence of the
armed force which had already invaded their country.
They must have considered the tribute a most insult-
ing, forcible imposition.

Waiving a statement of the charges which Ninigret made, or might have made, on the other hand,
against the English, we shall only observe in conclusion that whatever may be thought of his political
course, there are points in his personal character not
unworthy of esteem and even of admiration. It was
noble in him, according to the principles of a warrior
and king, to revenge, as far as he was able, the cool-
blooded massacre of his relative and predecessor
That purpose he pursued with undaunted courage
and indefatigable energy. He would gladly have

avoided a contest with the English; but he would not sacrifice his honor either to his friendship or his interest. The spirit with which he repulsed their attempts to interfere in his contest with the Long-Islanders, indicated a soul of the same stamp. His reasoning upon that occasion—assuming the truth of his premises, which we have no means either of proving or falsifying—appears to us wholly unanswerable.

I.—U

CHAPTER XIII.

The Pequot tribe—Their first chief-sachem known to the English, PEKOATH—succeeded by SASSACUS—An embassy sent to Boston in 1631—Residence and strong-holds of Sassacus—His earliest intercourse with the English—Murder of Captain Stone—Justification of it by Sassacus—He proposes a treaty of peace in 1634—Sends deputies to Boston twice—Treaty concluded—Anecdotes—His wars with the Narraghansetts—Fresh controversy with the English—They send an armed party to demand damages—Conduct of the party, and consequences of it—War with the Pequots in 1636—Political movements of Sassacus—English expedition against him in 1637—He is defeated—Driven from his country—Killed by the Mohawks—The English policy in his case briefly considered.

THE Pequots, or Pequods, inhabited that part of the southern coast of New England, which is now comprehended within the limits of Connecticut. They are said to have been originally an inland tribe, and to have gained possession by mere force of arms of the fine territory which they occupied at the date of their first acquaintance with the English. They were in the meridian of their glory and power about forty years previous to that period, and were then the most considerable tribe in New England, mustering as many as four thousand bowmen. Their principal settlements were now about New London and Groton ; the former of which was their chief harbor, and called by their own name. The Nipmuck Indians, on their north, were still tributary to them. So also were a part of the Long Islanders, and most of the Indians on the Connecticut river. The Narraghansetts alone of the neighboring tribes had been able to oppose them with success, and against that nation they waged an implacable and almost perpetual war.

The first great sachem of the Pequots known to the English was PEKOATH, from whom they probably derived the national name. He appears to have been a great warrior. He was going on conquering and to conquer, when the earliest settlements of the English were made upon the Massachusetts coast. Tribe after tribe retreated before him as he advanced, till his terrible myrmidons were at length in a situation to locate themselves at their ease on the best soil, and beneath the most genial skies, of New England.

As early as 1631, Waghinacut, a sachem of one of the expelled or subjected tribes just mentioned, travelled across the wilderness to Boston; and attended by a Massachusetts Sagamore, and one Jack Straw (an Indian who had formerly lived with Sir Walter Raleigh in England,) made application for the alliance or assistance of the Massachusetts government against Pekoath. He gave a glowing description of his native land; and promised, if some of the English would go there and settle, that he would supply them with corn, and pay them eighty beaver-skins yearly. This proposition being rejected, he desired that at least two men might be permitted to accompany him, with the view of examining the country. He showed great anxiety to effect that object, but to no purpose; the governor suspected some stratagem, and politely dismissed his visiter with the compliment of a good dinner at his own table.*

The successor of Pekoath, and the last as well as first great sachem of his tribe known personally to the whites, was SASSACUS, a warrior of high renown, who, when the English commenced their settlements in Connecticut, soon after the transaction last mentioned, had no fewer than twenty-six sachems or war-captains under his dominion, and could at that time muster, at the smallest calculation, seven hun-

---

* *Winthrop's Journal.* Waghinacut persevered, however, and succeeded. He went to Plymouth, and Governor Winslow sent out a party, at his suggestion, who are understood to have been the first discoverers of Connecticut river and the adjacent parts.

dred bowmen. The site of his principal fortress and residence, was on a most beautiful eminence in the town of Groton, commanding one of the best prospects of the Sound and the adjacent country which can be found upon the coast. Another strong-hold was a little farther eastward, near Mystic river ; and this also was finely situated upon a verdant swell of land, gradually descending towards the south and southeast.

Sassacus, and his warlike Pequots, are almost the only American chieftain and tribe who, in the light of history, seem to have been from the outset disposed to inveterate hostility against all foreigners. They were, as Trumbull observes, men of great and independent spirits ; and had conquered and governed the nations around them without control. They viewed the English especially, as not only strangers but mere intruders, without right or pretence of right to the country, who had nevertheless taken the liberty to make settlements and build forts in their very neighborhood, without asking their consent—and even to restore the Indian kings whom *they* had subjected, to their former lands and authority. Under these circumstances, it is no matter of wonder, that the whites had scarcely located themselves within the bounds of Connecticut, when " that great, spirited and warlike nation, the Pequots, began to murder and plunder them, and to wound and kill their cattle."*

And yet—setting aside the general offence committed, or at least by Sassacus understood to be committed, in the act of making settlements without leave— it does not clearly appear whether the first particular provocation was given on the one side or the other It is only known, that in the summer of 1633, one Captain Stone, on a voyage from Maine to Virginia, put into the mouth of the Connecticut river, and was there murdered by the natives, with all his crew

---

* Trumbull.

Three of them, who went ashore to kill fowl, were first surprised and despatched. A sachem, with some of his men, then came aboard, and staid with Captain Stone in his cabin until the latter fell asleep. The sachem then knocked him on the head; and his crew being at this time in the cook's room, the Indians took such guns as they found charged, and fell upon them. At this moment, all the powder on board the vessel, in the hurry of sudden alarm, was accidentally exploded. The deck was blown up; but most of the Indians escaping, returned, completed the massacre, and burned the wreck.

Such was the English account of the proceeding. The Pequots had a different story to tell. In October 1634, Sassacus sent a messenger to the Governor of Massachusetts, to desire friendship and alliance. This man brought two bundles of sticks with him, by which he signified how many beaver and otter skins his master would give, besides a large quantity of wampum. He brought also a small present. The Governor received it, and returned a moose coat of the same value; but sent word to Sassacus withal, that a treaty could not be negotiated, unless he would send men proper to negotiate, and enough of them.*

Accordingly, but a fortnight afterwards, (though the distance to the Pequot country was a five-days' journey,) two more messengers arrived at Boston, bringing another present of wampum. They were told, in answer to their renewed application, that the English would willingly come to amicable terms with Sassacus, but that his men having murdered Captain Stone, he must first surrender up the offenders to justice. The messengers readily replied, that the sachem concerned in that transaction had since been killed by the Dutch; and that all the other offenders had died of the small pox, excepting two. These, they presumed Sassacus would surrender, *if*

---

* Winthrop Vol. I.

the guilt were proved upon them. They asserted, that Captain Stone, after entering their river, had taken two of their men, and detained them by force, and made them pilot the vessel up the river. The captain and two of his crew then landed, taking the guides on shore, with their hands still bound behind them. The natives there fell upon and killed them. The vessel, with the remainder of the crew on board, was blown up—they knew not how or wherefore.

This—in the words of the journalist who gives the particulars—was related with so much confidence and gravity, that the English were inclined to believe it, especially as they had no means of proving its falsity. A treaty was concluded on the following terms.

1. The English to have as much land in Connecti cut as they needed, provided they would make a settlement there : and the Pequots to render them all the assistance they could.

2. The Pequots to give the English four hundred fathoms of wampum, and forty beaver and thirty otter skins ; and to surrender the two murderers whenever they should be sent for.

3. The English were to send a vessel immediately, 'to trade with them as friends, tho' not to defend them," and the Pequots would give them all their 'custom.'

The agreement was put in writing, and subscribed by the two messengers with their marks. The chief object proposed by Sassacus in effecting it, appears to have been, not the assistance of the English in his wars, but their commerce in peace. He thought himself competent to fight his own battles ; and perhaps would have made no attempt to conciliate even the English, but for having quarrelled with the Dutch of New York, who had hitherto supplied him, and thereby lost their trade as well as incurred their hostility.

Meanwhile, he was at deadly war, as usual, with the Narraghansetts. The very next morning after the treaty was concluded, and while the messengers still tarried in Boston, news came, that a party of two or three hundred of the tribe last named had come as far as Neponsett, (the boundary between Milton and Dorchester) for the purpose of laying wait and killing the Pequots on their way home. The English immediately despatched a small armed force, to request a visit from the Narraghansetts; and two sachems, with about twenty of their men, obeyed the summons. They said they had been hunting round about the country, and came to visit the Indians at Neponsett, according to old custom. However this might be, they showed themselves quite ready to gratify the English in their requests; and the Pequots were permitted to return home unmolested.

A passage in the Journal of Winthrop, relating to this occasion, illustrates the spirit of Sassacus and his subjects. The Narraghansetts were privately told by the Governor, that if they should happen to make peace with the Pequots, they should receive a goodly proportion of the wampum just sent.—"For the Pequots held it dishonorable to offer them any thing as of themselves, yet were willing we would give it them, and indeed did offer us so much to that end."

Thus matters remained until 1636. During that season one Oldham, an Englishman who had been trading in Connecticut, was murdered by a party of Block-Island Indians; several of whom are said to have taken refuge among the Pequots, and to have been protected by them. On the strength of this fact and this supposition, the Governor of Massachusetts—Mr. Oldham being a Dorchester resident—despatched a force of ninety men, under Captain Endecott, commissioned (as Mr. Winthrop tells us,) to put to death the men of Block-Island, but to spare the women and children, and bring them away, and take possession of the Island. Thence they were to go to the Pequots, " to demand the murderers of Captain Stone and other English, and *one thousand fathom of wampum for damages* &c. and some of their children as hostages, which if they should refuse, they were to obtain it by force."

The proceedings which ensued upon the attempt to execute these orders ought not to be overlooked. From Block-Island, the English sailed to Pequot harbor.   Here an Indian came out to them in a canoe, and demanded who they were, and what they would have in the country of the Pequots.   Endecott replied, that he came from the Governor of Massachusetts, to speak with the Pequot sachems.   The Indian answering that Sassacus was gone to Long-Island, he was directed to communicate Endecott's message to another sachem.   He returned to the shore, and the English meanwhile made a landing.   The messenger came back, and the Indians began to gather about the English.   Several hours passed in desultory conference, until Endecott, growing impatient, announced his commission to the crowd which surrounded him, and at the same time sent word to the sachem, that unless he would come to him or satisfy his demands, he should try forcible measures.   The messenger, who had been several times running to and fro between the parties, said that the sachem would come forward if the English would lay down their arms, the Indians also leaving their bows and arrows at a distance.

Endecott was incensed by the proposal, considering it a pretext for gaining time.   He therefore bade the Pequots begone, and take care of themselves; they had dared the English to come and fight with them, he said, and now he was ready for the battle. The Pequots withdrew peaceably to a distance. When they were beyond musket-shot, " he marched after them, supposing they would have stood it awhile, as they did to the Dutch,"*—but they all fled, letting fly a few arrows among the English, which did no damage.   Two of their own number were killed and

---

* Winthrop.

several more wounded; and the English then marched up to their village, and burned all their wigwams
and mats. At night, concludes the historian, they
returned to their vessels; and the next day they
went ashore on the west side of the river, and burnt
all their wigwams and spoiled their canoes in *that*
quarter; and so set sail and came to the Narraghansett country. There they landed their men, " and
on the 14th of 7ber they came all safe to Boston,
which was a marvellous providence of God, that
not a hair fell from the head of any of them, nor
any sick nor feeble person among them."

The sequel of the tragedy must be gathered from
other authorities. A detachment of Endecott's
party was appointed to reinforce the English garrison at Saybrook. Lying wind-bound off Pequot
harbor, after his departure, a part of these men
went on shore to plunder the Pequots, and bring off
their corn. Their ravages were interrupted by an
attack from these Indians. The skirmish lasted till
near evening, and then both parties retired, the English with one man wounded, and the Pequots with a
loss unknown. We have given the particulars of
this transaction, (according to the English version
of course) because it throws light upon the subsequent relations between Sassacus and the English.

Whatever was the disposition of the Pequots
previous to this date, there is no question about them
ever afterwards. They determined to extirpate the
whites from the limits of Connecticut; and to that
great object Sassacus now devoted the whole force
of his dominions and the entire energies of his soul.
The forts and settlements were assaulted in every
direction. In October, five of the Saybrook garrison
were surprised, as they were carrying home their
hay. A week afterwards, the master of a small
English vessel was taken and tortured; and several
others within the same month. The garrison just
mentioned were so pressed before winter, (1636—7)
that they were obliged to keep almost wholly within

10—17

reach of their guns. Their out-houses were razed, and their stacks of hay burned; and so many of the cattle as were not killed, often came in at night with the arrows of the enemy sticking in them. In March, they killed four of the garrison, and at the same time surrounding the fort on all sides, challenged the English to come out and fight, mocked them with the groans and prayers of their dying friends whom they had captured, and boasted they could kill Englishmen "*all one flies.*" Nothing but a cannon loaded with grape-shot, could keep them from beat ing the very gates down with their clubs.

Three persons were next killed on Connecticut river, and nine at Wethersfield. No boat could now pass up or down the river with safety. The roads and fields were everywhere beset. The settlers could neither hunt, fish, nor cultivate the land, nor travel at home or abroad, but at the peril of life. A constant watch was kept night and day. People went armed to their daily labors, and to public worship; and the church was guarded during divine service. Probably no portion of the first colonists of New England ever suffered so horribly from an Indian warfare, as the Connecticut settlers at this gloomy and fearful period.

Nor was the employment of his own subjects the only measure adopted by Sassacus against his civilized enemy. He knew them too well to despise, however much he detested them. He saw there was need of all the ingenuity of the politician, as well as the prowess of the warrior, to be exercised upon his part; and he therefore entered upon a trial of the arts of diplomacy with the same cunning and courage which were the confidence of his followers in the field of battle. The proposal of alliance offensive and defensive which he made to his ancient rival and foe, the chief sachem of the Narraghansetts, was a conception worthy of a great and noble soul. And such was the profound skill with which he supported the reasonableness of that policy, that, (as we have heretofore seen,) Miantonomo himself wavered in his high-minded fidelity to the English cause. But for the presence and influence of Roger Williams,* the consummate address of the Pequot must have carried his point.

The measures taken by the other colonies, in con sequence of the state of things we have been describ ing, and the minutiæ of the famous expedition of Ma son, are too well known to be repeated at length The contest was not long continued, but it required the most serious efforts on the part of the English; and not only did Massachusetts and Plymouth feel themselves under the necessity of aiding Connecticut in the suppression of this common and terrible foe, but many of the Narraghansetts also were called on to aid, with the Nianticks, the Mohegans and other tribes upon the river.

Sassacus must have felt, that the day of restitution and reparation was indeed come upon him for all his ancient victories and spoils. Every people in his neighborhood who had suffered, or expected to suffer, from his pride or his power, now gladly witnessed the onset of a new enemy against him; and large numbers availed themselves of the opportunity to do personal service. Not less than five hundred Indians of various tribes accompanied Mason in his march against the great Pequot fortress. Not a few of them, without doubt, remembered old times as well as Miantonomo himself, though they acted very differently in consequence.

These gallant allies were so eager to go against the Pequots, that nothing but the van of the army could satisfy them for their own station. "We hope,"

---

* That gentleman, in one of his letters preserved on the Mass. Records, writes—"That in ye Pequt Wars it pleased your honoured Government to employ me in ye hazardous and waighty Service of negotiating a League between Yourselves and the Narigansetts: *when ye Pequt messengers (who sought ye Narigansett's league against the English) had almost ended yt my worck and life together*"

said they, (—or something, no doubt, to that pur
pose—)
"We hope it will offend not you nor yours
The chiefest post of honor should be ours."
    Upon which
'Mason harangues them with high compliments
And to confirm them he to them consents.
Hold on, *bold men*, says he, as you've began ;
I'm free and easy ; you shall take the van."
    But,   —(" as we always by experience find,
Frost-bitten leaves will not abide the wind ")—

    These formidable veterans had gone but a few
miles, when every man of them fell in the rear, and
that unluckily to such a distance that not one could
be found.   They were in the enemy's country, and
the truth was, they
            —" Had so often, to their harm,
Felt the great power of Sassacus's arm,
That now again just to endure the same,
The dreadful sound of great Sassacus' name,
Seemed every moment to attack their ears,
And fill'd them with such heart-amazing fears,
That suddenly they run and seek to hide,
Swifter than leaves in the autumnal tide."*

    This was in the evening.   As the English ap-
proached the fortress about day-light, they halted at
the foot of a large hill, and Mason sent word for his
allies "to come up."   After a long time, Uncas and
Wequash† alone made their appearance.   "Where is

---

* Wolcott's Account.
† Vide "A BRIEF HISTORY OF THE PEQUOT WAR:
Especially of the *memorable Taking of their Fort at Mystic in Connecticut in* 1637, written by Major John Mason,
a Principal Actor therein, as the chief captain and commander of Connecticut Forces: Boston: Printed and Sou. by S.
Kneeland and T. Green in Queen St. 1736."   The following
is the motto of this tract.—" We have heard with our ears, O
God. * * * how thou didst drive out the heathen with thy
hand, and plantedst them: how thou didst afflict the people and
cast them out," &c.
    The author of NEW ENGLAND'S FIRST FRUITS calls th's

the fort ?" inquired Mason. "On the top of that nill," answered they. "And where are the rest of the Indians ?"—Uncas said, "they were behind, exceedingly afraid;" and the most that Mason could induce them to do, was to form a semi-circle at a particularly respectful distance, for the purpose of witnessing the attack of the English upon the enemy's fort, and waylaying such of the Pequots as might escape *their* hands.

The resistance was manly and desperate, but the whole work of destruction was completed in little more than an hour. The extent and violence of the conflagration kindled by the assailants, the reflection of this pyramid of flames upon the forest around, the flashing and roar of arms, the shrieks and yellings of men, women and children within, and the shouts of the allies without, exhibited one of the most awful scenes which the pens of the early historians have described. Seventy wigwams were burnt, and five or six hundred Pequots killed. Parent and child alike, the sanop and squaw, the gray-haired man and the babe were buried in one promiscuous ruin.

It had been Mason's intention to fall upon both the principal forts of the enemy at once; and finding it impossible, he says, "we were much grieved, chiefly because, the greatest and bloodiest sachem there resided, *whose name was* SASSACUS." The execution of this design would have saved him much subsequent loss and labor. That great warrior was

---

man a famous captain, a proper man of person, and of very grave and sober spirit. He became religious after the Pequot war, lived sometime among the whites, and then preached to ais countrymen until his death, which was occasioned by a dose of poison wherewith some of them repaid him for his labors. A Massachusetts clergyman says of him, in 1643: "He loved Christ, he preached Christ up and down, and then suffered martyrdom for Christ; and when he dyed, gave his soule tc Christ, and his only child to the English, rejoycing in this hope that the child should know more of Christ than its poore Fa ther ever did."

so little discouraged by the horrible havoc already nade among his subjects, that immediately on receiv ,ng the intelligence he despatched, perhaps led on in person, a reinforcement of three hundred warriors, who pursued the English very closely for a distance of six miles, on their march towards Pequot harbor.

But the reception which this body met with from the English, drove them to desperation. The whole remaining force of the nation repaired to the stronghold of Sassacus, and vented all their complaints and grievances upon his head. In their fury they even threatened to destroy him and his family: and perhaps nothing but the entreaties of his chief counsellors, who still adhered to him in his misfortunes, prevented his being massacred by his own subjects in his own fort. A large number deserted him, as it was, and took refuge among the Indians of New York. The fort was then destroyed, and Sassacus himself, with seventy or eighty of his best men, retreated towards the river Hudson.

To kill or capture him, was now the main object of the war; and the Pequots were pursued westward, two captured sachems having had their lives spared on condition of guiding the English in the surprisal of their royal master. The enemy were at last overtaken, and a great battle took place in a swamp in Fairfield, where nearly two hundred Pequots were taken prisoners, besides killed and wounded. Seven hundred, it was computed, had now been destroyed in the course of the war. As Mason expresses himself, they were become " a prey to all Indians; and happy were they that could bring in their heads to the English—of which there came almost daily to Windsor or Hartford." So Winthrop writes late in the summer of 1637—" The Indians about still send in many Pequots' heads and hands from Long Island and other places." &c.*

But Sassacus was not destined to fall by the hands

* Journal, Vol.

of the English, although thirteen of his war-captains had already been slain, and he was himself driven from swamp to swamp, by night and day, until life was hardly worthy of an effort to preserve it. Even his own men were seeking his life, to such extremities were they compelled by fear of the English. One Pequot, whose liberty was granted him on condition of finding and betraying Sassacus, finally succeeded in the search. He came up with him in one of his solitary retreats ; but finding his design suspected, and wanting the courage necessary for attacking a warrior whom even his Narraghansett enemies had described as " all one God,"* he left him in the night, and returned to the English.

The sachem was at last obliged to abandon his country. Taking with him five hundred pounds of wampum, and attended by several of his best war-captains and bravest men, he sought a refuge among the Mohawks. These savages wanted the magnanimity to shelter, or even spare, a formidable rival, now brought within their power by his misfortunes. He was surprised and slain by a party of them, and most of the faithful companions who still followed his solitary wanderings, were partakers with him of the same miserable fate. The scalp of Sassacus was sent to Connecticut in the fall ; and a lock of it soon after carried to Boston, ' as a rare sight,' (says Trumbull,) and a sure demonstration of the death of a mortal enemy.

Thus perished the last great sachem of the Pequots ; and thus was that proud and warlike nation itself, with the exception of a small remnant, swept from the face of the earth. The case requires but brief comment. However this tribe and their chieftain might have been predisposed to treat the English, and however they did treat their Indian neighbors, they commenced their intercourse with the whites, ostensibly at least, in a manner as friendly

---

* Mason's *History.*

and honorable as it was independent. **Previous to**
the treaty, indeed, complaints had grown out of the
murder of Stone ; but the English had no evidence
at all in that case, while the evidence of the Pequots
was, according to their own acknowledgement, cogent
if not conclusive, in support of their innocence.

We may add, that it was confirmed by what is
known incidentally of the character of Stone.   Governor Winthrop, speaking of his arrival at Boston in
June 1633, on board a small vessel loaded with
" corn and salt," adds, that " the governor of Plymouth sent Captain Standish *to prosecute against him*
for piracy."   The particulars of the accusation need
not be stated, for only a few months after this, we
find the same person mentioned as charged with another infamous crime ; " and though it appeared he
was in drink, and no *act* to be proved, yet it was
thought fit he should abide his trial," &c.   He was
fined a hundred pounds, and expelled from the
Massachusetts jurisdiction.

As to the next proceeding recorded—the expedition of the English in 1635—we have only to remark, 1. That the demand of one thousand fathoms
of wampum, with no justifiable nor even alleged
reason for it, was an imposition and an insult. 2.
The English should at least have taken time to
see Sassacus himself, his subjects having no more
authority than disposition to treat without him. 3.
The English, with no apparent provocation, not only
insulted but assaulted the Pequots, merely to see if
they would 'show fight ;' and then burnt their towns
and boats ; not a hair of their own heads being meanwhile injured, and Sassacus himself being still absent.

With such inducement, the chieftain began a war
of extermination ; and then indeed it became necessary that one of the two nations at issue should be
completely disabled.   No civilized reader entertains a
doubt as to the result which, under such an alternative, was most to be desired.   But he may nevertheless have his opinion, respecting the moral propriety

as well as the state policy of the measures whi
brought on that horrible necessity. Let the whole
truth, then, be exposed. If it shall be found, (as w3
believe it must be,) that under the influence of strong
and sincere though fatal excitement, a rashness of
the civilized party was the ultimate cause of the ruin
of the savage, let that injustice be acknowledged,
though it should be with shame and with tears.
Let it be atoned for, as far as it may be—in the only
way now possible—by the candid judgment of posterity and history, upon the merits and the misfortunes of both.

I — X

CHAPTER XIV.

The Pequot territory claimed by UNCAS—His tribe, family,
and early history—Services in the Pequot expedition re
warded by the English—Effect of their favor—His contest
with Miantonomo, and result—Subsequent wars and quarrels
with various tribes and chiefs—Assistance rendered him by
the English—Complaints brought against him to them—His
Christianity considered — His morality — Evidence of his
fraud, falsehood, violence, tyranny, ambition—His services,
and those of his tribe to the English—Manner in which he
met the accusations made against him—Cunning and servility
—His treatment of neighboring sachems—Various negotiations with the English —His death—Fate of his tribe.

ON the conquest of the Pequots, the whole of their
territory, about thirty miles square, was claimed by the
Mohegans. The best opinion is, that this tribe was
originally a part of the Pequot nation ; and that their
subsequent name was derived from the place of their
subsequent residence. The first chief sachem of
the Mohegans personally known to the English, was
UNCAS,* who was a Pequot by birth, and of the royal
line, both by his father and mother. His wife was
a daughter of TATOBAM, one of the Pequot sachems.
Probably he had been himself a war-captain under
Sassacus. But when the English began their settlements in Connecticut, he was in a state of rebellion
against him, in consequence of some misunderstand-
ing between them, for which either he had expatriated
himself, or Sassacus had expelled him from his dominions. At this time, his influence was inconsiderable ; but his great address and ambition soon made
him the leading Sagamore of the Mohegans, as they

---

* ONKOS.   *Mason's Pequot Expedition.*
UNCASS.   *Wolcott.*
OKACE.   *Roger Williams.*
ONKUS and OKOKO.   *Winthrop.*
UNCUS, UNQUAS, UNKOWAH, &c.   *Hazard.*

afterwards made that tribe the leading one in Connecticut.—[See Appendix No. I.]

The English were more indebted to Uncas for his zealous services in the Pequot war, than to all the other Indians together, though they at first entertained doubts of his fidelity. Governor Wolcott says:

'' T was here [at Hartford] that Uncass did the army meet,
With many stout Moheagans at his feet.
He to the general [Mason] goes, and doth declare,
He came for our assistance in the war.
  He was that Sagamore, whom great Sassacus' rage
Had hitherto kept under vassalage.
But weary of his great severity,
He now revolts and to the English fly.
With cheerful air our captain him embraces,
And him and his chief men with titles graces;
But over them preserved a jealous eye,
Lest all this might be done in treachery.'

But he was soon convinced, that his suspicions were unjust. The Mohegans embarked with Mason's ninety men, on board a pink or pinnace and a shallop, both which, the water being low in the river, fell aground several times. The Indians disliked this new species of navigation, and especially so much of it as pertained to the flats and sands; and Uncas was still more impatient to recommend himself by an active commencement of the war. He therefore requested, that he and his men might be set on shore, promising to join Mason again at Saybrook. His request was granted; and he not only redeemed his pledge, but, meeting a considerable party of Pequots on the route, he attacked them with great spirit, and killed seven of their number—"which," says Captain Mason, "we looked at as a special Providence; for before we were somewhat doubtful of his fidelity."

This good opinion was daily confirmed by the Sachem's conversation and conduct. "Indeed," our writer elsewhere adds, "he was a great friend and did great service—I shall never forget him." At the commencement of the campaign, the various

Indians who engaged in it, were in high glee. They
gathered into a ring, and one by one made solemn
protestations how gallantly they would demean
themselves, and how many men they would kill.
But Uncas said very little, until Mason inquired of
him what he thought these Indians would do.
"Nothing," answered he, gravely; "The Narraghansetts will leave you to a man. I can only say
for myself, that I never will." And he never did.
The Narraghansetts, who had vaunted themselves on
the example they should be obliged to set the English,
to encourage them in their attack upon the enemy,
soon fell into the back ground, and many of them
returned home.

The English marched on through the woods by
moonlight, until, finding themselves altogether abandoned by these spirited allies, they halted, and sent
messengers to know what had become of them.
At last,

> —'After long waiting for the same,
> Up trusty Uncass and stout Wequash came,
> Of whom the general in strict terms demands,
> Where stands the fort, and how their judgement stands
> About the Enterprise? and what's the cause
> They left their post [the van] against all martial laws '

From the answer given to these questions, it would
appear that, however it might be with the Sachems,
the Indians generally were in horrible fear of the
Pequots. The apology however was cogent; "when
once they were engaged," said they,

> "——'t is hard to get
> *A dispensation from them to retreat.*"

But no such reasoning influenced the resolution
or the fidelity of Uncas. Even after the great success which attended the assault, most of the Indians
deserted, or at least disappeared, in consequence of
an apprehension of falling in with the wandering
Pequots. But Uncas remained steadfast. He also
did active service afterwards, against a band of the

enemy who had settled themselves at Pawcatuck, contrary to the terms of their submission to the English; joining his friend Mason, on that occasion, with one hundred of his men and twenty canoes.

A small harbor in the southern part of the town of Guilford, (in Connecticut) has to this day a name derived from one of his achievements. He and his Mohegans, with a few of the English, having undertaken, when the enemy fled westward, to scour the shores near the sea for the purpose of cutting off stragglers, came up with a Pequot sachem and a few men, not far from this harbor, and pursued them. As the south side of the harbor is formed by a long narrow neck of land, the Pequots went out upon that point, hoping that their pursuers would pass by them. But Uncas, perceiving the stratagem, ordered some of his men to give chase, which the enemy observing, swam over the mouth of the harbor. There they were waylaid, and taken as they landed. A council being held, and the sachem sentenced to death, Uncas himself is said to have shot him with an arrow, cut off his head, and set it up in the crotch of a large oak-tree near the water. The skull remained there many years, and the name of the SACHEM's-HEAD has been ever since attached to the harbor.*

The remuneration to Uncas for the part which he took in this war, was a portion of the Pequot territory, (which he afterwards sold to the English,) and one hundred captives of that tribe; and this, with the honor of having subdued his great Pequot rival, and the reputation of being upon the most flattering and favorable terms of intercourse with the English, made him at once a character of high dignity and of no little influence. Indians began to collect around him from neighboring tribes, and he could now muster four or five hundred warriors. The state of Connecticut treated with him, and made him presents,

---

* History of Guilford, Mass. His. Coll.

and permitted him to exercise dominion and to give deeds of territory, in all respects like an independent and sovereign authority, while he enjoyed at the same time the benefit of their personal patronage and the protection of his tribe from *their* enemies.

In July, 1638, Uncas visited in person the authorities of Massachusetts at Boston—the only visit of mere ceremony which is recorded of him in history. Ostensible ceremony, we should perhaps say; for considering the time, the company, and especially the deportment on that occasion, there can be little doubt that the Sachem had an object in view which lightened the weariness of his long journey.

He came attended by thirty-seven men, and accompanied by Governor Haynes, whom he had called upon by the way. He offered the Governor of Massachusetts a present of twenty fathoms of wampum, which being in open court, the Council thought fit to refuse it, " till he had given satisfaction about the Pequods he kept," &c.* Upon this he appeared much dejected, and even affected to apprehend that his life was in danger. But he was not long at a loss. Evidence was produced which counteracted the main suspicions that rested upon him; and he promised to submit his controversy with the Narraghansetts to English arbitration, and to follow any arrangement they should make as to his Pequots.

The present was now accepted, and about half an hour afterwards, he went to the Governor, and addressed him in the following terms: " *This heart* "— he said, laying his hand on his breast—" *is not mine, but yours. I have no men. They are all yours. Command me any hard thing—I will do it. I will not believe any Indian's words against the English. If any man shall kill an Englishman, I will put him to death were he never so dear to me.* " The Governor gave him a handsome red coat, defrayed the ex-

---

* Winthrop.

penses of his visit, and furnished him with provisions for his return-journey, and a general letter of protection—and so " he departed very joyful."

This transaction throws some light upon what is far the most singular point in the history of the cunning Sachem, viz: that he invariably maintained at once the best terms with his civilized ally and the worst with his Indian .ieighbors. The latter circumstance indeed naturally ensued from the former; on account of which, as well as from other causes partially explained heretofore, the inveterate hatred which had so long existed between the Mohegans and the Narraghansetts, previous to their union with the English for the suppression of the common enemy of all, broke out again soon after the treaty of 1638, and continued from that time forward until the proud Narraghansetts in their turn fell beneath the power of the English. Ostensibly, (as we have seen in the life of Miantonomo,) the war was brought on by the quarrel of Uncas with Sequassen, of whose outrage he complained to the Governor and Court of the Colony. The high estimate he set upon his own dignity appears from his demanding six of Sequassen's men for the murder of his subject. With great difficulty he was finally persuaded to accept of the offender alone. But Sequassen objected even to these terms; for he would do nothing but fight. A con test ensued, and Uncas was the victor.

His subsequent war with Miantonomo, and the proceedings which ensued upon his triumph over that formidable chieftain, have been detailed. From this period. so long as the Narraghansetts remained able to send an army into the field, there was no rest for Uncas or his people, day nor night. Truces and promises were negotiated and passed between the parties by the English; but the power which imposed, or the influence which induced these obligations was scarcely withdrawn, when the unextinguishable flame blazed forth, the more furiously for its brief suspension. The Narraghansetts repeatedly invaded

the Mohegan country in the course of the year 1645,
assaulted Uncas in his own fort, killed and captured
numbers of his men, and finally so pressed him, that
both Connecticut and New Haven were obliged to
send troops to his assistance, as Hartford had done
before, to prevent the enemy from completely sub-
duing him and his country.

In 1648, the Mohawks, Pocomtocks, and other
tribes were induced to take part against him. Nine
years afterwards, he was again beset in his fortress,
and again rescued by the Connecticut forces; and so
late as 1660, the same emergency led to the same
measures. On that occasion, he was besieged until
his provisions were nearly exhausted, and he saw
that, without speedy relief, he and his men must soon
perish by famine or sword. In this crisis, he found
means of communicating his danger to the scouts of
the English, who had been sent out from Saybrook
fort. The case being urgent, one Leffingwell, an
ensign of the garrison, and a bold enterprising man,
loaded a canoe with beef, corn and pease, and paddled
it under cover of the night from Saybrook into the
Thames river, where he had the address to get the
whole into the besieged fort, which stood near the
water's edge. The enemy soon ascertained that
Uncas was relieved, and raised the siege. The
Sachem is said to have rewarded Leffingwell for his
services by a deed of the town of Norwich.*

And not open and honorable arms, (as civilized
foes would consider them,) alone, were employed
against Uncas. One of the Pequots, in 1643, shot
him through the arm, at the instigation, as was generally supposed, of Miantonomo; and the war with
that chieftain was brought on by similar attempts on
the part of Sequassen. The Narraghansett sachems
hired an Indian to assassinate him in 1649, and he
succeeded so far as to give him a wound in the
breast with a sword, which for some time was thought
mortal. Sorcery and poison were also tried

---

* Trumbull.

Attempts were meanwhile made to injure him in the estimation of the English ; his enemies believing, and with good reason, that the withdrawal of their protection would be fatal to him. Sequassen, whose hatred was inveterate, went so far, in 1646, as to form a plan for murdering Governor Haynes and other of the principal inhabitants of Hartford, with the view of having the crime charged upon Uncas. Watohibrough, a Waranoke Indian was engaged to do the business ; and he and Sequassen, after leaving matters in a proper train, were to take refuge among the Mohawks. The price of blood was already paid in girdles of wampum ; but Watohibrough wanted courage to perform what avarice only had led him to undertake. Having altered his mind thus far, he soon bethought himself that the English had given rewards to those who discovered a similar conspiracy on a former occasion ; and concluding they would do so again, he went to Hartford, and disclosed every thing he knew. Messengers were immediately sent to demand the attendance of Sequassen, for the purpose of clearing himself from the charge ; but he thought it more politic to avoid the messengers, and so escaped unpunished.

The English authorities invariably took cognizance of all these and similar proceedings ; and no doubt, but for their interference, and the expectation of it, many more of the same nature would have taken place, and might finally have succeeded. Thus it was the extraordinary good fortune of Uncas to be a favorite with his early allies, from first to last. He complained of no grievance in vain : and as a natural consequence, he uniformly complained upon good occasion, as well as frequently upon bad or none. The Mohansick Sachem, of Long-Island, committed trespasses on his men ; and forthwith " hee desires the commissioners that hee may be righted therein ;" and four persons are immediately appointed to examine the Mohansick Sachem, " and if proof bee cleare to labor to convince him thereof, require satis-

faccon, and in case of reasonable complyance en-
deauor a Composure thereof: but if no satisfaccon
will bee giuen for Iniuries, proceed then to lett him
know *they give the English just cause of offence, and
will bring trouble vpon themselues.*"*

The possibility of his giving false testimony against
his enemies and rivals, seems scarcely to have entered the Commissioners' minds.   Upon rumors of fresh
assaults by the Narraghansetts upon the Long-
Islanders, in 1653, they sent messengers to the former, requiring their attendance at Boston, for the
purpose of compromising the quarrel.   These messengers were farther instructed to notify, not only to
the Long-Islanders, but *to Uncas,* that if they or any
of them had any thing " to enforme charge or propound either in the foremencioned or any other,'
they were to send witnesses accordingly—" and by
Thomas Staunton or otherwise you are to giue notice
to Captaine Mason, *Vncus* &c. *that there may bee noe
fayling for want of Witnesse or Euidence.*"   It is not
wonderful, that Ninigret asked the messengers, on
this occasion, after being told of their errand—" Why
doe the English slight *mee,* and respect the Longe-
Islanders and the Mohegins, seeing all around mee
do love mee and are my frinds ? "†

In 1654, great complaints were made against Uncas
himself.   On that occasion, the same messenger
sent to the Mohegan sachem was sent also to Ninigret ; but although the former was the accused party,
it will be observed, that a peculiar provision was
made to accommodate *him,* while the only one made
in relation to Ninigret's visit was, that " hee may not
bring with him aboue twenty or thirty men ; nor
may Newcome, or as the Indians call him, Mattackist,
come with him whoe last yeare gaue offence att Boston."   It is clear, that the plaintiff in this suit was no
favorite ; and it is further remarkable, that the mes-

---

* *Records of the Colonies :* 1649.
† *Ibid* for 1653.

senger was directed to take the present occasion of reminding him of his old debts and defaults, and (as if to prevent his appearance) requiring satisfaction to be given at the time of his visit. The following are the messengers instructions :

" You are to informe both Vncus and his brother Woweque that the Commissioners haue receiued information of some purpose of theires to invade the Narraghansetts or Ninnigrett; they haue alsoe heard of some differences lately groune betwixt Vncus and his brother and betwixt them and theire men. They are not willing to receive reports without due enquiry; they haue therefore sent for Ninnigrett, the better to secure the longe-Island Indians, and to heare what hee hath to allege against the Mohegens, and compose all other differences. The Commissioners therfore desire and expect that both Vncus and his brother doe forthwith Come to hartford, &c. *You are alsoe to informe both Vncus and his brother* * *ana theire men, that the English doe oune Vncus so longe as hee carrieth himselfe well,* and shall bee loth hee suffer wrong." &c.

Next follow the " Instruccons for John Gilbert and John Baily *whoe were sent to continue att Vncus his fortt during his absence.*

" You shall Repaire to Mohegen, and acquaint Vncus and all other Indians that you are to reside att his fortt by the Commisioners of all the Collonies, to the Intent that Vncus and all others may know the realitie of the English to continnew his frinds whiles hee continueth faithfull to the English; and because the Commissioners have now sent for Vncus to speak with him concerning some affaires of concernment relating to himselfe Ninnigrett and Woweque, and being Informed some sturrs may arise in his absence to his prejudice you shall vse youer Indeauors to keep all things quiett and informe the

---

* WOWEQUE, a very troublesome fellow, elsewhere noticed under some ten or fifteen other names.

Indians that such attempts wil bee offenciue to the Englisł." &c.

No fears seem to have been entertained, that 'sturrs' would arise in the Niantick country during Ninigret's absence, although the message itself was founded upon the rumor of an attack to be made upon *him* by the other party. So, when Captain Mason had been commissioned to march against Ninigret with an armed force, on a former occasion, he was ordered "to advise particularly that Vncus Fort be secured when any strength is sent forth against the enemie, lest hee and wee recieue more damage by some Indian stratageme than the enemie." A multitude of other decisions and directions might be cited to the same purpose.

Uncas was in less favor with the English towards the latter part of his life than formerly, for reasons which will soon be mentioned. He did not however come to an open rupture with them at any time; and his subjects, though frequently insolent, were never hostile. On the contrary, they assisted their ally on many occasions, the Commissioners never hesitating to notify them when their services would be acceptable, and *they* never hesitating to attend a summons. For this zeal, directed as it invariably was against their Indian neighbors, and generally their old enemies, it would be easy to suggest more reasons than one. They thought themselves fortunate in these secure and sanctioned opportunities of revenge and plunder, even had they not also been richly repaid by the protection of the English, reciprocated to them in all emergencies of their own. Their last services during the life of Uncas were during Philip's war, when a party of them was commanded by Onecho, a son of Uncas, and by other sachems. The father was then too old a man to endure much more labor and weariness

It has been stated, that Uncas was at least convinced of the truth of Christianity, and that he died in the faith; but we fear this information can hardly be relied upon. The only proof of it we have seen is derived from the following anecdote.

In the summer of 1676, a great drought prevailed throughout New England, which was extremely severe in the Mohegan country. The corn was dried up in August, and the fruit and leaves fell from the trees, as in autumn. The Indians were alarmed, but knew not what to do. According to custom, they applied to their Powahs to intercede with the Great Spirit for rain, after their manner; but these men labored to no purpose. They then went to the English settlement at Norwich, and Uncas went with them. He told Mr. Fitch, the clergyman at that place, that it was a hard case with them—the Powahs could do them no service—they must apply to the English God. Mr. Fitch appointed a fast-day at these and other suggestions. The weather on that occasion proved to be clear; but about sunset, at the close of the religious services, some clouds arose. The next day also was cloudy. Uncas now went to the house of Mr. Fitch, with many Indians, and again lamented the great want of rain. "If God shall send it," said Mr. Fitch, "will you not attribute it to your Powahs? "No," answered the sachem; "we have done our utmost, but all in vain." The clergyman then told him, that if he would make this declaration before the Indians, they should see what God would do for them. Uncas then made a speech to the Indians, confessing with particular emphasis, that if God should grant this favor, it could not be in consequence of their powawing, but must be ascribed to the clergyman's prayers. Of the sequel we only know, that upon the day following there was so copious a rain that the river rose more than two feet.

This testimony proves but little. On the other hand, Mr. Fitch himself in a letter cited by Gookin gives a very clear opinion as follows:

"—Since God hath called me to labor in this work among the Indians nearer to me, the first of my time

was spent among them at Moheek, where Unkas,
and his son, and Wanuho are sachems.   These a
first carried it teachably and tractably ; until at length
the sachems did discern that religion would not con
sist with a mere receiving, and that practical religion will throw down their heathenish idols, and the
sachems' tyrannical authority.   Discerning this, they
did not only go away, but drew off their people and
would not suffer them to give so much as an outward attendance to the ministry of the word of
God. * *   At this time UNKAS and his sons seem as
if they would come on again.   *But it is no other but
in envy against these* [the converts] *and to promote
some present self-design.*"

When Mr. Gookin, with the Apostle Elliot, visited
the towns of the Massachusetts Praying Indians, in
1674, he says, that on one occasion, a large part of
the night was spent at Sagamore's wigwam, in com
pany with the principal Indians then at the settlement, in prayer, singing psalms and exhortation.
There was one person present, who sat mute during
all these exercises.   At length he arose and said, that
he was an agent for Uncas, the Mohegan sachem, and
that in his name he challenged a right to, and dominion over this people of Wabquissit.*   "Uncas is not
well pleased," added he, "that the English should
pass over Mohegan river, to call *his* Indians to pray
to God."   Mr. Gookin replied, that Wabquissit was
within the Massachusetts jurisdiction, and that no
harm need be feared at all events ; the English only
wished to bring the Indians to the knowledge of
Christ, and to suppress among them the sins of drunk-
enness, idolatry, powowing, witchcraft, murder, and
the like.

This was plainly a lecture meant for the benefit
of Uncas himself, and his agent was specially requested to inform him of the answer made to his protest.

---

* The South-East corner of Woodstock, and still called
Wabequasset.   It was in truth, as it still is, part of Connecticut, though claimed by Massachusetts, as well as by Uncas.

In another connexion, we find Mr. Gookin's opinion expressed to the same effect, without the same circumlocution. "I am apt to fear," is his language,* "that a great obstruction unto his [Mr. Fitch's] labors, is in the sachem of those Indians, whose name is Unkas; an old wicked and wilful man; a drunkard, and otherwise very vicious; who hath always been an opposer and underminer of praying ⟨ ⟩od—some hints whereof I have given in the narrative of my journey to Wabquissit, before mentioned." The Sachem once took the trouble to visit Hartford for the express purpose of complaining to the Colonial authorities of the attempts made to convert his subjects to Christianity.

His piety, then, will hardly bear rigid examination. Whether his morality was quite so objectionable as Mr. Gookin supposed, or whether that good man was unduly prejudiced against him for his opposition to the ministry, may not be easily decided. There is but too much reason for believing, however, that there was great truth in most of the charges, and a most pertinent application for the lecture referred to above. The United Commissioners themselves seem to pay but a sorry compliment to his previous habits when, so late as 1672, they directed a letter to be written to him, "to incurrage him to attende on the Minnestrey."

What is more to the purpose, we find a complaint entered against him before them, in 1647, by one of his Pequot subjects, named Obechiquod. The grievance was, that Uncas had taken possession of and detained the man's wife; and though Foxon, the deputy of the Mohegan sachem, ingeniously argued, that this accident had happened only in consequence of Obechiquod's having unlawfully withdrawn from the jurisdiction of Uncas, and left his wife behind him, to be of course appropriated, according to Indian law, by any other person who desired such a connex-

---

* His. Coll. Chapter X.

ion; yet even the Commissioners felt themselves obliged, upon a hearing of the whole case, to express their abhorrence "of that lustfull adulterous carriage of Vncus." He was adjudged to restore the complainant's wife, and allow the husband to live where he chose, on condition of his assisting Uncas in his wars whenever the English desired. He was discharged from another accusation of the same nature made by Sanops, a Connecticut Indian, at the same time—the evidence not being sufficient to convict him.

The proofs of fraud and falsehood are still more abundant. Miantonomo hesitated not to accuse him of foul play, even in the Pequot war; and the account given by Roger Williams of the reports which he rendered in to the English authorities, of the Pequot captives who fell into his hands, goes very far to establish the charge. Six, whom he had taken at one time, he represented to be Mohegans, although an Indian who gave information of the fact to Mr. Williams, knew them as Pequots personally, and perfectly well, and mentioned the names of all.

His conduct at the Hartford conference in 1637, has already been the subject of comment. Some time after Miantonomo's arrival, who had been delayed by his machinations, he sent in messengers to the court that he was *lame*, and could not visit them. Governor Haynes observed, that this was a lame excuse, at best, and immediately despatched a cogent request for him to attend without fail or delay. He came at length, and the Governor then accused him of the flagrant outrages which he and his subjects had committed on the Narraghansetts. Some altercation ensued between the rival chieftains, but, by the persuasion of the English, they were finally induced to shake hands. Miantonomo then cordially invited Uncas to sup with him, his men having just killed some venison: but he would not consent. The sachems were now called upon to make returns of their Pequot prisoners. Mianto-

nomo made his promptly, and no fault was found.
" Okace [Uncas] was desired to give in the names
of his. He answered, that he knew not their names.
He said there were forty on Long-Island; and that
Juanémo [*alias* Janemoh] and three Nayantaquit
Sachims had Pequts, and that he himself had but
twenty. Thomas Stanton [Interpreter] told him
and the magistrates, that he dealt very falsely : and it
was affirmed by others, that he fetched thirty or forty from Long-Island at one time. *Then he acknowledged that he had thirty*, but the names he could not
give. It pleased the magistrates to request me to
send to Nayantaquit, that the names of the Pequts
might be sent to Cunnihticut; as also to give Okace
ten days to bring in the number and names of his
Pequts and their runaways, Mr. Haynes threatening
also (in case of failing) to fetch them."* This transaction speaks clearly enough for itself.

The Sachem's treatment of the Pequots surrendered to him on this occasion, does him little more
credit. In 1647, ten years after the conquest, these
unfortunate people sent in a complaint to the commissioners, in which they stated that Uncas had
drawn wampum from them unjustly, on all manner
of pretexts, and without any pretext. When his
child had died, for example, he made, or pretended
to make, a present to his wife, and ordered the Pequots to do the same. Frightened by his threats,
they collected one hundred fathoms of wampum, and
gave it as directed. Uncas appeared to be pleased,
and promised to treat them from that time forward
as his own ancient subjects. But only a few days
afterwards, his brother (Woweque) came and told
them, that Uncas and his Council had determined to
kill some of them. They now thought it necessary
to appeal to the English protection, and they set
about collecting a quantity of wampum to be sent
in to Connecticut with that view. Uncas received

---

* Letters of Williams in *Mass. His. Coll. Third Series*

I.—Y

a hint of their movements; and the next morning
he came to the fort where they were, with a body
of warriors, armed, and apparently bent upon killing
some of their number. They however escaped safe
to Connecticut. It was farther alleged, that they
had given Uncas wampum forty times. Twenty-
five times they had sent it by him to the English,
in payment of tribute; but they knew not that any
part of it was delivered.—Also, that Uncas favored
the Mohegans to *their* prejudice. If they won any
thing of one of them in play, it could never be collected.—Also, that he had cut all their fishing nets
for not aiding him—as they were not bound to do—
in certain of his forays against the Indians of Long
Island.

The reply of Foxon to these charges—no doubt
by instruction from his master—is full of his usual
ingenuity. 1. As to the wampum—" he belieueth
the Pequats haue for tribute and vpon other occasions at sundry times paid wampam to Vncus, but
denyeth that they in particular had giuen him any
for the English; but the Moyhegens and they had
sometimes joyned togeither to giue in wampam,
which had been sent as a presente twice into the
Mattachusets, and sometimes to Mr. Haynes at
Hartford, but he thinckes the nomber of twenty-fiue
times to be altogeither false."

2. " He concieues that the Pequats being an vnder
people might haue some wrong from the Mohegens
in play and durst not presse for their right, but
denyeth that Vncus had any hand therein."

3. " He acknowledgeth that the Pequats did bring
in 100 fathome of wampam at the death of Vncus
child, and were promised favoure as is expressed,
but the latter was only a treacherous plott of Vncus
brother perswading the Pequats to withdraw from
Vncus into theire oune Country, and there he would
come vnto them, and to prouoke them thereunto he
tould them (though falsly) that Vncus had determined to kill some of them."

4. " Though Vncus at first apprehended noe in-
convenience in such a present to the English, yet
being after informed it was a plott on a fruite of
crooked counsell giuen them by Tassaquanott, Sassacus his brother, who had suggested vnto them that
most of the cheife Sachems were cutt off, Vncus to
them but a stranger, why should they serue or giue
wampam to him, herewith Vncus was justly offended."

5. " He had heard some of the Mohegans tooke
fish from them, but knoweth not that hee cutt theire
netts, though he cannot deny it."

The Commissioners decreed, that the Pequots
should return to the dominion of Uncas, who should
recieve them without charge or revenge for the manner in which they deserted him ; and on the other
hand, that he should himself be reproved for his
tyranny, and seriously informed, that the English
would not support him " in any unlawfull, much less
treacherous and outrageous courses."

Unquestionably, this 'brother' of Uncas was quite
as troublesome to himself as he was to the white
people. Mr. Winthrop complained, at this very
meeting, that he had fallen upon the Nopnet Indians
entirely without provocation, with one hundred and
thirty Mohegans, and carried off wampum, copper
kettles, great hempen baskets, bear-skins, deer-skins
and many other things to a great value. These facts
were admitted by Foxon, who also asserted that
Uncas had no part either in the assault or the spoil,
he being at New Haven when the affair happened.
Other complaints being brought forward and proved,
the Commissioners directed that Uncas should either
disown his brother entirely, or else regulate him in
a more suitable manner for the future. This was
correct. It is clear that he either instigated these
flagrant outrages, or at least connived at them by
sufferance. He was able to prevent them, as far as
he thought proper.

It would be tedious, though not wholly without
matter of amusement, to detail at large all the accu-

sations brought against the Mohegan Sachem by various complainants at various times. Massachusetts and Connecticut arraigned him. The English settlements nearest to him accused him of insolence and violent assaults. The Mohawks quarrelled with his tribe. The Narraghansetts and Nianticks charged him repeatedly with inroads and insults upon them. Necwash Cooke, a Pequot under English protection, complained of being plundered with open force. Sanops, an Indian mentioned heretofore, was robbed of his corn and beans, (perhaps hardly less valuable to him than his *wife*.) Mr. Winthrop stated, in behalf of a Long Island Sachem, that *he* had sent sixty fathoms of wampum to the Governor of Massachusetts by Uncas; and though he made the bearer himself a present of twenty at the same time, he had embezzled the whole.

Again, one Apumps "complained against Vncus, that about sixe weekes since hee tooke sixe of his people at Quinnapauge, killed one, and wounded another."

"Pomham [a Massacusetts Sachem] appearing before the Commissioners [at the same meeting] said that about a month agone Vncus or some of his men killed a man and two wemen at Cawesett, the one of them belonging to himselfe, the other vnto Tupayamen, both without provocation."

"Wee desire the English Sachims"—wrote the Pocomptocks in answer to an English message of inquiry — "not to perswade vs to a peace with Vncus; for though hee promiseth much yett will hee performe nothinge. We have experience of his falcenes" &c.

In 1656, he, or his brother, invaded the Norwootucks; and he even joined arms with Ninnigret against a Sachem of Long Island. About two years before this, he had taken occasion to push his conquests beyond the river Connecticut by quarrelling and then fighting with Arrhamámet, Sachem of Mussaúco (now Simsbury, near Hartford.) He sent one of his warriors to take and burn a wigwam in the outskirts of the village, killing a few of the inhabitants, and then leaving marks *of the Mohawks.* His orders were executed, and the stratagem took effect. Arrhamámet ascribed the mischief to the Mohawks, and, burning with resentment, fitted out a war-party, and went in pursuit of them to the Northwest. Uncas thus gained time to equip his men, and fall upon the enemy's town in his absence. Arrhamámet was subjugated and his tribe, the Podunks, were ever afterwards tributary to Uncas.

The season before this, Meeksaw [probably Mexham] a Narraghansett Sachem, complained that Uncas had killed one of his men, and also that he had " afronted him by abusiuely naming and jeering his dead ancestors, and sending him a challenge this summer to fight." The Commissioners inquired of Foxon the truth of the charge, "and hee not giuing a satisfactory answare, they tooke the matter into consideration." &c. Soon afterwards the same person complained " of a gun taken from a Narraghansett Indian by Vncus his son, which some of Vncus his men acknowlidged to bee true." The Commissioners' judgment in this case was, substantially, that although Mexham had not sufficient proof, yet, knowing that Uncas out of his pride and folly was apt to insult people, they would send him a suitable reprimand. In some other cases, they went so far as to adjudge, and perhaps enforce restitution.

Not to examine the records farther, it is only necessary to observe, that though all these accusations were not strictly correct, many of them, and many others, were proved; and perhaps a tithe of the truth never appeared after all. Some of the sufferers were too proud to complain. Others had no evidence to offer but their own. Many supposed it impracticable to obtain a fair hearing or decision of the Commissioners, against a chieftain regarded as their ward; and many more were too much irritated not

to right themselves in a more customary and summary manner upon the spot.

The secret source of this extraordinary series of
wars, forays, challenges, robberies and adulteries, like
that of the Sachem's inveterate opposition to Christianity, was in his lawless appetites and passions;
but especially an inordinate and uncontrolled ambition. It might be with justice that Miantonomo was
accused of a design to make himself UNIVERSAL
SAGAMORE—as the phrase was—of New England.
But the Naraghansett took no measures for the
attainment of his object which were in his own view
either mean or malicious. He neither kept back part
of the captives, nor embezzled the tribute which
they deposited in his hands, nor plundered his
neighbors in time of peace, nor unduly availed himself of foreign assistance for the annihilation of his
rivals. He sent a few of his men, it is true, to aid
in the Pequot expedition—or rather did not, perhaps
could not prevent them from going—but these were
only two hundred, out of two thousand; and he
neither headed them himself, like Uncas, nor even
engaged personally at all in the contest. Indeed,
he at most only continued, on this occasion, the hostilities which had existed between the two nations
for a long series of years; and all historians admit,
that he was very near joining Sassacus at one time
against the English themselves. Uncas, on the other
hand, made the most of the opportunity, to revenge
himself upon Sassacus, and to exalt his reputation
and power upon the wreck of the Pequots.

Miantonomo became in his turn a victim to the
same over-reaching spirit. He began the war, indeed—or rather the campaign—and Uncas, on the
other hand, was encouraged in *his* course by his
allies;—but a magnanimous soul would never have
permitted either circumstance to affect the treatment
of a sovereign like himself, who had fallen into his
hands by the chances of battle.

Ninigret next became the grand object of his scrutiny. He went forward as often as practicable to prejudice the character of that chieftain in the eyes of the English, as well as to reduce his resources by direct attacks. No man was so zealous as he in furnishing evidence—such as it was—to convict him of a conspiracy with the Dutch against the colonies; and though he is understood to have been ostensibly at peace with him at that period, he carried his interference to such a length as to lay wait and intercept a Niantick canoe which, as he pretended to suspect, was laden with certain palpable evidences of the hostile coalition. So we find him falling upon Mexham, Necwash, Cooke, Woosamequin, and last of all, King Philip. No doubt, he had sagacity enough to perceive, that such a course must prove unfavorable, if not fatal to his race; but patriotism, honor, friendship, generosity, truth, every nobler feeling of his nature was merged in a barbarous, ferocious ambition.

There is a curious illustration of this weakness upon record:—" Vncas complained that SEQUASSON som yeares sence as is well knoune began hostile actes vpon him to the desturbance of the publicke peace. Whervpon hee was ocationed to fight and in the Issue ouercame him and conquared his Country, which though hee gaue to the English and did not oppose the fauor they were pleased to shew him in sparing his life, *yet hee cannot but look vpon himselfe as wronged, in that Sequasson, as hee is informed, is set up and endeauoured to bee made a great Sachem,* notwithstanding hee hath refused to pay an acknouledgment of Wampam to him according to engagements."

Of this acknowledgement, no proof appears but the Sachem's own assertion; and whether true or not, no real cause of complaint can be gathered from the whole context. The Commissioners, with their usual complaisance, " disclaimed any Endeauors of theirs *to make Sequasson great,* and are ignorant of

what hee afeirmes concerning the other [acknowl
edgement] yet recommended it to the Gouernment
of Conecticot to examine the case, and tc provide
vpon due proofe Vncas may be owned in what may
be just and equall, and Mr. Ludlow was entreated
to promote the same." This passage will be found
in the Records for 1651. No subsequent mention
is made of the suit.

It might be a subject of some speculation, what
were the causes of the extraordinary partiality of
the English for Uncas; and especially what were
the means whereby he counteracted the strong current of reproach which set against him from all other
quarters. Different opinions have been entertained
upon this point. We suppose, however, the Commissioners considered it good policy, to select some
one among the principal uncivilized and unsubject-
ed Indian chiefs, to be made a channel of intercourse
and influence with and over all. This one would
naturally be the most ambitious, and at the same
time least scrupulous of the number. Such was
Uncas; and hence it was, that with his shrewdness,
he found no difficulty in maintaining a tolerably
good understanding with them under all circumstances. The 'Proud Ninigret' disdained the
English interference. Massassoit protected rather
than courted them. Sassacus fought them at the
first provocation. Philip hated them and kept aloof:
and Miantonomo, though he met them and treated
them as friends, yet forgot not a soul of his own,
more sovereign than his royal blood. But Uncas
was neither more nor less than their humble servant.
He fought for them, and gave evidence for them,
with about the same alacrity, and the same indiffer-
ence as to subject or occasion, antagonist or defend-
ant.

Whenever complaints were made against himself,
he of course had resources for defence. There was
something in the testimony he could generally
bring forward in his favor; and still more in the in-

genuity of his explanations, or the humility of his acknowledgements and apologies. Other Sachems, irritated by suspicion and accusation, frequently committed themselves in reality by rash speeches and rude acts. But Uncas never lost sight of his interest in his pride.

The pliability of Indian evidence, and the manœuvres of Indian politicians, appear singularly in the case of Necwash Cooke. Uncas was at New Haven, attending a meeting of the Commissioners, in 1646, when one William Morton came forward, and charged him with having hired Wampushet, a Pequot Powah then present, "by himselfe or some other with a hatchet to wounde another Indian *and lay it vpon Neckwash Cooke.*" The consideration for the bargain was said to be fifteen fathoms of wampum, and the Indian was assaulted according to the terms. After some inquiry into the evidence, Wampushet himself was brought upon the stand, and questioned by the English interpreter. Much to the astonishment of Mr. Morton, and of the Pequots who came into court with him, he cleared Uncas and cast the plot upon Cooke himself, and Robin, Mr. Winthrop's Indian; and though the other two Pequots, whereof one was Robin's brother, were much offended, "and after [afterwards] *said* Uncas had hired him to withdrawe and alter his chardge, yet hee persisted and said Necwash Cooke and Robin had giuen him a payre of breeches and promised him twenty-five fadome of wampam to cast the plott vpon Uncas."

As to the main allegation in Cooke's case, which *was* proved, the Sachem acknowledged some miscarriages or misdemeanors in vindicating what he called his right, so near the English plantations,—but alleged provocation. Then follows the sentence.

1. That it was an error to quarrel with Cooke to the public disturbance, without consent of the English.

2. That to do it near an English plantation was worse still; and the Commissioners required him to

10—19

acknowledge his fault to that plantation, (as he did to themselves) and by promise to secure them from any such disturbance for the future.

For Uncas it was an easy matter to make such satis-faction. But as if it was thought too harsh by those who decreed it, they took occasion at the same time to sweeten the dispensation with promises of protec-tion and professions of respect. After all, so strong was the additional testimony advanced against him on the same matters, at the next session, that they were induced to modify their decision as follows:—"All which being duly considered the insolency and outrage of Vncus and his men appeared much more heinous than the complaints at Newhaven the last yeere imported. The Commissioners (having the last yeere ordered that Vncus should acknowledge his fault to the English plantation, which they heare he performed in Captain Mason's presence) thought fitt now to add that vpon the return of the Pequots to his subjection Vncus foorthwith pay into the hands of Mr. Jo. Winthrop, to be by him divided to the English and ould Pequots and other innocent Indians, towards the repaire of theire losses in pro-portion as he shall finde cause, one hundred fathome of wampam."

We conclude these expositions with a literal copy from Hazard, of one of the last formal messages of complaint sent by the Commissioners to Uncas, together with his answer. The date is 1661:

"Vncus

We have Receiued Information and Complaint from the Generall Court of Massachusetts of youer hostile Invading of Wosamequin and the Indians of Quabakutt whoe are and longe haue bine Subjects to the English killing some and Carrying away others captiues spoyling theire goods to the vallue of 33lb. as they alledge, and all this contrary to youer couenant and promise to the Comissioners seuerall times Renewed. not to make warr against any of our

Tributaries without the allowance of the Comissioners wee alsoe vnderstand that the Generall Court of
Massachusetts whose subjects the said Indians are,
haue formerly signified theire offence vnto you Requiring the Returne of youer Captiues and Satisfaction for the wronge you haue done to which you
haue not returned any answare *which seemes to bee
an Insolent and proud carriage of youers* wee cannot
but wonder att it and must beare witnes against it
and doe heerby will and require you forthwith to
returne the said Captiues with due Satisfaction for
other wrongs done them or to make out sufficient
grounds and Reesons for youer Invading the said
Indians the which you are speedily to send to the
Governor of the Massachusetts and if it appeer they
haue done you any wronge vpon due proofe wee
shall take care that they may make you satisfaction
if you shall neglect to obserue our order and Injunc-
tion herein contained ; wee must leaue the Massachusetts to Right themselues as formerly signifyed
vnto you : in which case wee must oune and if need
bee assist our Confederates ;

The Comisioners of the Vnited Collonies ;"
(Signed)
SAMUEL WILLIS	THOMAS PRENCE *Presedent*
Plymouth the 13th.	WILLIAME LEETE SIMON BRADSTREET
of September 1661.	BENJAMIN FEN	DANIEL DENISON
THOMAS SOUTHWORTH."

Then follows the answer given in on behalf of
Uncas by Major Mason. As nothing more is heard
of the affair, it may be presumed that the reasons
alleged were considered sufficient.

"Whereas there was a warrant sent from the
Court of Boston dated in May last to Vncus wherein
it was declared upon the Complaint of Wosamequen
that the said Vncus had offered a great violence to
theire Subjects at quabauk killing some and taking
others captiue ; which warrant came not to Vncus
aboue 20 daies before these presents whoe being summoned by Major John Mason in the full scope of the

said warrant wherin hee was chardged if hee did not
Returne the Captiues and thirty-three pounds damage then the Massachusetts would Recouer it by
force of armes which to him was very grieuous;
*professing hee was altogether ignorant they were sub-
jects belonging to the Massachusetts* and further said
they were none of Wesamequen's men but belonging to Onopequin his deadly enemie whoe was there
borne; one of the men then taken was his oune
Cousin, who had formerly fought against him in his
oune person; and yett sett him at libertie and further
saith that all the Captiues were sent home alsoe that
Wesamequin's son and diuers of his men had fought
against him diuers times this hee desired might bee
returned as his answare to the Commissioners."

Concessions of this nature it was—which no other
Indian Sachem of equal power ever submitted to—
that went farther than anything else to keep Uncas
secure in the English favor. His actual services,
which were considerable, have been alluded to. His
tribe were an out-guard for the settlements in Connecticut. After selling the town of Norwich, that
place being first colonized in a period of general excitement and hostility among the tribes, the Mohegans
kept out spies and runners to give the inhabitants
intelligence of their enemies' movements, and were
a continual defence against them. In times of greater
danger, they often moved, and pitched their wigwams
near the town. On one occasion, a hostile party of
savages approached the outskirts, on the Sabbath,
with a design to make a descent upon the village;
but viewing it from an eminence, and seeing the Mohegan huts, they were intimidated, and retreated
without doing the least damage.

The sale just mentioned was but one of a large
number with which Uncas was always ready to
oblige his civilized friends, and which constituted
another claim to their good will. In 1648, on receiving presents to his satisfaction, he conveyed to the
Governor and Magistrates of the English on Con

necticut river all his lands, called by whatever name, reserving only the ground then planted by him for himself and his tribe. In 1641, he granted to Henry Whitefield and others, certain lands near Guilford, in consideration of four coats, two kettles, four fathoms of wampum, four hatchets, and three hoes. In 1659, he granted all his lands, with all his corn, to his old comrade and friend, Major John Mason, who the next year surrendered it to the Colony of Connecticut. Trumbull says, that the individual towns in this great tract were very generally purchased, either of him or his successors, a second or third time.

It is remarkable, that a very late mention made of Uncas in history, casts an imputation upon his friendship for the English. " It is suggested by them who know him best "—says Hubbard in his Narrative— " that in his heart he is no better affected to the English, or their religion, than the rest of his countrymen, and that it hath been his own advantage hath led him to be this time," &c. This was written in 1677. Only two years previous, at the commencement of Philip's war, it was reported to governor Winslow of Plymouth, that the Mohegan Sachem had sent twenty men to join his Pokanoket brother, with a message that if Philip would send him six English heads, all the Indians in *his* territories would go for him.* Uncas is last heard of in 1680, when he must have been a very old man, though still likely, we are told, to survive all his enemies.†

The best comment on the Sachem's husbandry of his own interest is perhaps, after all, in the fact that a remnant of his tribe exists to this day, (on a reservation of about three thousand acres of land,) in the neighborhood of Norwich; and are the only natives yet lingering within the limits of the state. The last sachem of the tribe was Isaiah Uncas, once a pupil in the famous school of Dr. Wheelock, at Lebanon.

---

* *Sixth Vol. Mass. Coll. First Series.*
† Hubbard's General History.

The following epitaph, copied by President Stiles from a grave-stone in the old Indian burial-ground at Mohegan, indicates the end of the genealogy :

Here lies the body of SUNSEETO,
Own son to Uncas, grandson to ONEKO,
Who were the famous sachems of MOHEAGAN;
But now they are all dead, I think it is WERHEEGEN *

---

* The Mohegan term for *All is well* or *Good-news.*   Oneko, or Onecho, is the same who commanded in Philip's war

CHAPTER XV

.rdians who submitted to Massachusetts—The Gortonists—
Pomham, Sachem of Shaomet, and Saconoco complain of
them—Submit to the Government—Their examination and
entertainment—Policy of Massachusetts in the case of Pom-
nam—He and Saconoco much harassed by their neighbors
—Subsequent history—Pomham takes part in Philip's war
and is killed—Canonchet, son of Miantonomo—His agreement of October, 1675—Weetamore, Squaw-Sachem of
Pocasset—Canonchet's career during Philip's war—Particulars of his surprisal and death—His character—Anecdotes
—His reputation with the English—Defence of his conduct

Among a considerable number of chieftains who
submitted to the Massachusetts Government, were
several whose territory was without their jurisdiction, and in some cases within that of other Govern-
ments. The most notorious case of this kind is
connected with that much-discussed transaction in
which the notorious Gorton and his associates were
engaged; and by which they brought themselves into
a disagreeable collision with civil and martial authorities in all directions.

To explain that affair very briefly,—Gorton, having
become obnoxious as the founder of a new religious
sect, left the Massachusetts jurisdiction for Plymouth.
Here he met with much the same treatment. He
was whipped for disturbing the Church, and required
to find sureties for his good behavior; which not
being able to do, he either removed or was driven to
Rhode Island. There he treated the Court with contempt, and by order of Governor Coddington was
imprisoned and again whipped. He then took refuge in Providence, where Roger Williams, though
he disliked his principles, yet gave him shelter. But
he had hardly located himself, and begun to gather
a company of disciples around him, when the neigh
boring English settlers complained of him to *Massa-*

chusetts, under the apprehension that he was about
to supplant their own possessions by purchasing the
Patuxet territory from the Narragansett original
owners.   Massachusetts issued a warrant to the
Providence people to submit to *their* jurisdiction
Gorton denied their authority to interfere with him
or his company, where they now were. and signified
this opinion in a contemptuous letter.

But, perhaps for the sake of being still farther
out of the reach of Massachusetts, or from discord
among themselves, the Gortonists soon removed
to a tract of land called by the Indians Shaomet
or Showamet, (since Warwick in Rhode Island,)
having previously purchased it of Miantonomo, for
the consideration of one hundred and forty-four
fathoms of wampum, " with the free and joint consent, [as the deed itself is expressed] of the present
inhabitants, being natives." The instrument was
dated January 12, 1642-3, and was subscribed with a
bow and arrow as the mark of the grantor, and of a
hatchet, a gun, &c., as the marks of " the Sachem of
Shaomet, POMHAM," and other Indians.   Possession
was given upon the premises, at the same time.

From this moment, Pomham,—who, though he
signed the deed of conveyance, and was offered a
share of the consideration, (which he would not
accept,) affected to consider himself aggrieved,—
neither gave rest to his neighbors, nor found any for
himself.   Whether, according to the relation which
existed between himself and Miantonomo, and the
customary degree of subjection attached to it, he had
reason to complain of that chieftain in the present
case, cannot well be decided.   But it may be safely
said, that the part soon afterwards taken by Massachusetts, was at least an unusual stretch of authority,
however it might correspond with the general policy
of that government wherever the formidable Narraghansett Sachem was concerned.

Whether at his own suggestion or that of others,
Pomham, and SACONOCO, a Sachem equally interest-

ed in the land, but otherwise of no note in history, went to Boston a few months after the sale, and by an interpreter, made complaint of the manœuvres of the Gortonists whereby, as they alleged, Miantonomo had been induced to compel them to an arbitrary disposal of their territory. They further desired to be received under the protection of Massachusetts, and withal brought a small present of wampum. The matter being referred to the next Court, and Gorton and Miantonomo notified to attend, the latter made his appearance. He was required to prove the interest he had claimed in the Shaomet Sachems and territory, but it is said he could prove none; and upon the testimony of Cutchamequin and other Indians who were present, it appeared that the Shaomet chiefs were not tributary to the Narraghansett, though they sometimes made him presents,—a mark of deference and not of subjection. Upon this an order was passed, authorizing the Governor and certain magistrates to treat with the applicants at their discretion.*

These Commissioners soon after conferred with the Sachems; and, giving them to understand upon what terms they should be received, "they found them very pliable to all." So, indeed, it might be inferred from the answers made by the Sachems to the requisitions touching the ten commandments. The servility which some of them indicate—as represented in the Commissioners' report, at least,—is hardly redeemed by the shrewd simplicity of others.

Being asked if they would worship the true God, and not blaspheme him, they waived the first clause, and replied thus to the latter. " We desire to speak reverently of the Englishman's God, and not to speak evil, because we see Englishman's God doth better for them than other Gods do for others."

As to 'swearing falsely,' they replied, that they never knew what swearing was, or what an oath

---

* Winthrop's Journal, Vol. II.

was. As to working unnecessarily on the Christian Sabbath,—"It is a small thing," answered they, "for us to rest on that day, *for we have not much to do any day, and therefore we will forbear on that day.*"

In regard to honoring parents and seniors, they said, "It is our custom to do so, for when if we complain to the Governor of the Massachusetts that we have wrong, if they tell us *we lie*, we shall patiently bear it." The following articles are also part of the report :

5. Not to kill any man but upon just cause and good authority, &c. *Answer*. It is good, and we desire to do so.

6. Not to commit fornication, stealing &c. *Answer* Though they be committed among us, we allow it not, but judge it evil.

8. For lying, they say it is an evil, and shall not allow it. And finally, as to being christianized, they said, "as opportunity serveth by the English coming among us, we desire to learn their manners."

Whatever may be thought of the right of Massachusetts to interfere in this case, and especially of the policy of interfering as regarded the Narraghansetts and the other colonies, it must be admitted, that the submission itself, so far as concerned the applicants, was conducted with the honesty, as well as civility, generally characteristic of the intercourse of that Government with the natives.

The Governor having sent for the Sachems to appear at Boston on the 22d of April, (1643) they attended, with their interpreter. The submission was then explained to their entire satisfaction. They were also expressly informed, that they were not to be considered confederates, but subjects, to which they manifested their assent. So, adds the historian, they dined in the same room with the Governor, at a table by themselves, and having much countenance shown them by all present, and being told that they and their men should always be welcome to the English, provided they brought a note from Benedict

Arnold (their interpreter,) and having some small things bestowed upon them by the Governor, they departed joyful and well satisfied. The submission was as follows:

"This writing is to testify, that we, POMHAM, Sachem of Showamet, and SACHONOCHO, Sachem of Patuxet, have and by these presents do voluntarily and without any constraint or persuasion, but of our own free motion, put ourselves, our subjects, lands and estates under the government and jurisdiction of Massachusetts, to be governed and protected by them according to their just laws and orders, so far as we shall be made capable of understanding them; and we do promise, for ourselves, our subjects, and all our posterity, to be true and faithful to the Government and aiding to the maintenance thereof to our best ability; and from time to give speedy notice of any conspiracy, attempt, or evil intentions of any we shall know or hear of against the same, and do promise to be willing from time to time to be instructed in the knowledge of the worship of God. In witness whereof, we have hereunto put our hands the 22d of the 4th month, 1643.

The Y mark   The 9 mark
of SACONOCO.   of POMHAM."

Thus was consummated the title of Massachusetts to the jurisdiction of the Shaomet land. It was at this very time, as well as afterwards, claimed also by Plymouth, and by Rhode Island.* Gorton always alleged, that it belonged to Miantonomo, and that Pomham was secretly influenced by Massachusetts to withdraw from him and seek protection under their authority. No doubt that Government was sufficiently aware of the interest they had, not only in humbling the Gortonists, but in extending their jurisdiction as far as possible towards or into the territory of the Narraghansett chieftain, then, as Hutchinson

---

* Winthrop, Vol. II. pp. 251. and 317.

calls him, the greatest and most powerful sachem of
New England. Speaking of the petition of certain
settlers, in 1645, for permission to begin a plantation,
where Gorton and his company had erected three
or four small houses "on the land of Pomham, who
had submitted himself," &c. Mr. Winthrop himself
states, that the Court readily granted their petition,
promising all encouragement, &c.—"for it was of
great concernment to all the English in these parts,
*that a strong plantation should be there, as a bulwark
&c. against the Narraghansetts.*" It may be, that this
consideration assumed, in the view of the Massachusetts Government, the imperious interest of what is
commonly called State-necessity.

Hence the measures occasionally adopted subse
quent to the submission, for affording Pomham the
promised relief; a policy which certainly accorded
better with their stipulations to him, than with their
relations to some other parties. The Gortonists
harassed him beyond measure, but they were at
length subdued. The Narraghansetts, (after Miantonomo's death,) threatened and frightened him still
more. In April 1645, "that it might really appear
that the Massachusetts did own and would protect
him," which would seem to have been heretofore
doubted, an order was taken for sending men and an
officer to Shaomet, to stay there a few days, and act
on the defensive against the Narraghansetts.* These
men being *volunteers*, however, refused to go, unless
they were each paid ten shillings a week, furnished
with arms and ammunition, and allowed such booty
as they might be able to collect in case of fighting.
Whereupon the Court, not choosing to establish such
a precedent, sent word to Pomham, that the required
force would be at his disposal, whenever he should
forward sufficient funds to enable them to perform.
On the earnest importunity of the Sachem, early in
May, his request was finally granted; and, with the
aid of the English, he erected a fort upon his lands

---

* Winthrop.

This was in 1646. But Pomham and Sacono
to were not destined quietly to enjoy their possessions, as the following detail from Mr. Winthrop's
records for 1647, will abundantly illustrate. The
Gortonists had at that period returned to Shaomet,
which they now named Warwick; and, as the
Sachems alleged before the Commissioners of the
United Colonies, manifested a decided disposition
"for eating up all *their* corn, with their cattle," &c,
These functionaries hereupon wrote to certain persons in the vicinity of the premises, to view the
damages, and require satisfaction; which process,
however, had scarcely been commenced, when Jus ·
tice Coggleshall and others from Rhode Island came
to Shaomet, claimed jurisdiction for that colony over
the land in question, and forbade the appraisers to
proceed. Upon this, the latter returned home.
Another warrant was issued, with the same result.
Pomham was reduced to extremities; but still undis-
couraged, he renewed his complaints once more.
Massachusetts now sent three special messengers, to
demand satisfaction of the trespassers, and to warn
them to leave the territory. The application did no
good; and therefore, "as we could do no more at
present," writes Mr. Winthrop, "we procured the
Indians some corn in the mean time." The measures subsequently taken for redress, it would be
alike tedious and needless to enumerate.

As to Pomham, with whom we have chiefly to do,
it must be confessed, that his character assumes but
little dignity throughout this proceeding. In after
times, his career was occasionally more independent,
while at the same time it gave evidence that his early
attachment to the English was by no means one of
indissoluble affection, or of principle sacred in his
own eyes. It is not a little remarkable, that after
all the trouble and expense taken and incurred by
and between the colonies, and especially by Massa
chusetts, for his protection; and notwithstanding the
authorities of the latter government fondly and we

trust sincerely represented his submission as the frui
of their prayers, and the first fruit of their hopes, in
the great process of civilizing and christianizing
the natives ;* this incorrigible savage not only loosen-
ed his connexion with the English, but engaged
against them, with his whole force and influence, in
the great war of King Philip.

That course, fatal as it was to himself and his interests, was upon the whole the most creditable
passage of his life. And once adopted, he pursued
it with an energy that altogether sets aside any
doubts which his former course might suggest, in
regard to his real temperament and genius. Even
Philip was scarcely more feared than Pomham.
Historians universally, while they *now* call him a
Narraghansett, as evidently he had determined to
consider himself, place him in the highest rank
among the Sachems of that warlike and powerful
tribe. He did not even *pretend* to neutrality in the
early part of the war, as they did. He did not sign
either the treaty of July, (1675) negotiated at the point
of the English bayonet in his own territory, or the
submission executed in October following at Boston,
although upon the latter occasion one of his fellow-
chieftains affected to sign for him. This, at best, like
every other part and circumstance of the compro
mise, was a mere artifice, meant to divert the Govern
ment by a show of satisfaction and amity.

During Philip's war the territory of Pomham was
ravaged far and wide, and one hundred and fifty
wigwams destroyed by fire at one time, in December, 1675. Whether this chief was in the decisive and bloody battle of the 19th, or in what other
engagements he was during the war, history does
not determine. He was finally slain in July, 1676,
a few weeks previous to the death of Philip, and
the consequent close of that contest, the most critical and the most furious ever waged between the

---

* Winthrop

red man and the white. Great was the exultation of the conquerors over this first success, so encouraging to themselves, and so disastrous to their savage and terrible foes. The event took place in the neighborhood of Dedham, (in Massachusetts) where Pomham, with a small band of faithful warriors, half-starved and desperate, were still roaming the woods in the close vicinity of the English settlements. About fifty Indians were captured ; and the Sachem seems to have been the only man of the company who would not be taken alive. "That which increased the victory," says Mr. Hubbard, " was the slaughter of POMHAM, which was one of the Stoutest Sachems *that belonged to the Narraghansetts.*"*

His spirit and strength were such, that after being mortally wounded in the fight, so that he could not stand, he caught hold of an English soldier who came near him, and had nearly destroyed him by his violence, when the poor fellow was rescued by his comrades, and the dying chieftain relieved at once from his agony and his foes. He had little to live for, had there been a disposition to spare him His territory was long since subjected to a foreign power by his own act, and afterwards desolated. His subjects were dispersed and destroyed. His grandson had been slain in the field within a few months; and among the captives at the time of his own fall, historians particularly notice one of his sons, "a very likely youth, and one whose countenance would have bespoke favor for him, had he not belonged to so bloody and barbarous an Indian as his father was." This unfortunate lad was probably executed, by order of the Plymouth government, together with the other principal captives of the last months of the war. At best, he was spared, like the son of Philip, only to be enslaved in a foreign land.

* Narrative of Indian Wars. It will be observed in what erms the true allegiance of the Sachem is mentioned.

Among other distinguished chieftains of the Narraghansett tribe, who perished much in the same manner, and about the same time with the last named, was NANUNTENOO or QUANANSHETT, commonly call ed by the English CANONCHET. He was the son of Miantonomo, and probably, after the death of Mexham and Pessacus, succeeded to his father's high rank,—being generally entitled by historians the Chief-Sachem of his tribe. His reputation, both with his countrymen and his foes, was worthy of the noble blood in his veins. Mr. Trumbull observes, that he inherited all his father's pride, and all his insolence and hatred towards the English. What is still more conclusive in his favor, Mr. Hubbard calls him a 'damned wretch,' enlarges upon his cruelty and blasphemy, and exults over his final destruction. This—not the facts alleged, (which are wholly without proof,) but the assertion—furnishes, as a modern writer has aptly remarked, irresistible evidence of his heroic character.

There is abundant other evidence, however, to the same effect. The only ostensible deference of any description which he ever paid to an English authority—detesting, as unquestionably he did, their very name—was the act of subscribing the celebrated treaty of October 1675, negotiated at Boston. The object of it was to quiet the jealousy of the English, who suspected him of having contracted engagements with Philip. One provision went to ratify a treaty executed at Hartford during the month of July previous, (by four of the Narraghansett Sachems, nominally in behalf of all.) Another and the principal one, was expressed thus : *

' And wheras a considerable Number of people both men weomen and Children appertaining to those Indians who haue bin in actuall hostillitie against the English are now fled to the Narraghanretts Countrey; and are vnder the Custody of the

---

* Records of the Colonies.

said Sachems there; after a full and long Conference had concerning that matter, wee doe in the Name and by the Power to vs giuen and betrusted in the behalfe of the Sachems of the aboue said Countrey fully and absolutely couenant and promise to and with the abouenamed Comissioners att or before the 28th Day of this Instant month of October to deliuer or cause to be deliuered all and euery one of the Said Indians, whether belonging vnto Phillip: the Pocasset Sqva* or the Saconett† Indians Quabaug hadley or any other Sachems; or people that haue bin or are in hostilitie with the English or any of theire Allies or abettors; and these wee promise and Couenant to deliuer att Boston to the Gouernor and Councell there by them to be disposed in the behalfe of and for the best securitie and peace of the Vnited Collonies.

Sealed and deliuered in
the presence of vs. QUANANCHETTS   marke.
RICHARD SMITH Sachem in the behalfe of himselfe and
IAMES BROWNE *Conanacus* and the old Gueen and Pom-
SAMUEL GORTON IUNR. ham and Quanapeen. (Seal)
  Interpretors MANATANNOO *Councellor*
JOHN NOWHENETTS *marke* his   marke.
Indian Interpretor : and Canannacus in his behalfe
         (Seal)
    AHANMANPOWETTS marke
    Councellor and his (Seal)
    CORNMAN cheiffe Councellor to
    NINNIGRETT in his behalfe and a (Seal.)"

---

  * Weetamore, Weetamoe, or Weetanno, a kinswoman of Philip, and the active ruler of the tribe, though married to an insignificant fellow named Peter Nunnuit. All her subjects joined Philip with herself, excepting Alderman, who had the honor of shooting that Sachem with his own hand. Weetamore was drowned in August, 1675, attempting to escape from the English over a stream in Swanzey; and her head, in the barbarous style of the times, was set upon a pole at Taunton, much to the chagrin of such of her tribe as were compelled to witness the spectacle. Pocasset, now Tiverton, was on the coast, opposite the north of Rhode Island.

  † Or Sogkonate; a tribe on the same coast with the Pocassets, governed also by a Squaw-Sachem named AWASHONKS, or Awasunck, somewhat celebrated for her masculine qualities,

It is well known, how speedily the execution of this instrument was followed up by sending a strong English force to invade the Narraghansett territory, and subdue that spirited people at the point of the bayonet. Canonchet is supposed to have been engaged in the great swamp-fight, the most fatal to the Indians, and they most desperately fought upon their part, of the whole war. It continued to rage with the utmost violence for three hours from the moment of assault, until the enemy's wigwams, to the number of five or six hundred, were fired, and the field of contest became almost instantaneously an immense mass of terrific conflagration. The Savages, inspirited by their leaders, defended every wall and post with the fury of maniacs; and when they at length slowly retreated, they left the ground behind them encumbered with heaps of the slain. Quarter was neither asked nor given. Three hundred of the Narraghansetts, at the least estimate, are supposed to have been killed, besides more than double that number wounded, and an unknown multitude of women, children and old men burnt in the wigwams.

But the victory was dearly bought. Of the one thousand English soldiers of which the civilized portion of the invading army consisted, according to their own statement, eighty were killed and one hundred and fifty wounded. Abandoning the captured fort, they retreated sixteen miles the same night—and that in the depth of winter—leaving the enemy to return the next day to their former position.

It is not our intention to discuss at length the propriety of the summary course adopted by the colonies in this case. The principal offence of the Narraghansetts, as set forth in the Manifesto, was their evasion and delay in surrendering the hostile Indians

and for the part she took in Philip's war, first against the English and then with them. Captain Church, who effected this change in her politics, has given a minute account of his interviews with her. Ten of her tribe were living in Compton, as late as 1803.

who took refuge in their country. This refusal was
certainly inconsistent with the stipulations of July
and October preceding ; but these stipulations were
enforced in the first instance by the presence of an
English army, which had already invaded the Narraghansett territory.

Those of the tribe who made proposals of peace,
immediately after the swamp-fight, imputed the
blame of hostilities wholly to Canonchet. He had
made them believe, that by the former treaty they
were not obliged to surrender Philip's followers, until *his* brother, (who, with three other Indians of
rank, was detained as a hostage at Hartford,) had
been released. Probably, Canonchet did not himself misunderstand the plain provisions of that instrument, although, as he does not appear to have
been present at the execution of it, it might be misrepresented to him. It is more likely, that he considered it an absolute nullity, as having been obtain
ed by force, unjustly and insultingly imposed. The
construction referred to by his subjects, he counte-
nanced with the view of overcoming scruples on
their part in the protection of Philip's Indians.
Whether that protection—independently of the forced promise to surrender the refugees—was or was
not a sufficient cause for the war which ensued, it
must be allowed at least to do no dishonor to the
humanity and honor of Canonchet, and the other
Sachems, who persisted in that policy at every hazard
and almost in the very face of their enemy. With
him and them it was unquestionably a measure of
sacred principle. No noble-minded chieftain upon
the Continent, educated as an Indian chieftain always is, would have given up men who appealed to
their hospitality—their own brethren, in distress and
nakedness, driven before the bayonet of a mortal
enemy of a distinct race and of vastly superior power—and least of all, when, if surrendered, they were
surrendered to a certain alternative of slavery or
death. Some of his tribe would have compromitted

their dignity through fear, but not the son of Miantonomo. " Deliver the Indians of Philip!" said the
haughty Sachem at one time—"Never! Not a Wampanoag will I ever give up.   No!—Not the paring of
a Wampanoag's nail!"

Those who are familiar with the history of the
war will recollect, that the most critical period of it
was immediately subsequent to the swamp-fight.
This was owing to the desperate exertions of the
Narraghansetts, and especially Canonchet and their
other Sachems. They were indeed driven about the
country far and wide, and reduced to such extremities for food, that corn sold for two shillings a pint;
but their sufferings only made them the more ferocious, and the more bold. "That young insolent
Sachem, Canonchet, (writes Mr. Hubbard, in his
usual complimentary style,) said they would fight it
out to the last man, rather than they would become
servants to the English."

The destruction of Lancaster took place early in
February. Medfield was desolated ten days afterwards; and in March happened that memorable
engagement, not far from Providence and upon ancient Narraghansett ground, in which Captain Pierce
with his detachment, to the number of fifty English
soldiers, were cut off to a man. Canonchet commanded in this affair. The spirit of his warriors, as
well as the superiority of the English skill in the use
of their arms, appears from the fact that the Indians
lost between one and two hundred killed. Warwick,
Seekonk, and Providence were next successively
ravaged by the victorious foe. Plymouth was assaulted, and eleven of the inhabitants slaughtered; and
another party had the courage to commit horrible
ravages within eleven miles of Boston itself. The
prospects of Philip were never so flattering to himself and so disastrous to the English, as at this memorable juncture, when the exasperated and fearless son
of Miantonomo was supporting him with the whole
force of his dominions.

The manner in which the Narraghansett Sachems treated Roger Williams, at this period, amid all the excitement of suffering on the one side and success on the other, is worthy of everlasting remembrance. That gentleman was one of the few English who remained at Providence, exposed to the full torrent of war, and with no other security than such as he attributed to long acquaintance, friendship, and good faith, with those who were now become the inveterate enemies, and were openly calculating upon the utter extermination of his race. He had even the hardihood to reproach some of the Sachems who frequently came to converse with him, for their cruelties; and to threaten them with the sure, though it might be lingering vengeance of the English. "Massachusetts," said he, "can raise thousands of men at this moment; and if you kill them, the King of England will supply their place as fast as they fall." "Well!" answered one of the chieftains, "let them come. We are ready for them.—But as for you,—Brother Williams,—you are a good man,— you have been kind to us many years.—Not a hair of your head shall be touched." This noble pledge, bearing upon the face of it the mark of the chivalrous spirit of Canonchet, was regarded throughout the war with the most sacred fidelity. It was not in vain that the young Sachem remembered the warm affection which his father had entertained for his English neighbor and confidant.

But to resume the narrative;—"It was now full sea with Philip's affairs," says Mr. Hubbard, "for soon after the tide of his successes began to turn about the coast, which made way for the falling of the water up higher in the country." The disasters of the Pokanoket Sachem commenced with no less a misfortune than the death of Canonchet. And a matter of rejoicing indeed it was to the Colonies of the English—if we may credit the historian last cited— "that the ring-leader of almost all this mischief, and the great incendiary betwixt the Narraghansetts and us, died himself by that sword of war which he had drawn against others." The last assertion might perhaps have been spared to advantage, but the epithets furnish the best evidence in favor of the subject of them which the case could be supposed to present.

Early in April, it seems, Canonchet, weary of desolating the towns of the English, had betaken himself to the Indian haunts on the Connecticut river. Here he continued to take a most active part in the war; the whole body of the savages to the Westward trusting, (as our eulogist expresses himself,) under the shadow of that aspiring bramble. Nor was it in battle only that they placed reliance on his courage and genius. It was necessary, as it was difficult, to provide the means of sustenance, from day to day, for something like one thousand five hundred warriors, with their women and children. Canonchet suggested the plan of planting the lands on the West bank of the river, recently taken from the English. But how should even the means of planting be obtained? A council was summoned to solve this question; but not a man could be found who would hazard his life, at this season, in that section of the country where corn must be procured. The Sachem himself went forward, and proposed, with the assistance of thirty volunteers, who soon found courage to second him, to undertake a journey to Seekonk, in the immediate vicinity of Montaup, the old residence of Philip.

The adventure proved fatal to him. On the 27th of March, Captain Dennison, of Connecticut, had commenced a volunteer expedition against the enemy, with about fifty English soldiers, and eighty Niantick, Pequot and Mohegan Indians, severally commanded by Catapazet, Casasinamon and Oneco.* By the time Canonchet reached Seekonk, where

---

* The son of Uncas. The Pequot Sachem was a man of no particular note. Catapazet was subordinate to Ninigret.

he encamped on Blackstone river near the Pawtucket falls, Dennison's party, following the sea-coast, had arrived in the same neighborhood. The former was so little apprehensive of danger, that he dismissed all his thirty attendants but seven. The English, on the other hand, received the first intimation of his being near them, from two old straggling squaws, who confessed, on being captured, that Canonchet was not far off. The intelligence put new life into the weary soldiers, and they pressed forward till they came upon fresh tracks, and these brought them in view of a cluster of wigwams on the bank of the river.

In one of those wigwams Canonchet was at this moment reposing from the fatigues of his journey. His seven remaining followers sat around him; and he entertained them with the recital of the bloody victory over Pierce's detachment, which had taken place but a week or two before.* Suddenly the speaker suspended his narrative. His silent audience started to their feet, and stood aghast. The trained ear of the savage had already detected the approach of an enemy. Two of the company were immediately despatched to the summit of the hill, at the foot of which the wigwam was situated. These men, frightened by the near approach of the English, who were now (says Hubbard,) mounting with great speed over a fair champagna on the other side of the hill, ran by, as if they wanted time to tell what they saw. A third was sent, who executed his errand no better. But of two others who were sent up, one had the courage to return and inform the Sachem, in great

---

* So writes Mr. Hubbard, and Trumbull and others follow his authority. Baylies (Memoir of Plymouth Colony,) doubts the correctness of the statement, alleging that Canonchet did not leave the Connecticut river until April, whereas Pierce's defeat happened on the 26th of March. We do not however conceive that the distance was so great, but it might have been traversed more than once after the battle and before the surprisal

haste and trepidation, that the whole English army
was upon him.

Canonchet had no means of defence, and no time
for deliberation. He could only attempt an escape
by running round the hill opposite his pursuers ; and
he had not gone far in that direction, when Catapazet,
with twenty of his followers, and a few of the English who were lightest of foot, nearly intercepted him
as they descended the hill, and immediately commenced a vigorous and close pursuit. Canonchet
was a fleet runner, but the swiftest of Catapazet's
men began to gain upon him. He threw off his
blanket, and then a silver-laced coat which had been
given him on the renewal of his league at Boston.
His wampum belt was finally abandoned ; and this
betraying his rank to his pursuers, they redoubled
their efforts, until they forced him to betake himself
to the river, in which he plunged forward with great
haste. Unluckily, his foot sliped upon a stone, and
this not only delayed him, but brought him down so
far at to wet the gun which he still carried in one
hand ; "upon which accident, he confessed soon
after (we are told,) that his heart and his bowels turn
ed within him, so as he became like a rotten stick,
void of strength."*

Thenceforth he submitted to his destiny without a
struggle. He was a large, muscular man ; and as
Hubbard himself allows, of " great courage of mind,"
as well as strength of body ; but the foremost of the
hostile party, one Monopoide, a Pequot, laid hold
of him without his making the slightest resistance.
The first Englishman who came up was Robert
Stanton, a young man of some twenty years old ; yet
adventuring to ask him a question or two, (continues
the historian, with a touch of feeling which does
him credit,) the manly Sachem looked somewhat
disdainfully upon his youthful face, and replied in
broken English, "you much child—no understand

---

* *Hubbard's Narrative, p.* 129.

war---let your chief come---him I will talk with."
The English offered him his life if he would submit
to their government, but he would make no submission of any kind. They suggested his sending one
of his men to propose terms to his Narraghansett
warriors in the west; but he refused with scorn. He
was then told of the enmity he had manifested towards the English. "And many others," he replied
haughtily, " will be found of the same mind with myself. Let me hear no more of that." When informed
of what his fate must inevitably be, he only answered,
"It is well. I shall die before my heart is soft.—I
shall speak nothing which Canonchet should be
ashamed to speak.—It is well." Even those who
have censured the Sachem most, touched with the
fine dignity of his last hours, would fain search in
the theory of a Pythagorean Metempsychosis for the
secret of his greatness. Some old Roman ghost, say
they, must have possessed the body of this Western
Pagan.*

He was soon afterwards taken to Stonington, in
Connecticut, where Dennison's expediton had been
fitted out; and there was executed upon him the
sentence of death. That all concerned in the capture of so proud a victim might be gratified with a
share in the honors of his slaughter, the English
contented themselves with being spectators of the
scene, while the Pequots were permitted to shoot
him, the Mohegans to behead and quarter him,† and
Ninigret's men to kindle the pile upon which he
was burned. As a token of love and fidelity to their
civilized allies, his head only was reserved, to be presented to the English council at Hartford. It is
remarkable, that Oneco, on this occasion, took the
same part in the execution of Canonchet, and under
very similar circumstances, which, near forty years
before, his father Uncas had taken in that of Miantonomo, the father of Canonchet.

* Hubbard.
† Baylies' Memoir of Plymouth Colony.

Thus fell, in the prime of his manhood, the last Chief-Sachem of the Narraghansetts, the grand-nephew of Canonicus, and the son of Miantonomo The English historians of his own period may be excused for the prejudice with which they regarded him (as they did all who fought for the same cause with the same courage,) and which nevertheless affords to the reader of these days the most satisfactory proof of his high reputation and formidable talents. "This," says one writer, "was the confusion of a damned wretch, that had often opened his mouth to blaspheme." Again:—"as a just reward of his wickedness he was adjudged by those who took him to die."

It were useless to dispute these positions, for every reader of history possesses the means of forming a just opinion whether or not they are sound. But at all events, (as an author of a more liberal period has observed,)* we may surely at *this* day be permitted to lament the unhappy fate of this noble Indian, without incurring any imputation for want of patriotism. In the entire compass of Indian, and we might perhaps add, civilized history, there is no finer instance of that generous and chivalrous character, which—whatever it might be termed under other circumstances—in the situation of Canonchet, and with his sincere and strict principles, can only be approved and admired, as humanity to the suffering who sought his protection; as fidelity to his own and his father's friends; as a proud and lofty sacrifice of royalty, liberty and life itself to honor; as patriotism to his country, and as religion to his gods.

---

* Baylies' Memoir of Plymouth Colony.

CHAPTER XVI.

Account of the Pawtucket confederacy in New Hampshire—
PASSACONAWAY, their Chief Sachem—He is disarmed by
order of the Massachusetts Government. His residence,
age and authority—He maintains a good understanding
with the English—Visits Boston—The Apostle Elliot's ac
quaintance with, and notice of him—His views of Christianity—Festival, and Farewell speech to his tribe in 1660—
Death and character—His son and successor, WONOLAN
SET. Anecdotes of the family—Legend of Passaconaway's
feats as a Powah.

TURNING our attention to a part of the country and
to a people which have not yet been the subject of
special notice, we shall now introduce, with the fol
lowing passage from Winthrop's Journal, an indi
vidual of far too much distinction to be wholly over
looked. The date is of July, 1642 :—

"There came letters from the court at Connecticut,
and from two of the magistrates there, and from Mr.
Ludlow near the dutch, certifying us that the Indians
all over the country had combined themselves to cut
off all the English—that the time was appointed
after harvest—the manner also they should go, by
small companies to the chief men's houses by way
of trading &c. and should kill them in the house
and seize their weapons, and then others should be
at hand to prosecute the massacre. * * Upon these
letters the Governor called so many of the magistrates as were near, and being met they sent out
summons for a general court to be kept six days
after, and in the meantime it was thought fit, for our
safety, and to strike some terror into the Indians, to
disarm such as were within our jurisdiction. Accordingly we sent men to Cutshamkin at Brantreé
to fetch him and his guns, bows &c. which was
done, aud he came willingly, and being late in the
night when they came to Boston, he was put in the

prison, but the next morning, finding upon exami
nation of him and divers of his men, no ground of
suspicion of his partaking in any such conspiracy,
he was dismissed. Upon the warrant which went
to Ipswich, Rowlye and Newberry to disarm PAS-
SACONAMY, who lived by Merrimack, they sent forth
forty men armed the next day, being the Lord's-day,
but it rained all the day, as it had done divers days
before and also after, so as they could not go to his
wigwam, but they came to his son's and took him,
which they had warrant for, and a squa and her
child, which they had no warrant for, and therefore
order was given so soon as he heard of it, to send
them home again. They fearing his son's escape,
led him in a line, but he taking an opportunity, slipped his line and escaped from them, but one very
indiscreetly made a shot at him, and missed him
narrowly."

The Sachem here mentioned, and commonly called PASSACONAWAY,* was generally known among
the Indians as the Great Sagamore of Pannuhog, or
Penacook—that being the name of a tribe who in
habited Concord, (New Hampshire) and the country
for many miles above and below, on Merrimac river.
The Penacooks were among the most warlike of the
northern Indians ; and they, almost alone, seem to
have resisted the occasional ancient inroads of the
Mohawks, and sometimes even to have carried the
war into *their* territories. One of their forts, built
purposely for defence against these invasions, was
upon Sugar-Ball Hill, in Concord; and tradition indistinctly preserves to this time the recollection of
an obstinate engagement between the two tribes,
which occurred on the banks of the Merrimac in that
vicinity.

The Penacooks were one member of a large con-

---

* Hubbard writes Passaconnawa : Mr. Elliot, Papassaconaway: Wood, in that most singular curiosity, NEW ENG-
LAND'S PROSPECT, has pointed out Pissaconawa's location
on his map, by a cluster of marks representing wigwams.

federacy, more or less under Passaconaway's control, which, beside comprising several small tribes in Massachusetts, extended nearly or quite as far in the opposite direction as the northern extremity of Lake Winepissiogee. Among those who acknowledged subjection to him were the Agawams (at Ipswich,) the Naamkeeks (at Salem,) the Pascataquas, the Accomintas, and the Sachems of Squamscot, Newichwannock and Pawtucket,—the latter being also the National name of all the confederates. Passaconaway is supposed to have resided, occasionally, at what is now Haverhill (Mass.) but he afterwards lived among the Penacooks.

He must have been quite advanced in life at the date of the earliest English settlements on the coast, for he is said to have died, about 1665, at the great age of one hundred and twenty years, though that statement indeed has an air of exaggeration. The first mention of him is in the celebrated Wheelwright deed of 1629—the authenticity of which it is not necessary to discuss in this connexion. In 1642, Passaquo and Saggahew, the Sachems of Haverhill (Mass.) conveyed that township to the original settlers, by deed sealed and signed,—the consideration being three pounds ten shillings, and the negotiation ex pressly " wth ye consent of Passaconaway."*

It was about the time of this conveyance that the measures already mentioned were taken for 'disarming' the old chieftain. That was clearly a most unexampled stretch of prerogative, especially as Passaconaway had hitherto maintained his independence equally with his apparent good will for the English. There is some apology for the outrage in the excitement of the period, which was so powerful, it appears, even with the well-informed and well-meaning citizens of Boston, that they hesitated not to entertain the Braintree Sachem, their most obedient servant

---

* The original is still in the possession of a gentleman in Haverhill. See Mirick's History of that town.

on all occasions, in the town-jail. Even the report of a gun, in the night-time, in the neighborhood of the town, was now sufficient to rouse the good citizens far and wide ; and the shouts of a poor fellow at Watertown, who, having lost himself in the woods, cried out somewhat lustily for *help !—help !—*against an apprehended assault of the wild-cats round about him, produced an alarm hardly less serious than would probably have followed an actual foray of the Mohawks.

This excitement. we say. furnishes an apology for the harsh treatment of the Grand-Sachem. The government, upon cool reflection, appears to have been sensible of having gone too far, and what is creditable to them, they were not ashamed to make such explanations of the matter, promptly and politely, to the injured party, as were fitting their own true dignity as well as his. Governor Winthrop, speaking of the treatment of the Squaw and the Son as ' an unwarranted proceeding,' and conceiving " that Passaconamy would look at it as a manifest injury," called the court together, and proposed measures of reparation. Cutchamequin was accordingly sent to the old Sachem, to disclaim any order for kidnapping the woman and child, and discharging a musket at the boy, and to explain to him the real purpose and principle of the warrant. Passaconaway listened with composure, and returned answer that whenever the two absent members of his family should be returned, he would of his own accord render in the required artillery,—(and this, it would seem, the war-party which went out from Boston on the Sabbath, had not after all been able to effect.) One of them was still in custody, and the other had taken refuge in the woods. "*Accordingly*," adds our authority, " about a fortnight after, he sent his eldest son, who delivered up his guns, " &c. The fair inference is that the conditions made by the Sachem were performed to his satisfaction.

At all events, he considered it a good policy to

maintain peaceable relations with his much excited neighbors; he was too old, as most of his near relatives—children or grand-children—seem to have been too young. On the other hand, the English movements in this case, taken together, certainly indicate a respectful estimate of his character; and in fact the policy by which he was gained over, was so much valued, that either Mr. Winthrop alludes to his one act of submission repeatedly, or else the Government troubled itself to have the scene actually rehearsed as many times :—

"At this Court," says the Journal, for the spring of 1644, "Passaconamy, the Merrimack Sachem, came in and submitted to our Government, as Pumham &c. had done before."

And again, in 1645—"At this Court, in the third month, Passaconamy, the Chief Sachem of Merrimack, and his sons, came and submitted themselves and their people and lands under our jurisdiction, as Pumham and others had done before."

One of the most distinct notices of the old Sagamore occurs in that ancient tract, "THE LIGHT APPEARING &c." most of which was written by the apostle Elliot, in 1649. He preached about that time at Pautucket, that being "a fishing place where from all parts they met together."

"The Chief Sachem at this place," says Mr. Elliot, and of all Mermak, is Papassaconaway, whom I mentioned unto you the last yeere, *who gave up himself and his sonnes to pray unto God;* this man did this yeere show very great affection to me, and to the Word of God." The writer adds, that the Sagamore even urged his solicitations importunately using withal many "elegant arguments, with much gravity, wisdome and affection." He observed, among other things, that the preacher's coming there once a year did them but little good, "because they soone had forgotten what he taught, it being so seldome, and so long betwixt the times." Another sound suggestion was, that the Sagamore had many subjects who

"would not beleeve *him* that praying to God **was**
so good," whereas as no doubt they might be convinced by the preaching itself. Nor did Mr. Elliot,
he thought, allow himself leisure enough to *explain*
and *prove* what he asserted. It was "as if one
should come and throw a fine thing among them,
and they earnestly catch at it, and like it well, because
it *looks* finely, but could not look into it, to see what
is within,—whether something or nothing,—stock,
stone or precious jewel." So it was with praying;
it might be excellent, as it seemed,—but on the other
hand it might be hollow and empty,—he wished to
see it *opened*.

Whether this sensible advice was followed as far as
it could be, is uncertain ; but there can be little doubt
that the Sagamore himself became, if not almost a
Christian, yet strongly prepossessed in favor of the
English. In 1660, an English gentleman, who had
been much conversant among the Indians, was invited to a great dance and feast, at which among
other ceremonies, Passaconaway, now very old,
made a farewell speech to his people. He cautioned
them especially, as a dying man, to take heed how
they quarrelled with the English. He said, that
though they might do the whites some damage, it
would prove the sure means of their own destruction ;
and that, as for himself, he had formerly tried his
utmost by the arts of sorcery to hinder their settlement and increase, but all to no purpose.

It is remarkable, that when Philip's War broke
out, fifteen years after this transaction, WONOLANSET,
the Sagamore's son and successor, withdrew both
himself and his people into some remote place,
where he wholly escaped the disasters and excitement of the times. Probably there was no other
instance of the kind among all the tribes.

The allusion made by Passaconaway to the arts of
sorcery should be explained, by observing that he
had formerly been, for a long term of years, one of
the most noted Powahs, or Conjurors, ever heard of

among the Indians of New England. Perhaps his dominion itself, and certainly the greater part of his influence, was acquired by his talents exercised in that capacity. He indeed excelled his contemporaries, as all historians allow, in general sagacity and duplicity, as well as in moderation and self-command ;* but these were the very qualities proper for playing off that game on the extreme superstition of the Indians, which has so frequently been tried among them, and yet so rarely with a very prevalent or very permanent success.

But Passaconaway's attempt was no failure. He induced the savages to believe it in his power to make water burn, and trees dance ; to metamorphose himself into a flame ; and to raise, in winter, a green leaf from the ashes of a dry one, and a living serpent from the skin of one which was dead. Few modern practitioners, we presume, have surpassed the old Sagamore in the arts of legerdemain. These, however, were not his substantive profession, or at least not long. The politician soon emerged from the slough of the juggler. The Priest became a Sachem ; the Sachem, the Grand Sagamore of Penacook ; and the Sagamore preserved not only his own power, but his son's after him, by a series of diplomatic demonstrations, and a few words of ' elegant' civility, which, without disparaging his importance with his countrymen, made him the most agreeable neighbor to the English.

That Passaconaway was living as late as 1662, appears from the following annecdote of that date. Manataqua, Sachem of Saugus, made known to the chief of Panacook, that he desired to marry his daughter, which being agreeable to all parties, the wedding was soon consummated, at the residence of Passaconaway, and the hilarity was closed with a great feast. According to the usages of chiefs, Passaconaway ordered a select number of his men to

---

* See Hubbard, Hutchinson, Belknap, &c.

10—21

accompany the new married couple to the dwelling
of the husband. When they had arrived there,
several days of feasting followed, for the entertainment of his friends, who could not be present at the
ceremony in the first instance, as well as for the escort; who, when this was ended, returned to Penn-
akook.

Some time after, the wife of Manataqua expressing
a desire to visit her father's house and friends, was
permitted to go, and a choice company conducted
her. When she wished to return to her husband,
her father, instead of conveying her as before, sent
to the young Sachem to come and take her away.
He took this in high dudgeon, and sent his father-in-
law this answer: "When she departed from me, I
caused my men to escort her to your dwelling, as
became a chief. She now having an intention to
return to me, I did expect the same." The elder
Sachem was in his turn angry, and returned an
answer which only increased the difference; and it
is believed that thus terminated the connexion of the
new husband and wife.*

In the Third Volume of Farmer and Moore's Historical Collections, may be seen an account of the
death of an Indian called SAINT ASPINQUID, May 1st,
1682, at Mount Agamenticus on the coast of Maine,
where his tombstone is said to be still visible. It is
also stated, that he was born in 1588, and of course
died aged about ninety-four; that he was over forty
years old when he was converted to Christianity
that from that time he employed himself in preaching
the gospel among the Indians; and that his funeral
obsequies were attended by many Sachems of various
tribes, and celebrated by a grand hunt of the war
riors.†

---

* Manuscript documents, cited in Drake's Indian Biography.

† At which were slain "ninety-nine bears, thirty-six moose,
eighty-two wild-cats, thirty-eight porcupines," and a long list of
other animals of various names.

We are inclined to hazard the hypothesis, that this
Saint was no other than our Sagamore; that Agamenticus was the retreat of Wonolanset, or at least
of his father, during and subsequent to Philip's war;
and that the latter obtained his new name from his
new friends, and the title attached to it from an
English source. It certainly would be remarkable,
that so many and such particulars should appear of
the death of a man never before heard of. And on
the other hand, the reputation and the age attributed
to Aspinquid, agree strikingly with those of Passaconaway. By his 'preaching' must be meant his
sacred character and the great exertions he made to
keep peace with the English; and the date of the
alleged 'conversion,' we suppose to have been the
same with that of his first acquaintance with the
whites in 1629.

Our sketch may be fitly concluded with one of
those popular traditions concerning the old Chief,
which happens still to be in such preservation as to
form now and then, in some sections of the country,
the burden of a fireside tale. It is probably a fair
illustration of the opinion entertained of his abilities
by the credulous of his own era.

He said, that Sachem once to Dover came,
From Penacook, when eve was setting in.
With plumes his locks were dressed, his eyes shot flame;
He struck his massy club with dreadful din,
That oft had made the ranks of battle thin;
Around his copper neck terrific hung
A tied-together, bear and catamount skin;
The curious fishbones o'er his bosom swung,
And thrice the Sachem danced, and thrice the Sachem sung

Strange man was he! 'T was said, he oft pursued
The sable bear, and slew him in his den;
That oft he howled through many a pathless wood,
And many a tangled wild, and poisonous fen,
That ne'er was trod by other mortal men.
The craggy ledge for rattlesnakes he sought,
And choked them one by one, and then

O'ertook the tall gray moose, as quick as thought,
And then the mountain cat he chased, and chasing caught

A wondrous wight!   For o'er 'Siogee's ice,
With brindled wolves, all harnessed three and three.
High seated on a sledge, made in a trice,
On mount Agiocochook,* of hickory,
He lashed and reeled, and sung right jollily ;
And once upon a car of flaming fire,
The dreadful Indian shook with fear, to see
The king of Penacook, his chief, his sire,
Ride flaming up towards heaven, than any mountain higher.†

---

* The Indian name applied to the White Mountains.   There is a curious tradition, preserved in Josselyn's New England, of the veneration of the Indians for the summits of these mountains They considered them the dwelling places of invisible beings, and never ventured to ascend them.   They had also a tradition, that the whole country was once drowned, with all its inhabitants, except one Indian with his wife, who, foreseeing the flood, fled to these mountains, were preserved, and afterwards re-peopled the country.—*Ed.*

† See F. and M His. Coll

END OF VOL. I.

INDEX for THATCHER'S
INDIAN BIOGRAPHY VOL. I